Lamplighter and Son

Lamplighter and Son

CRAIG SKINNER

BROADMAN PRESS/NASHVILLE. TENNESSEE

© Copyright 1984 • Broadman Press
All rights reserved
4257-05
ISBN: 0-8054-5705-4
Dewey Decimal Classification: B
Subject Heading: Spurgeon, Thomas // Spurgeon, Charles Haddon
Library of Congress Catalog Card Number: 82-82947
Printed in the United States of America

Unless marked otherwise, Scriptures are quoted from the King James Version of the Bible.

Scriptures marked NASB are from the *New American Standard Bible*. Copyright © The Lockman Foundation, 1960, 1962, 1963, 1968, 1971, 1972, 1973, 1975, 1977. Used by permission.

Library of Congress Cataloging in Publication Data

Skinner, Craig.
  Lamplighter and son.

  Bibliography: p.
  Includes index.
  1. Spurgeon, Thomas—Fiction.   2. Spurgeon, C. H.
(Charles Haddon), 1834-1892—Fiction.   3. Baptists—
History—Fiction.   I. Title.
PR9619.3.S498L3   1984   823   83-25227
ISBN 0-8054-5705-4

He was walking one day up Norwood Hill with a friend. Some distance ahead of them, moving up the hill, they could see a lamplighter, lighting lamp after lamp until he disappeared over the brow of the hill. Turning to his friend, Spurgeon said: "I hope my life will be just like that. I should like to think that when I've gone over the brow of the hill I shall leave lights shining behind me." *Spurgeon left many lights behind him. More than any other great preacher he fashioned and molded others after his own model. His influence will not leave the earth until they all have left it; perhaps not then. That is the greatest of tributes to his ministry.**

Ronald W. Thompson

This biography centers on one of C. H. Spurgeon's preacher sons. The story cannot be disentangled from that of his father, and it declares how some of the light that Spurgeon kindled shone to one of the far corners of the world. It also reveals how that light ultimately came to shine again, in continued strength, from Spurgeon's own pulpit in the heart of London, through that beloved son. The elder Spurgeon traveled on, amid what he believed was an encroaching and malignant darkness. But the beams of that light still shone out from that dynamic century and into this one. Beneath and above and beyond it all, one discerns the omnipotent hand of *a frowning Providence*, behind which he hides *a smiling face*.

---

*Quoted from Ronald W. Thompson, *Heroes of the Baptist Church* (London: Carey Kingsgate Press, 1937) p. 145.

Foreword

My friend Craig Skinner has produced an enthusiastic study of Thomas Spurgeon, son of Charles Haddon Spurgeon and his successor as the pastor of the Metropolitan Tabernacle in London.

While there is much detailed research still to be done on the period—concerning James Spurgeon, for example, and the training provided by the four English Baptist seminaries which existed before Spurgeon founded his own—Craig Skinner's work will have immediate interest for many readers today.

I find the book particularly valuable for three reasons. First, it brings Thomas Spurgeon out from under the long shadow cast by his father. To be a great preacher's son is difficult enough; to be his successor as pastor of a divided congregation is almost too much for mortal flesh to bear. Yet Thomas Spurgeon proved himself not only a considerable preacher and pastor in his own right, but also a brave and good man who was forced to fight chest illness and bouts of black depression. No wonder the preacher in Dr. Skinner emerges, as he finds a message for lesser men in God's use of Thomas!

The second strength of Dr. Skinner's work is his depiction of the remarkable work which Thomas Spurgeon did in Australia and New Zealand, especially among evangelicals in general and Baptists in particular in Auckland at the end of the last century. There, with the shadow of his father much less apparent, he was able to be his own man. Of course, while his doctrinal stance remained fundamentally that of Charles Haddon Spurgeon, his preaching style was different. But in Auckland there were few who knew or cared to whisper the comparisons—or the contrasts.

Third, Dr. Skinner may well be making an interesting contribution to the debate about the nature of "fundamentalism." His work suggests that historians and theologians in the future may need to take careful note of the suggestions that the theology behind the publications of the first "Fundamentalist" groups grew, in part, from Spurgeonic circles. Furthermore, he suggests that "fundamentalism" was much more typical of the moderate evangelicalism of recent decades than of the wilder dispensationalist views and statements about biblical authority which have sometimes been identified with that term.

Lastly, may I, as a rather old-fashioned and straitlaced historian, add a footnote: while some of Craig Skinner's imaginative reconstructions of inner thoughts and private conversations may make his book more readable to some than to others, I want to say that they in no way affect the central truth of what he wants to say!

Barrie White, Ph.D., principal
Regent's Park College, Oxford, England

CONTENTS

1 Footsteps in the Sea (1877-1878)

God moves in a mysterious way,
  His wonders to perform;
He plants His footsteps in the sea,
  And rides upon the storm.

"We left Gravesend with 107 persons on board the trim English barque, *Meridian*, on June 4, 1853. Our fair progress as far as the Cape of Good Hope changed dramatically then to rough weather with a succession of sudden, heavy squalls, and one or two smart gales, until we crossed the Equator.

"On August 24, steering hard upon a fast wind, we came to the Island of Amsterdam in the centre of the Indian Ocean. The Island rose abruptly from the sea, and a dense cloud enveloped it so that it had the appearance, at a distance, of a heavy squall. For such, "alas!" it was mistaken by the second mate, who, on leaving his watch at six-o'clock, said to his successor, "There is a tremendous squall ahead; you had better keep a sharp look-out!"

"Had this caution been heeded it might have been much better for us. At the moment there were few steps betwixt us and death; yet all was comparatively peaceful below. We were regaling ourselves with tea, not much more discomposed than, from the heavy lurching of the ship, we had for some hours previously been. Towards seven preparations were made for putting the children to bed; and, while attending to this, a furious battery commenced without; wave after wave with unwonted violence and rapidity struck the ship, and a great wave of water swirled between decks and down the hatches into the hold.

"Immediately after that great sea struck the vessel we felt the first mortal blow, and it would be impossible for me to describe to you the incredible and fearful sensation it conveyed to our minds and hearts. One tremendous shock beneath set the ship a-quiver from stem to stern, shaking her like a reed in the wind. Another, and another shock succeeded, accompanied by a fearful crashing noise, as if we were in the jaws of some fearful sea-monster bent on crushing us to nothing. At every blow the vessel sank deeper into the water, until at the last she settled fast on the rocky bed of the Island reef (where she lay until finally, completely smashed to fragments) while the ocean poured in and out of skylights and every other aperture with the noise of a thousand thunders.

11

"Ours was a stern cabin on the lee side of the ship. The scene frightened us beyond all description. Crashing timbers, the tumult of the elements, and the wild darkness of the night, combined to induce moods of common terror and despair. With destruction appearing inevitable we gathered our little ones around us and, amid mutual embraces, took our last farewells.

"It seemed but an unfortunate change of fates, for the ledge, on which we stood just above the beach, was both rough and narrow. Behind us the cliffs rose for two hundred feet like a perpendicular wall. The moon, which shortly made its appearance, gave sufficient light to expose the terrors and dangers of the place, and our thought was, that standing under the forbidding shadow of that unclimbable cliff, it was certain, unless the sea abated, that we would soon all be swept away to our doom.

"Wet through, cold, and in many instances all but naked, there, with our unfortunate companions, we gathered in little clusters along the ledge, presenting a complete contrast to the comfort and respectability of appearance which had marked us all just a few hours before.

"At this point a gracious Providence cast bales filled with warm clothing from the ship's cargo holds right at our feet! Jersey frocks, ready-made trousers, boys' jackets, and large-red shirts and pieces of warm flannel, destined no doubt for some Sydney haberdasher, all came riding upon the breakers onto the beach, and in such profusion to supply all. We had great reason to be thankful for this plentiful supply, very little dampened by the sea air, and we rapidly covered ourselves against the bitter cold.

"In addition we found one cask and a part of a barrel of biscuit, more soggy and stale than we ordinarily would consume, but a delight to us in this hour. Also some herrings in cases, tough and very salt, but likewise welcome. A slow spring of fresh water bubbled up at our feet from a crevice in that towering cliff behind us, so we had much for which to thank God. These provisions, along with a few nuts, raisins, and dried apples, we calculated could barely sustain us for about five days, at the rate of half a biscuit and one herring a man per day. Some of the seamen found barrels of spirits also washed over from the wreck, and thus the lust of plunder now was added to the excitement and riotousness occasioned by the drink, as some fine cases of money and jewelry consigned to the banks and merchants in the colony had now broken open on the beach.

"For two whole days we remained in this perilous position. Men were sent around the cliffs in every direction but could find no points by which we could ascend. At last one plucky man managed to climb to the top, ropes were rigged aloft, and, after a day and a half of struggle, all were safely above. We were among the first up and found that those who had preceded us in the ascent had set fire to the long grass of the plateau to clear a place for our settling, and we found that, as it was the season when the birds on the Island were breeding, some of the young ones being overcome by the smoke, we collected their bodies, finding them about the size of small English pigeons, and a soup was made from them in a footpan which we had fortunately preserved. It was a poor refreshment as we had no salt to season it with, and there was but a quarter of a gourd for each individual, we had no spoons or knives and forks to assist us at our meal, but we found it very delicious.

"At night we had again to lie down on the grass, cold and exposed to rain and tempests. Saturday night passed away thus, and Sunday and Monday. It then became evident to all that our only chance of life was in being taken off by some ship; but who could hope for any ship to come near such a place, while boundless searoom invited them to avoid its dangers! And suppose one should come? Could that only augment our tragedy? All hope except in the power and goodness of God, was cut off; many among us turned to Him in a prayerful and resigned spirit, and He in return looked upon us with pity.

"Our condition rapidly became most painful from excessive fatigue, hunger, cold, and sleeplessness, when at midday on Monday after four weary nights on that towering clifftop, suddenly, in the midst of our brooding silence, the cry rang out, "A ship, a ship, a ship!" The word was shouted by my dear wife so frantically excited that her wild and eager gestures made some think she was frantic, and the children became excessively frightened at her intense insistences. Soon, however, all saw the sail, which turned out to be an American whaler, *Monmouth*, of Long Island, under Captain Isaac Ludlow, and immediately all was tumult and excitement.

"The grass, wherever it could be found, was again set on fire. Every child who stood enveloped in one of the red flannel shirts which we had rescued from the beach and which had been so useful to us, tore his off and waved it with abandon. The smoke drifting from the Island attracted attention, and the waving from the almost hysterical group on the plateau told our coming saviours our sad story. Soon a boat rowed around the Island, finally finding an inlet suitable for our embarkation some many hours distant by foot for us on the farther side. From there, eventually, we all were rescued."[1]

Tom lifted his eyes abruptly from the absorbing narrative before him. A quick glance past the flickering cabin lamp and through the misty porthole revealed the dim outline of the fretted Victorian coast, less than a mile beyond. He walked to the brass-framed window, opened it a crack to feel the bite of the morning wind, and gazed more intently. To his left the craggy extremities of a rugged bluff reached out as if to touch him. One gigantic rock stood at the cliff base, baring its squat jaw to the foaming surf line. Others sat like attendant junior brothers ringing a slow curve around a golden beach just beginning to awaken to the sun.

So this is Australia at last! he mused. The excitement of the coming arrival now drove away the weariness of the eleven long weeks of sail which lay behind. His hands folded the pages he had been mechanically reading and stuffed them back into a long brown envelope. His thoughts were of his father and of home. Smiling, he recalled how C. H. Spurgeon had blundered into his sickroom, tossing those pages into his lap. "Now, here's a sea yarn you'll enjoy m'boy!" his father had chuckled. "I know your mind always is filled with ships, and sailors, and sea stories! This is a shipwreck story, and a true one, what's more! It will convince you that truth is often stranger than fiction!" In a year filled with illness, this absorbing narrative had been just what a bored fourteen-year-old had needed.

Tom had devoured the report eagerly, and turned to it again many times over the years. Today he was almost twenty-one, and nearly a man. Yet he often found his pencil straying to nautical subjects, like the sailor sketch which he had copied from the *British Workman* for his mother when he was a thirteen-year-old school-boy.[2] Strange, how a shipwreck story like this, now a quarter century old, could still hold his interest in 1877! Strange, too, the compulsion which drove him to ask for these pages to be his own, and to carry their detached inconvenience to his mother six years ago to be bound so daintily with the needle and thread which seemed ever to be at her side.

When his cough had improved enough to allow a return to daily tasks, he took great pains to preserve the little pages. They were the first items to be packed into his sea chest, and the treasure had been read, and reread, on the voyage.

What compulsion drove him again to this ancient record? Its perusal dulled the predawn boredom of his final day afloat, but was there more than this behind it all? Why such an urge, on this crisp Australian morning, to relive the maritime stresses of one among those early Baptist pioneer-pastors who struggled so hard to serve God in Sydney? Did this interest infer his own subconscious desire so also to minister once he had disembarked?

Never! Lay preacher he might be, but clergyman he most certainly was *not*! His plan to capitalize upon the South Kensington College art studies, by becoming a wood engraver in the new land, left no room for that alternative. A small engraving business should go well in Melbourne, with sales of weekly illustrated papers mushrooming across the nation from that center. If some chapel in the new land lacked permanent pastoral oversight and sought his occasional honorary presence in the pulpit, he would be glad to oblige. The past year or two of similar service in the little Baptist mission at Clapham, with his twin brother Charles, had been satisfying. It was good preparation for some permanent lay preaching. (His health could not stand normal employment in the English climate, let alone anything extra. He planned the Australian move for restoration and recovery.) The hope of a full theological course at his father's London Pastors' College was a dream for somewhere in the future. For now the dream stood in indefinite postponement.

All Australian honorary service must, then, be conditional upon his return to full health. The doctors assured him that this was a bright hope, considering the long sea voyage and the many months yet to be spent in the warm Australian sun.

Carefully he checked the coat pocket in which his father's letter lay. Glancing at the address, *Pastor Bunning, Aberdeen Street Baptist Church, Geelong, Victoria, Australia,* Tom tried to remember all that his father had told him of this former student. "A warm man, Tom. Cold and gruff exterior, mind you, but a heart of pure gold. He'll help you get set up!"

Perhaps some full-time study lay in the future if he could return to England in a year or so. Then there was his father's oft-expressed desire that both his sons serve alongside him in the manifold ministries associated with the Metropolitan Baptist Tabernacle in London. Well, it all sat squarely in God's hands, and was probably best left there.

Come to think of it, though, he confided to himself, *I really did enjoy reading those theological works Father picked out for me to study on the voyage. Enjoyed them far more than I thought I would. And the informal Sunday services Captain Jenkins encouraged me to lead in the dining saloon were an undoubted blessing to some and the brightest hour of each week for me!*

Suddenly the Captain's gruff voice boomed down the narrow stairwell, almost deafening him with its ricocheting echo. "Hey! Below there! Thomas! Are you awake yet?"

Tom bounded from the bunk, his reverie broken, thankful he was already dressed. He leaped up the stairs, taking two at each long-legged stride. But he grabbed his scarf and jacket from the hook over the door so fast that he tripped and landed in a heap at the captain's feet. With a laugh he blurted an embarrassed apology for such untimely haste. The two men stepped smartly to the deckside rail, joking over his discomfiture. Their verbalized breath, hanging in the chill morning air, reminded him of the sharp spurts of steam which heaved from the old iron kettle on the hob beside the fire in his mother's warm kitchen.

"Well, did you finish that gigantic letter home to your folks yet?" the Captain queried. "Twenty-two, four-page sheets, no less," Tom bragged. "All in my best copperplate hand, and finished before I slept last night!" "Good work," his companion chuckled, "that should convince your father that I have looked out for his son as I promised, and that you have enjoyed yourself over these past weeks.

"I shall truly be sorry to see you go," Captain Jenkins continued. "Particularly because I shall have to go back to reading some of your father's *Penny Pulpit* series to the men for their Sunday worship. They are always popular, of course. But to have a *real* Spurgeon to preach to us each week has been a rare treat indeed."

"It seems such a mystery to me that my father's sermons have such popularity everywhere," Tom replied. "I know of country chapels and village churches at home that have no minister. Many read a Spurgeon's sermon together when they gather on the Lord's Day. But I had no idea these penny sermons were so prized on the high seas."

"Well, you are in for some interesting surprises about those sermons when you get to Australia," the Captain laughed. "So many who have migrated to Australia once sat under your father's London ministry, or have sermons sent them from relatives at home, or have stumbled across them unexpectedly. So they read your father's sermons widely in all the colonies. Any religious publications are rare out here, and evangelical ones very rare."

"I'm sure that many know of my father's work in London," Tom responded. "The Metropolitan Tabernacle can hold 6,000 and it has been filled twice on Sunday, and almost filled each Thursday evening now, for sixteen years. Visitors from across the world are often present. The great meetings he has addressed all over England—at the Crystal Palace and the Surrey Gardens Music Hall—have made his reputation as a popular preacher known everywhere. But what do you mean about surprises concerning his sermons here in Australia?"

The Captain spoke with deep respect. "Tom, I am thrilled with some of the stories I have heard about your father's ministry out here. That's what I meant when I said 'some have stumbled across them unexpectedly!' One of your father's admirers has actually paid for the insertion of those sermons as advertisements for the gospel in many secular papers—like that sporting weekly, *The Australian.*"

"And are they well accepted?"

"I should say so! After six months of publication at full advertising rates, the sponsor asked for a reduction, contingent upon a favorable reaction from the readers. The paper asked for expressions of opinion and four hundred letters of enthusiastic support came in from all parts of Australia and New Zealand.[3] And many of them were written by far-off dwellers in the bush, who looked for the weekly sermons as regularly as for their daily meals. In some cases lonely believers were encouraged and helped by the preacher's message. In other instances, little companies gathered together while one of their number read to them. Although they were first delivered thousands of miles away, these sermons seem as fresh and fragrant as ever.[4] . . I recall hearing of an Australian hobo (they call them 'swagmen') who had traveled the country for about five years, able to hold only an occasional job because of his drinking. He found a sheet of torn newspaper outside a public house on which one of Mr. Spurgeon's sermons was printed. Led to an experience of conversion, he became a changed man, holding steady employment. I know of other documented cases where some lives have been transformed from violence and tension to peace and happiness by these sermons.[5]

"I believe you will find your father's name and ministry as widespread and beloved on these shores as in England. When folks find out you are C. H. Spurgeon's son, I am sure you will never lack friends!"

Tom's thoughts leaped quickly from the captain's testimony (a prophecy he would well remember in future days) to the coming embarkation. "But what exactly is Victoria like these days?" he queried. "I know it is no longer a pioneer colony. I have heard of the gold rushes and the frontier life, the huge sheep properties, and the lonely roads which lead to the outback areas through the eucalyptus forests. But tell me about Melbourne! Is it a true city? Or just an overgrown country town?"

"I'm sure you'll have some surprises there also, my lad!" the captain nodded. "Melbourne is truly a 'little London'! It boasts itself a commercial center and a businessman's delight. Even Queen Victoria herself could make her home there and want for nothing. You can buy the finest goods from all over the world. Opulent hotels offer services to match those of any of the leading hotels in Europe. If you want a grand time and smart clothes, modern inventions, the latest books, Melbourne is the place. Banks on every corner. Financial houses like those in London and Paris.

"You are right to say that Australia's gold rush began it all, but those days are at least twenty years behind us now. Mark my words—*Australia now rides to a new prosperity on the sheep's back*. Last year they exported over 300,000 bales of wool from the Melbourne exchange alone! That's where the future is. Did you know that some of the fast wool clippers can get from Melbourne to London in forty-five days? They sail the dangerous polar route, right past the Antarctic ice caps, in order to get the Australian wool early to the London market for the best prices."

The two chatted on for a few more minutes about the development of steamships, the invention of the screw propeller, and other changes which affected ocean transport. Captain Jenkins opined that the new land line telegraph from Adelaide, South Australia, to Darwin, on Australia's South-East Asian extremity was a great blessing. Opened in 1872, and now linked to the submarine cable from Ceylon to London, the telegraph meant that news could move across the world in about two hours. Reminded of the cable he had sent Mr. Bunning from Adelaide advising their time of arrival in Melbourne, Tom looked up to see that Port Philip Bay was now plainly in view. He hurried to the cabin to make ready to disembark, grabbing a sea biscuit to munch as he worked. It was now

10:30 AM, but this was all the breakfast he wanted today.

Expertly now, after many weeks of practice, Tom stowed his books and larger clothing in the stout cabin trunk which had been his brother Charles's parting gift. As he slipped the remaining belongings into the slim portmanteau on the bed, he wondered again at the relative ease with which the seventy-four-day voyage had passed. He recalled his father's quip on the closeness of cabin life as he had departed: "Life on a ship is like going to prison, with the added chance of being drowned!" But he had not found it too confining. Certainly now his breathing was smoother, and his cough was almost gone. The sea air had obviously worked wonders. Also he felt much more energetic. That dreadful lassitude, his constant companion over these past six years, had disappeared.

The last item he packed was the bright bundle of cards and letters which he had received at his departure. The top one was a simple word of encouragement over C. H. Spurgeon's signature:

> "You will preach, I am sure, but without good training you cannot take the
> position which I want you to occupy. Theology is not to be learned in its
> amplitude and accuracy by one destined to be a public instructor without
> going thoroughly into it, and mastering its terms and details. Perhaps a
> voyage may give tone to your system and prepare you for two years of steady
> application. Only the Lord make you a great soul-winner, and I shall be more
> than content."[6]

The ship glided into the dock amid the forest of tall masts and busy water traffic of the inner harbor. There, standing at the pier edge, was a tall, full-bearded, brown-eyed gentleman. Pastor Bunning looked every inch the nonconformist minister, with his white cravat and long black frock coat. Beside him panted a fine mare, harnessed to a hansom cab.

With a quick wave to the crew and a brief handshake with Captain Jenkins, Tom was down the walkway. "I am so glad you are here at last!" Bunning exclaimed. "We have been watching your progress up the harbor for the past forty-five minutes. Now we must be quickly away, for we have a noon appointment in the city."

The customs official gave only a cursory glance at Tom's baggage, tipping his hat deferentially to the Baptist minister at his side as he waved them on. Within minutes the little cab had cleared the quay side, the sharp tattoo of the mare's clipped heels on the timber wharf decking rapidly giving way to the quieter clop clop of the gravel road leading toward the city proper. Lady Melbourne sat every inch like a bejeweled dowager (in regal majesty) on the bank of the river Yarra as it stretched back toward the Bay. She revealed herself increasingly, to Tom's interested gaze, as an immense and stately metropolis, just as Captain Jenkins had promised. An elaborate tramway system snaked past them, branching off in a multitude of directions to the hidden suburbs. The Grand Lady herself seemingly almost buried her amid a swath of enveloping parklands of verdant green.

The inner city displayed even more attractive charms. Imposing masses of sandstone and granite buildings in pleasant designs grouped in noble clusters cheek-to-cheek in a connubial association which gave the whole mass an air of familial congeniality. Green banks and flowered gardens glowed under the brilliant sunshine, combining with the metropolitan sprawl to imply an air of comfortable affluence. The whole scene suggested a young giant resting quietly in the noonday sun, whose muscular vitality lay poised for later exploits. Astonished at the magnitude of it all, Tom inquired if the potential was as large as the panorama suggested.

"We're riding a business boom and everyone is optimistic about the future," Mr. Bunning smiled. "Melbourne has everything—colleges, schools, public gardens, museums, libraries, theaters, clubs, banks, churches, commercial enterprises. A great flow of British capital supports us. We possess a Wool Exchange that rivals any overseas. Sydney and Brisbane are more provincial in style. In Melbourne, the wives of our most prominent businessmen can choose the best Parisian styles. Mrs. Bunning says that the young ladies who serve in the Bourke Street stores appear more like those in the most aristocratic parts of London than anywhere else she has been.

"The sons and daughters of our gold rush generation have now settled into city life. Some of these newly rich are unable to handle their prosperity, of course, but many have invested heavily in real estate, as you will see when you view the grand mansions at St. Kilda and Toorack. Melbourne sets the pace for everything in Australia, from the size of its Chinatown to the strength of its Trade Unions. The magnificence of the city residences of our farmers may surprise you. They call them 'squatters' here, because of the cheap government land which they have gobbled up greedily by staking claims of huge dimensions. But many of them spend more time in Melbourne than in their vast sheep stations in the North and the West.

"We publish a bewildering mass of newspapers and journals. You should find that your talents as an illustrator and wood engraver will not go unused, Tom. Melbourne offers stock and station agents who claim they can market the farmer's crops and provide him everything needed to build a house from cement to timber and nails. They will engage servants for his household, appoint book-keepers and shearing bosses, roustabouts and boundary riders, and, in fact, provide any form of food or goods any squatter ever may require."

"Some old sailor on the ship tried to tell me that one of the cooks on a certain sheep station had so many mouths to feed that he had to go out in a boat to stir the soup!" Tom grinned. Mr. Bunning chuckled.

"Well, that is a bit much, Tom, but don't laugh too quickly! One of those properties is the size of all Wales, and many would stretch beyond two or three counties in England. Wool will be Australia's major export for many years to come, but we also are becoming a highly-industrialized nation, just like England."

Bunning waved a casual hand, indicating the rows of town houses which marched in orderly terraces to the right and the left of the cab. Tom noticed their bright timber fences, iron-lace trims, and cool verandas. The slim houses were grouped in pleasant suburban settings, behind narrow footpaths dotted with modern gas lamps. The children, bowling hoops and playing hopscotch on quiet front sidewalks, seemed models of contentment.

"These terraces have risen close to the factories and workshops which now penetrate the whole city," his host declared. "We manufacture everything in Melbourne from chocolates to agricultural implements, and unfortunately our breweries grow each year, with a consequent alcoholic addiction at all levels of society. Some real poverty exists. Many of the unlucky diggers returned from the fields and populated our slums, bringing vices worse than those of London itself. I can take you to areas where barefoot and unkempt children mix with Chinese hawkers, opium smokers, and gamblers in scenes reminiscent of Charles Dickens's scenes."

By this time they had reached the central shopping area, honeycombed with restaurants and arcades. After paying the cab fare, and tipping the driver to deliver Thomas's luggage to the rail station for shipment to Geelong, Bunning ducked quickly into a small doorway. This led to a large second floor hall, filled with clerks, apprentices, and other young men. They were noisily enjoying their lunch hour around long wooden tables. A handful of volunteer ladies served steaming cups of hot tea and huge slices of homemade cake to accompany each man's sandwich lunch. The whole happy assembly busied itself under a long banner which proclaimed, "YMCA Luncheon Fellowship Hour." Tom and his companion found a spare corner at a table and, after a brief word of thanks, he gratefully drank the hot, oversweet and overstrong black tea and shared the roast beef and pickle sandwiches Bunning had brought with him for the occasion.

In a few moments Tom learned that this was a regular monthly meeting and that the young men gathered for the occasion were served by the ladies from various churches, in order that Christian fellowship could be provided in the city. By then, Reverend Bunning had left him and was on the platform being introduced as that day's guest speaker.

The pastor began by acknowledging the honor of the occasion and launched immediately into his lecture which, to Tom's surprise, was entitled *The Life and Labours of C. H. Spurgeon*. Tom listened to the recital of familiar facts, noting how Reverend Bunning enlisted attention after his opening remarks with a relevant story about the sermons which had been printed in *The Leader, The Australian*, and other local papers:

Just as a specimen of the work done in our own colony, let me mention a fact which came under my own notice years ago. I had to preach for a Presbyterian brother in a church at the centre of a great pastoral district. After the morning service a group of squatters gathered around me making enquiries about Mr. Spurgeon. They told me that all up that valley, in the villages and towns, as well as at the homestead, Mr. Spurgeon had preached for more than fifteen years! Godly elders had read the sermons, both to the edification and conversion of souls, to the congregations which had regularly assembled through all those years. All the shepherds and others who had to spend the Lord's Day in watching the flocks were supplied with the sermons. I asked those gentlemen if they had, in acknowledgement of the obligation of the whole district to God's blessing on those printed pages of his servant, ever done anything to aid the College, Orphanage, or other great works carried on under Mr. Spurgeon. They said it had not occurred to them to do so. I pressed the matter on their consciences and left them. Some months after I received a cheque for one hundred and one pounds from one of those gentlemen, stating that the one pound was from a shepherd, who had been a profited reader of the sermons for more than fifteen years. I know that several hundreds of pounds from that district have since gone to aid Mr. Spurgeon's many institutions.

Mr. Bunning outlined his facts succinctly:

"Mr. Spurgeon came to London from a small but most successful pastorate at Waterbeach, Cambridge, to the church at New Park Street, Southwark, London, in 1853; when he had just completed his nineteenth year. Some time before his coming I was a regular attendant at that place and I remember how poorly the congregation was. Six weeks after his coming I found the place so full on a Sunday evening that in a few months it became so crowded that they had to go to Exeter Hall. Then the Surrey Music Hall was engaged. In 1861 the building known as the Metropolitan Tabernacle was opened free of debt. Its cost was thirty-one thousand and five hundred pounds. It seats 5,500, but every seat has a flap and a bracket, so there is room for about 7,000 persons. To that number the pastor of the tabernacle has regularly preached.

"In 1855 he began to publish the weekly sermon which speedily reached a circulation of 25,000 each issue. In 1856 the Pastors' College was established. It has educated hundreds for the ministry. In 1856 Mrs. Hillyard asked Mr. Spurgeon to take charge of twenty thousand pounds to establish an orphanage. Over 500 fatherless boys and girls are fed, clothed, educated, and housed. Seventeen almshouses for aged Christian men and women, and two day-schools accommodating four hundred scholars, were all part of the burden the Church and pastor undertook when they moved to the Metropolitan Tabernacle.

"The princely and self-forgetful generosity of this servant of God often amazed me and filled my heart with joy. The deacons make no secret of the fact that for many years Mr. Spurgeon gave back to the Tabernacle and its work far more than he ever received as income from the Church. Of course he could not have done this had not the proceeds from his books and sermons supplied him with such ample means of support."

The good pastor continued giving many instances of Spurgeon's freshness, naturalness, wholehearted friendship, and realistic faith. He concluded by saying:

"Just before I came to this colony I was going down to the Tabernacle with him on a Sunday morning. I remarked that he must sometimes think of the welcome home that awaited him from the thousands to whom God had blessed his testimony. He said, "I really have no time to think about it, for if I get a lift-up one minute, I get a knock-down in the next. So the welcome in that land I anticipate with joy is that of a very unworthy servant from an infinitely gracious Master." With thousands of others I bless God forever for bringing me within the influence of this servant of His. His warm way, his passionate love of Jesus was a new revelation of the Gospel to me. His willingness to undertake all sorts of burdens that Christ might be magnified is sublime. His fidelity to the truth, even though it cost him a bleeding heart, I cannot but admire and wish to emulate. We glorify God in him."[7]

Tom, somewhat embarrassed by the effulgence of Reverend Bunning's praise for his father, nevertheless joined in the general applause. Afterwards, as the two of them walked briskly to the railroad station, he asked, "Brother Bunning, were those young men *really* interested in such an address?"

"Well, you heard the extent of their applause, Tom! They have a committee which selects speakers and topics in advance. I was chosen to bring today's address because I am a graduate of your father's Pastors' College."

Tom grew silent after they had entered the railway carriage, thinking about the experiences of the past few hours. "Captain Jenkins was right," he thought. "Surprises at every turn indeed!"

The thirty-nine-mile journey to Geelong, closest port to the Ballarat gold-fields, passed quickly. Apart from a few words from his host about the rivalry between Geelong and Melbourne, the journey slipped by in silence. But as they came to the first outskirts of the city, Mr. Bunning drew the letter out of his pocket which Tom had brought from home and read it aloud. After the usual commendations, greetings, and assurances from his father that Tom would find congenial employment under Mr. Bunning's sponsorship, the recipient noted that C. H. S. had added one of his traditional postscripts. "P.S.," he read, "He can preach a bit!"[8] "Is that true?" Bunning asked with a twinkle in his eye.

"A very *little* bit, I assure you, sir," Tom blurted. He then told him of the lay services which he and his brother Charles had given to start the little mission in the gardener's cottage at Bollingbroke over the past year. "Capital! Capital!" Bunning exclaimed. "Then you shall preach for me at the Aberdeen Street Church this Sunday night!"

Over his feeble protests Reverend Bunning assured him that the plan was a good one. Saturday's *Geelong Advertiser* would publicize his presence, and "might draw a few of his father's admirers to hear his son, from the districts round about." But it was with somewhat mixed feelings that Tom settled into a fitful sleep that evening.

Sunday September 3, 1877, dawned bright and clear. Tom enjoyed the 11 AM service admiring the commodious brick and bluestone of Bunning's New Baptist Church in Aberdeen Street. The edifice was half-filled with about 350 persons. Mr. Bunning's sermon was one of those good, hearty slices of biblical exposition which was typical of C. H. Spurgeon's students. The *Advertiser* had published Tom's evening opportunity, and linked his name with C. H. Spurgeon's, so he was prepared for some expressions of affection for his father which might come from those who attended the evening worship. When the hour came, however, the experience quite overwhelmed him.

Worshipers packed the sanctuary, cramming into every pew, and overflowing the aisles. Windows stood ajar with young men crowding around to peer through them. The vestries, platforms, and foyers were packed so densely with women and children that it seemed as if they could hardly breathe. After the service, hundreds of lonely Australians rushed to welcome him. They showed him prized and tattered copies of C. H. Spurgeon's sermons which they had read and reread in weary travels through the outback. Many wept openly in the service as memories of England and home were revived by the presence of another bearing the Spurgeon name and image who stood before them proclaiming the evangelical gospel. Within a week he had written to his father:

> Mr. Bunning is a right good fellow, so thoughtful, and so kind. I didn't intend preaching my first Sunday ashore, but, as I expect to be in Ballarat next sabbath, I seized what may be my only opportunity of helping my dear brother. We had a grand time, the chapel was crowded, and God was in the place. Dear Father, I believe I have the way open to many hearts in this colony. I have seen them weep as I spoke. I suppose because of the recollections raised . . . Mr. Bunning . . . has given me kind advice in various matters, telling me that, from last Sunday's service, I need not mind facing any audience.[9]

The *Geelong Advertiser's* report of the occasion under the heading, "Mr. Spurgeon at the New Baptist Church," filled several columns:

> About 900 persons crowded into the New Baptist Church in Aberdeen Street

last evening, to hear Mr. Thomas Spurgeon, son of Rev. C. H. Spurgeon, preach for the first time in the colony. The name of Rev. Mr. Spurgeon is so well known in this part of the world that it cannot be wondered at that curiousity prompted a large number of persons to attend to hear his son expound the Scriptures. Mr. Thomas Spurgeon, who has come to this colony on a visit, and for the benefit of his health, appears to be about 22 years of age, is clean shaved, and consequently has a very youthful look about his face. As a preacher, however, Mr. Spurgeon showed surprising ability, and delivered his theological arguements in a clear and agreeable voice, every word of his discourse being plainly heard in all parts of the church.

The text was taken from the first epistle general of John, 3rd chapter and 2nd verse, but Mr. Spurgeon confined his remarks to the first line of the verse, "Beloved, now are we the sons of God." He did not think they should look more to the future than to the past that evening, but rather glance at what they had passed through, and at their present state, for "now are we the sons of God." Like tired excursionists, who had attained the top of a hill which had afforded a great deal of pleasure, those who felt that they were the sons and daughters of God could look back upon the path on which they had journeyed with pleasure.

Many of them could look back upon their past lives, and recognise the hand of God their heavenly father who had plucked them away from the paths of sin, by leading them, perhaps, to attend different places of worship, and hear various ministers. In that respect they would look back with pleasure, and praise God for lifting them out of wrath to love Him, and this showed the wondrous love of their Father, who brought them into His family and called them His children. There were privileges and responsibilities connected with the family of God which none of them should lose sight of. For the privilege of being one of his family they might be content to serve God, who was the great Master of all; and yet, although He was their Master, still they had the right to appeal to Him as their Father for were they not instructed by the Saviour when they prayed to say, "Our Father who art in Heaven"?

The angels of God delighted to do His bidding, but the angels could not call Him their Father, and in that respect the people on earth enjoyed a greater privilege by a closer relationship to the Almighty. The angels worshiped God with their faces veiled, and could not talk to him as the people on earth could. Although the people of this world were once children of wrath, heirs of perdition, and sons of sin, yet "now we are the sons of God," a fact still more wondrous, which should make them feel joyful for having obtained an inheritance, and show to their Father their full appreciation of His kindness and goodness towards them by loving Him with all their heart, soul and spirit.

Whilst preaching to the congregation before him, he (Mr. Spurgeon) was preaching to himself. In knowing that they were the sons of God they might become indifferent and wander from the proper course through sluggish inactivity and callousness. They should, therefore, be active and energetic in loving their Father and doing what they could to get others to become members of His family too. In spite of all the differences that they manifested towards God, they were still His sons and His daughters, although they must confess in their calm moments that they did not love God as sons and daughters had a right to, and they must acknowledge that they were not as dutiful as they should be.

The honor and dignity of the title which they could lay claim to was still more a cause to make them wonder at the goodness of, and be proud of the Almighty. They were frail creatures, and it was to them Christ came and gave that blessed privilege of calling them their elder brother, and his Father their Father. It was rather pleasing at the present hour to know that they were the sons of God, and yet they were promised in the Scriptures something more, for "it doth not yet appear what we shall be, but we know when He shall appear, we shall be like him, for we shall see Him as He is."

They could then rejoice that they were the sons of God. He urged them to grasp the privilege and to avail themselves of the opportunity whilst it presented itself of testifying to their Father their true love for Him. They had not to wait until the other side of the grave, but to rejoice now that they were the sons of God; and all that they were asked to do as to love, honor, and obey their Father, to serve Him in spirit and in truth. The relationship between them and God was an abiding one. Once a son, a son forever. Although they sinned often against the Father, still God cherished them as His children, and true repentance met with forgiveness.

The more they felt that they were God's children the more they would be inclined to serve the Father, and it was wrong for them to suppose that because God called them His sons they could treat Him with indifference. Those who did so would receive their punishment, whilst those who followed His advice would receive their reward in Heaven, as the text promised. The sonship led to heirship. There was a future, still unrevealed. Sonship was only a preliminary step to something higher, for which all should strive. There was a place in Heaven, at the right hand of the Father prepared for them, and as they were His sons on earth, they would be His heirs in Heaven.

The drunken father, who beat his child, and dealt harshly with him, had still a tender regard for his offspring, and when in his sober moments would fondle and caress his child. But how much better was the love of God their Heavenly Father, who could do no wrong. God loved those who did His bidding, and attended to their every want; for, although hidden from their sight, they still had the blessed assurance that they were His sons and had the privilege of asking from Him what they required.

Parents separated from their children desired to see them again, and have them in their company. Well, God saw His children, and although not seen by them, was ever ready to grant them what they asked for, and after a time He took them to Himself, so that they might see and love Him in His heavenly kingdom.

As children were taught to obey their earthly parents, so the children of the Heavenly Father should learn to love Him who attended to all their wants. God wanted them to assist Him, and said "My sons, come work in my vineyard," and they should obey this command if they wished to enjoy the fruits of their labour and love in a future and better state. They should show their likeness to God by loving all those who belonged to the same family. There was not a sadder sight in the world than that which presented itself by members of the same family falling out with themselves.

They must not be ashamed of their relationship; there were times in their lives when they felt most ashamed of being called a Christian. This was decidedly wrong, for it should be their greatest pride, to be called a son of God, and a Christian. They were to become sons of God by obeying the teachings of their Father, and striving to their utmost strength to serve the Lord their God with all their hearts.[10]

Carefully Tom folded the long news clipping and included it in the letter he wrote that week to his parents. But he had not slept at all after that service on Sunday night. Somehow that surprise in this new land had not only been the greatest he had experienced, but also the most troubling. Was this to be God's plan? Was he to be a preacher, now, after all, so far away from England and home? The program he had planned did not include such tasks. A few years here, using his artistic skills in a free-lance manner—perhaps even a small engraving business of his own—this was all he envisaged. What did the Lord mean by thrusting such an unasked for and unanticipated experience as this upon him? Still, he was thankful for his experience of spiritual life and service from his earliest years. The discovery of personal faith through his mother's quiet witness, the prayer meetings he and Charles had organized among the boys at Mrs. Olding's school in Brighton,[11] and the Bollingbroke mission services—all these had helped him aquit himself well tonight.

But he was also aware of the immensity of the task he had faced a few hours before. Who was he to proclaim the Word of God to settlers in this exciting new land? He was not yet twenty-one, and boldly declaring mature matters which seemed, at this juncture, beyond his ability to grasp, or to communicate! But what a service it had been! What a clear sense of God's Spirit seemed to mingle with the tears and smiles of all! How graciously so many had spoken, not just about his father, but also thanking God for *him*! At last he settled down, but not before opening his Bible for a final brief devotion of the day. His gaze never got past the flyleaf, for there, in his father's big, bold, black handwriting, was the memorial text given to him at his baptism, two years back. He remembered his confession of faith before the vast Tabernacle throng. Again he saw his brother Charles affirm his own faith, and heard the call of his father's words as he himself stepped forward. He traced the words now written before him: "ye are not your own, for ye are bought with a price: therefore glorify God in your body, and in your spirit, which are God's."[12]

Pensive, Tom closed the black cover of the Bible, breathed a quick prayer of fresh surrender to God's will, and tried to rest. Insomnia, an unusual companion, pestered him for hours. As the weary minutes of the night ticked away, he pondered on the Providence that brought him across half a world to face the challenge of that evening, which had so surprisingly blessed him. He slept fitfully until the early morning hours and awoke about 7 AM to find the morning sunshine streaming through the window and across the counterpane. But William Cowper's dramatic lines sang sharply in his memory, just as they had in those last moments of consciousness before he finally had slept:

> God moves in a mysterious way
> His wonders to perform;
> He plants His footsteps in the sea,
> And rides upon the storm.

*   *   *

Geelong nestled among gently sloping hills thirty-nine miles southwest of the larger port of Melbourne. Now a center for wood and grain sales for the London market and a place of woolen mills, tanneries, iron workshops, factories, and general commerce, she was a busy and gracious lady. Wide, shaded streets bracketed fine brown sandstone mansions in the upper levels of the town. Two Roman Catholic, three Anglican, six Presbyterian, and ten Wesleyan churches served a citizenry totaling 120,000. The numerous tall spires proclaimed a city in which faith was prominent. Aberdeen Street Baptist Church began in 1849. The church began by Baptists in Fenwick Street in 1852 fell on such hard times by the 1860s that Charles Andrews had bought their building to preserve its existence and allowed the congregation to pay back the debt over several years. By 1876 matters improved so much at the original location that a second and larger building of commodious local bluestone arose beside the original, and became known henceforth as the *New* Aberdeen Street Baptist Church. Two other healthy groups also developed in the suburban areas of the city, making four Baptist causes in all.

With such a large Christian constituency, the gatherings associated with Thomas's twenty-first birthday in Geelong seem less surprising. On Thursday, September 20, 1877, 200 invited guests celebrated his coming of age at a banquet offered in his honor at the Aberdeen Street Church. Five hundred gathered for the public meeting which followed. Speakers included some of his father's former students now pastoring in the colony, who had known Tom from infancy, and Charles Andrews, a former schoolmate of his father's. Mr. Andrews presented Tom with a fifteen-jewel gold watch to mark the occasion. Tom's remarks in response were both jocular and serious. He kidded about visiting the mining districts the week before while he was still a *minor*, and testified to his own faith as being discovered through his mother's quiet teaching, and his father's clear witness.[13]

When C. H. Spurgeon responded to Tom's cable announcing his safe arrival he included, along with birthday congratulations, the news that he had himself been invited to Australia by that same mail. He seemed grateful to have a son there to represent him, as he felt convinced he should refuse that invitation because of the tasks which anchored him in London. Knowing nothing, at that stage, of the turn of events which had thrust Tom into a preaching ministry, he wrote:

> Give them the Gospel. Study all you can, preach boldly and let your behaviour be with great discretion, as indeed I am sure it will be. . . . You will, I trust, find the Lord open up ways and means for you to see the country and do good and get good.[14]

The Ballarat *Courier* praised Tom's sermon in that city on September 10.[15] Reports in the press at Bendigo, and in other Victorian towns, described him as exhibiting "much originality, humour, and force,"[16] and as "possessing great confidence, and a good command of language and earnestness,"[17] although still a young man. They noted his lucidity of thought and clarity of vocal projection, even among large assemblies.[18] The state government operated railroads to Bendigo and Ballarat, using comfortable cars designed after the fashion of the best European and American models. Tom's travel was inexpensive, as a member of parliament had presented him with a free pass over the entire state system.[19]

Gideon Rutherford, a strong supporter of the Aberdeen Street Church, invited Tom to accompany Pastor Bunning for an extended visit to Quambatook, his country residence, immediately after the twenty-first birthday celebrations concluded. The family lived for most of the year on this vast sheep station, thirty miles west of the rapidly growing country town of Kerang. Mrs. Rutherford, desiring believers' baptism, wished to confess her faith among friends and neighbors in the district where she lived for most of the year. Pastor Bunning agreed to administer the ordinance. He and Tom boarded the Cobb and Company coach late in the afternoon, knowing that a full night's travel lay before them. The journey involved a total of twenty-five horses, and four stops en route. The two men passed much of the time in agreeable conversation.

"You asked about Reverend George Slade, our pioneer missionary in the Kerang district," Bunning began. "He is an amazing fellow. Raised on a farm in England, and converted at nineteen, he studied at Bristol College, and came out to this colony in 1858, at the invitation of the Baptist Missionary Society. He has been a faithful pastor of our Fenwick Street Church but just this year responded to the invitation to lead the new Baptist Bush Mission, which is part of our denominational outreach plan to evangelize this great state. Already he has established Baptist fellowships in Kerang, and in other places. Do you know that he walks out to Quambatook and many other scattered townships around here to bring some ministry to folks who otherwise are totally neglected? Mr. Rutherford has recently given him a horse, and he is known far and wide as a loving and effective pastor. The Rutherfords have begun an association with our Geelong Church largely through Mr. Slade's efforts, and Mr. Rutherford, who is really quite wealthy, has given some large gifts for your father's orphanage work which I have forwarded on to him in London."[20]

"Tell me about Quambatook," urged Tom. "What is a sheep station, and what on earth is a squatter?"

Bunning laughed. "I'm sure they do seem strange words to an English ear. A *station* does not mean a railroad stop—in fact there is yet no track laid to Quambatook. It simply means a large sheep run, usually totaling many thousands of acres; I guess our American cousins would call it a ranch, but it is far, far larger than any ranch I know of, and than any 100 sheep farms in England. Each station has its own character, but most were started from unauthorized settlement by ex-convicts.

"After the 1830s, men of wealth began investing heavily in the raising of wool. The name squatter remains now for any authorized sheep farmer who pays ten pounds for the right to graze on as yet unsurveyed and undeveloped land. Year by year more and more land is carved up and sold to selectors for more permanent development. But anyone who is willing to live there, buy a minimum of land, and invest his time and money in the surrounding acreage, is allowed to "squat" with government approval, particularly in the far country areas.

"In the countryside the squatter is king. Usually they have a central piece of legally-owned land and upon them many build elaborate houses. Some have huge ballrooms, where they entertain friends from the city for gala vacations. Many homes possess all the comforts money can buy. They feature large sweeping driveways and parklands, timbered lawns, wide, cool verandas, and cool summer houses. The forms and fashions of England have been established by a social aristocracy here in this colony, although we are still so young. Many squatters keep very elaborate homes also in the city. Even Mr. Rutherford has a holiday cottage at Lake Como, just out of Geelong."

"I know that," responded Tom. "He has invited me to spend a few weeks there next year."

"You will enjoy that, I'm sure," the pastor replied. "The whole area is cooler than Geelong. The heat out here is almost unbearable in the peak of summer, so the Rutherfords certainly need a place like that. We are always glad when they come, because we see them then regularly in the Aberdeen Street services."

"Is Rutherford very affluent then?" Tom queried.

"By normal standards I suppose so," Bunning responded, with obvious hesitation in his voice. "But don't think he is as some others are. Gideon Rutherford learned his farming in the rigorous winters of Scotland. He proved his capacities in the south of our state for many years before locating here. When they began Quambatook it was a primitive settlement. Now it gleams as a place of great charm and beauty."

"What do you mean by primitive?"

"Well, when a settler opens up country like this the work is rugged. Now the Rutherfords live right beside the fertile flats of the Avoca River, but they began in the north end of the property. Rough timber sheds roofed with bark still stand where they first settled. Beginning sheep farmers often start with rough mud-brick farm buildings, and bush camp conditions. They use pine wood tables with split-log benches, and every other inconvenience for living you can imagine. Nowadays the Rutherfords employ a station manager and a whole group of jackaroos [ranch hands] to herd the sheep. But when they began, believe me, it was all hard uphill sweat and struggle.

"A squatter's lot is still far from easy when you consider some of his problems. Properties must be huge, as it takes from one to three acres of natural grasses just to feed one sheep! And the men and dogs needed to move huge numbers out to graze and back to water are expensive, and often hard to obtain and retain. Sheep wander off. Lambs die. Shearers arrive late. And the bullocks pulling all the needed supplies from the south take their own sweet time about traveling.

"And what about the wild dingoes [dogs] who savage the young lambs? Huge grass seeds injure the wool, working their way into the sheep's sensitive skin. Maggots are blown by the bush flies into the slightest cut or scratch. Poisonous grasses may kill a whole flock. Mice, grasshoppers, and rabbits often breed in plague proportions. Past seasons and droughts dry up feed and water, and sometimes the bush fires race through, leaving incredible damage. The vegetable gardens die in the summer heat. The pale, powdery dust cakes your clothes, your eyes, your ears and your tongue, and almost everything else in sight."

"You mean the sheep farmer puts up with all of this, and works all that land, seldom owning anything but a small part of it?"

"Exactly! So don't let anyone tell you that these affluent men have not earned their wealth. And I haven't yet mentioned all the problems associated with the actual sheep breeding, doctoring, and wool-selling. There's also the hiring, feeding, and supervision of the shearers, who travel from property to property during the season. The bookkeeping tasks alone on a normal station will usually involve one man full time, and another one or two part time! If children need educating, their mother has to be teacher, and she has to be the doctor as well. Every station carries a stock of homeopathic remedies. Every woman in the bush must have some skill at setting a broken leg, and in nursing an injured stockman. Most squatters are constantly in debt to the wool brokers and merchants who finally wholesale their clippings. All year they depend on these financiers to bankroll the whole operation. Often, little is left when these costs finally are deducted from the sales check."

Tom grew quiet for some minutes. He thought how easily he and his mother had purchased a woolen coat or some yarn for a sweater over the counter of one of the drapery stores in London, without thinking of all that lay behind their availability. He took a moment to relax and enjoy the coach ride. These Cobb and Company vehicles, imported from America, were indeed far superior to the English bone shakers! Leather springs improved the ride.

The change to fresh horses every ten miles improved the pace. These coachmen possessed great skill. They could steer around the road ruts, and skate down the steep hills and gullies, with an aplomb that astonished him.

He gazed out the window in the gathering dusk at the long, low hills that glided past him as they drove. The graceful white limbs of the eucalyptus trees reflected some of the pale pearls and pinks of the setting sun. Earlier he had seen rabbits, goanna lizards, and an occasional wallaby or two in the distance, as they journeyed. He laughed out loud at the remembrance of the ungainly pair of emus which had raced beside the coach a few miles back, mesmerized by its movement. The enormous flocks of ibis and waterfowl nesting among the reeds in the creeks and lakes surprised him, but not so much as the maniacal laughter of the kookaaburras, perched in the high gum trees saluting the passing of the day. Croaking crows circling the carcass of some bush animal were not new to him. These he had seen at home many times. This strange country, so young, yet seemingly so ancient, caught him unaware at every turn.

As the dark shadows of the night finally closed, he gazed with interest at a group of drivers camping by the side of the road. They were boiling a billy of tea to accompany their evening meal. Tom remembered that the bullock wagons they directed provided a lifeline for these far-flung bush communities.

After a late breakfast in Kerang, Mr. Bunning stood with him on the long veranda of the hotel. He smiled broadly at a tall gray-haired horseman dismounting at 10 AM, precisely as he had promised.

"Mr. Rutherford, this is Tom Spurgeon!"

"God bless you, Mr. Spurgeon," came the warm response, thick with a Scottish burr. "Welcome to Kerang, and soon to Quambatook." Within a few moments Tom and Mr. Bunning were seated in the double buggy behind the station hand who had driven in with Mr. Rutherford. They set off at a smart pace, their host riding ahead on a slim-legged black stallion. Tom admired the horse's wine-red saddle, silver harness, and tightly-trimmed mane, and other obvious signs of special attention for what seemed to be a favorite animal. He watched the grace and ease with which Rutherford sat, thinking, *Well, here is a man who is no city squatter. He is obviously a man of the land, from his broad-brimmed hat to his jackaroo boots. I'll warrant that Quambatook will be outstanding in its efficiency and production.* And so it proved to be.

They soon covered the thirty miles, crossed the Loddon River bridge, and approached the long tree-lined driveway leading to the Quambatook homestead. On the journey, he saw flock after flock of sulphur-crested white cockatoos and pink and gray galahs, wild parrots of the Australian bush. Usually a group of 100 or so would be feeding in a field beside the road as the buggy approached. Long before the sound of its wheels could alert them the whole flock would wheel off into the bright blue sky as if under some specific command. From the station hand he learned how each group placed two or three of their number as lookouts in two directions, and that their movements came in response to signals given by these sentinels.

"The Quambatook children have tamed two or three bush parrots, as you will see, Mr. Spurgeon. They talk and dance, and will perch on your wrist for a cracker biscuit and ask you if you 'want a cup of tea?'" their driver said, "We estimate old Baldy, as we call him, is about forty! He has no head feathers left, and very few body feathers—in fact he almost looks like a living plucked chicken! But I have heard of some cockatoos living to seventy years!"

They pulled into the driveway before a stately Victorian homestead, set amid shady trees, with cool, iron-pillared verandas wrapping around three of its sides. To the left a quiet rose garden led to the wide river flowing gently several hundred yards away. A well-filled vegetable plot and a copper sundial graced by a small lily pond, completed the setting. Honeysuckle and some bush wildflowers struggled over the chimney walls on the shadiest side of the home. The whole scene suggested peaceful relaxation and a grace somewhat unexpected this far out into the country.

Mrs. Rutherford greeted them at the front door, and ushered them along the hallway and into a comfortable bedroom which the two visitors would share. On the way, Tom noted the walnut hat and umbrella stand, obviously an English import. Passing the dining room he glimpsed a massive cedar sideboard, a marble-topped chiffonier, and a spacious oak table ringed with twelve blue upholstered chairs. "Why, this *is* a quality place," he muttered to himself.

As they went into the sitting room for hot scones and tea, his glance fell on the rosewood cottage pianoforte with its gold escutcheon, proclaiming it to be manufactured by Broadwood and Sons. The range of wool-fringed rugs underfoot, the gleaming silverware and crystal on the sideboard, and the tall kerosene lamps, complete with buxom lamp glasses etched in delicate floral designs, impressed him even more. "I could be sitting in my dear mother's London living room amid such surroundings!" he exclaimed.

"We do try to be as comfortable as possible," Mr. Rutherford responded, "But these touches reflect my wife's finesse. These drapes, and most of the children's clothes, as well as some of her own, are the products of her skill with the new Singer sewing machine!"

Just then the Rutherford children trooped in to be presented to the visitors. Tom glanced with approval as they ranged in front of the fireplace. He laughed with them as the Ansonia clock on the mantel behind them suddenly buried all conversation amid a torrent of chimes. The eldest girl, Lila, a mass of gingham and giggles, with tightly braided hair and a saucy smile, captured his interest immediately. She possessed a pair of lustrous eyes which seemed to dart everywhere at once. At all of twelve years, she was obviously the queen of the little tribe, and the delight of both her parents.

When the introductions were complete and the children had returned to their play, Lila's face and presence seemed to linger in Tom's memory. Perhaps it was that bubbling energy she seemed to exude. He was unsure. Certainly he had no presumption at that time of all that this chance meeting would portend for them both in the years ahead.

After a restful night, Tom awoke to the haunting sounds of currawongs and the early-morning cackle of kookaburras, high in the trees outside his window. After a quick wash from the china jug and bowl in his room he presented himself in the kitchen at 7 AM, as instructed, for a breakfast almost as hearty as the dinner of the evening before. Hot Scottish porridge and bacon and eggs tasted superb as his appetite awoke to the briskness of the fresh morning air.

The big station kitchen featured a walk-in pantry, a safe, a mincing machine [grinder], and a brick oven. Through a doorway leading to the yard he glimpsed a corner of the outdoor laundry, with its large mangle mounted between two galvanized iron tubs beside a bricked-in copper boiler. After breakfast he strolled the great veranda for half an hour, enjoying the cool of its iron-roofed shade and the sweet scents of its climbing vines. Later, Rutherford found him in a lattice chair, among Mrs. Rutherford's ferns and potted plants, quietly rocking away, while several of the younger children played fetch and carry with the soft-eyed brown kelpie pup who had adopted Tom as a new companion.

"Time for you to see the property!" Rutherford beckoned. "Let's take a walk around the home paddock together." Tom scratched a few horses' noses, glared back at the bull, and then found himself entering a large shed with a high-pitched roof, surrounded by what seemed to be an almost endless chain of fenced yards.

"This is one of the largest woolsheds in the colony," Rutherford boasted. "We have twenty-three shearing pens, and have shorn 64,000 animals in one season!" On every side the bleating of the animals mingled with the shouts of the shearers. Some called for a fleece to be collected for the wool classer's table. Others shouted for a tar boy to bring his pot to dab a bleeding animal where the shears had slipped and cut the skin.

Tom learned that the sheep were well dipped with disease-preventative chemicals after the fleece was removed. He also realized that they were glad to be rid of their winter overcoats by the time summer came. An outer shed housed the bale presses. Beside this stood a small loading dock where the 400-pound bales could easily be winched onto the huge flat wagons later to be pulled to Geelong by a ten-bullock team. He learned that the shearers and wool classers were the aristocrats of labor in the bush and that the huge shed, so busy now with the bustle and hustle of shearing, only came to life for a few short weeks in each year.

"They work in expert teams, traveling across the country from one station to another," Rutherford told him. "We pay twenty shillings for each 100 sheep sheared, some men can even earn twenty-five shillings a day. We demand strict order in the woolsheds. I'll have no alcohol, or swearing, or fighting. Sometimes things get out of hand, as they always will with a bunch of tough men. But, in general, they are a pretty cooperative lot. You'll get a chance to preach to them Sunday!"

Tom soon learned that there were many hearts of gold, easily touched by the gospel, among these hard-faced men. Several evenings during the week he came as a welcome guest to their camp fires, enjoying the yarns they spun, and listening to their comments about Mr. Rutherford and about the station provisions. Food was the major topic of most discussions. Apparently the squatter provided sugar, flour, tea, mutton, pickles, jam, boots, shorts, and shoes from the station store, while they served in his employ. The men brought their own Chinese cook, whose constant concern was finding enough onions for the soup and enough currants for the cake. The men termed his supper offering *Railway Cake*, because they said the currants in it were "as scarce as stations on a country railroad."[21]

The days passed rapidly, full of pleasant company and good fellowship. On

Sunday morning the whole station complement gathered at a quiet bend of the Avoca River, behind the homestead, for Mrs. Rutherford's immersion. Shaded by the weeping willows and framed by the tall reeds at the river's edge, the ceremony was natural and moving. Tom offered prayer before Mr. Bunning administered the ordinance.[22] His petition not only sought blessing on her confession, but also asked that the children might find a faith of their own in the years which stretched ahead.

Mr. Bunning preached that morning. Tom's chance came in the evening. Many of the shearers stood quietly in the cool darkness, just outside the range of light streaming from the veranda, as he gave a strong gospel message. Tom could not see their faces, but was reminded of their presence by the glow of the men's pipes. With the meeting completed, several dozen came by to shake the young preacher's hand and express appreciation for "them good words from the good Book, Guv'nor," or to share some similar expression of awkward thankfulness for his presence.

Later, Tom remarked on the fine collection of volumes which overflowed the fireplace bookshelves. Mr. Rutherford was pleased. "Yes, Tom, you see we have some Shakespeare, all of Sir Walter Scott's novels, *Henry and Scott's Bible Commentary*, and some volumes of the *Sunday Magazine*. These are all our favorites. And I always read one of your father's sermons, from the half-dozen volumes of the *Metropolitan Tabernacle Pulpit* you see we have there, for our Sunday morning devotions. We seldom have a minister of any denomination to visit with us, so we go to church with C. H. Spurgeon, mostly! I am not a great preacher, but I certainly have preached some great sermons by reading those to my family, and to some of the permanent station hands, over these years!"

Tom knew that he would never forget the colorful experiences of those days, especially the impromptu camp fire concerts outside the shearers' huts in the evenings. He had even been encouraged to sing an old English song for them, accompanied by a wheezing concertina and a strumming Jew's harp. They had listened well to his stories of his father's London ministries and to his own testimony of faith.

The rough swagmen, itinerant farm workers, who came regularly to the homestead back door asking for a handout had frightened him at first. Later, he appreciated their willingness to chop firewood or to perform some other chore in exchange for a bed in the shearer's hut and a simple meal. Occasionally one would fix a broken sheep pen, or dig the vegetable patch for a little flour and meat to roll up into his blanket swag. Tom admired the carefree way in which each swagman would depart, hoisting the blanket roll (always affectionately termed *Matilda*), and waltz off down the road. Occasionally he envied their cabbage-tree hats, not only for the shade they offered, but for the efficient manner in which bobbed corks on strings, with which they ringed the rims, kept away the flies. He had never seen so many flies as he saw in five minutes at Quambatook! Sometimes they were so thick on a man's back they gave the appearance of an ink blot stretching between his shoulder blades, or a huge black collar dropped six inches below the neckline. Well, that was one Australian wonder he would never miss when he returned home to England!

The last day of his stay remained the most pleasant memory of all. Lila insisted on riding with her new English uncle to a gentle slope several miles behind the house. There they picnicked on a huge sandstone outcrop that stretched like a giant finger across the river, enjoying the wild budgerigars and parakeets that swooped and swung from the branches of the overhanging willows on the bank.

As the evening shadows fell, they rode homeward to the melancholy sounds of bush magpies, and paused at the gate to turn aside to a well-kept corner where she pointed out a tombstone. "See," she said with quiet affection, "I picked some daisies today for my sister's grave. She was accidentally killed when our kangaroo-hunting dog knocked her down during a rabbit chase, just before Christmas nine years ago. Agnes was eight, and I was then only four. I barely remember her. But I *do* remember how hard it was for Dad to read the burial service, because we had no pastor way out here then." She smiled quickly at him, "We'll all be at Lake Como for the summer's end. Will we see you then in Geelong?" "I hope so, indeed I hope so—in fact we must agree to see each other again!" Tom smiled, surprising himself with his enthusiasm.

That evening his sleep was filled with dreams of Lila's glowing complexion and pert, poised personality. She was bright, sweet in disposition, and altogether innocent of her fragile beauty just beginning to bloom. In the morning, try as he might, he could not escape from the disturbing maturity with which she seemed to look clear through him as he took his farewells.

And Lila swung pensively on the garden gate for a full twenty minutes after the buggy drove away, gazing intently at the swirling dust rising from the horses' hooves as they clopped into the distance.

At Kerang Tom asked Mr. Rutherford to wait while he dashed into the local grocery for a bright red tin filled with delicious candies. Quickly he thrust a card into the paper sack before handing it to his host to take back to Quambatook: "To the bairns who stole our heart."[23] Quite the proper thing to do under the circumstances.

But he told no one of the first card he had written, now crushed in his jacket pocket, where that good Scottish word for children had first been written as *lass*. "What on earth prompted me to do that?" he worried. It looked all right when first he had written it, yet he still blushed now at the thought of how it could have been interpreted. "She is but a child," he remembered, "and nine years my junior! The thought is preposterous! I must remove all trace of it from my mind."

* * *

But Lila of the laughing eyes remained with him. How was he to know that they would meet again after eleven years? And how could he imagine that one day he would see those bright orbs reproduced in the luminous faces of three little bairns of his own?

2 His Bright Designs
(1878-1881)

Deep in unfathomable mines
Of never-failing skill,
He treasures up His bright designs,
And works His sov' reign will.

om promised to return to Geelong for the twenty-sixth anniversary services of the Aberdeen Street Church scheduled for November 20. Mr. Bunning, pleased at the extent of Tom's reception six weeks before, booked the spacious Mechanics' Institute for the services. He reasoned that his own church would be inadequate for the occasion. One thousand gathered for the public meeting and anniversary tea on the Monday evening. Eight hundred had attended the 11 AM service the day before, and between 1,200 and 1,300 on the Sunday evening.[1]

Tom's addresses concerned the themes of God's blessings and pardon, materials he repeated in the weeks ahead many times. He complained, in a letter to his father, that fresh sermons came with great difficulty: "I never see a commentary, and rarely get sufficient time to prepare as I like. On the other hand there is this to be said, that going about as I do I need not hesitate to redeliver sermons."[2]

By November 24, Tom commenced an eight-week itineration in and around the city of Adelaide, South Australia. Experiences included a visit to preach to the Cornish miners in the copper ore center of Moonta in the Upper Yorke peninsular. The majority of residents were Bible Christians and Wesleyans, as befitted their Cornish ancestry. They had experienced a great religious revival three years prior to Tom's coming.[3]

Salvation Army and Baptist ministries were also there in strength and the interdenominational sense of evangelical fellowship was high. In announcing a special service one Methodist brother stated, "Addresses will be given by Salvation Army Cap'n and Baptist minister—and I tell'ee, when Salvation fire and Baptist water do get together tedden long before steam's up!"[4]

In such an environment Tom's welcome was hearty. The *Moonta Advertiser* stated, "He has found himself welcomed for his father's sake and liked for his own."[5]

A large open-air service led him to tell his parents that

> We had a blessed season beneath a clear Australian sky, among the gum trees,[6]

39

and to exclaim with delight about the bright moonlight which had enabled those from long distances to drive to and from the district gathering. On Sunday January 13, 1878, he preached to overflow crowds in the Adelaide Town Hall, and the following evening to a large gathering at the Flinders Street Baptist Church, also in that city.[7]

Letters from that period also tell of his delight that his father had added his name alongside his twin brother's on the roll of preachers sent out from the Tabernacle membership.[8] C. H. Spurgeon rejoiced at the ministries which so suddenly had opened up for his Australian son. He declared that he was overwhelmed at Tom's reception, taking this as a token of the acceptance his father's works had among the people.[9]

Journeying to the island of Tasmania, approximately 300 miles south of Melbourne, in late January, Tom wrote his father describing the pleasant week he had just spent again with the Rutherfords. This time he had been with them at their vacation home at Lake Como, outside of Geelong.[10] But he carefully avoided all mention of Lila to his father.

Just outside of the city of Launceston, in northern Tasmania, there lived a remarkable lady, an avid lover of C. H. Spurgeon's writings since her youth. Mary Ann Gibson, wife of William Gibson, Sr., had an evangelical experience of faith through the reading of the London pastor's sermons, while she was a girl in England. She emigrated to Tasmania to live with her uncle, Reverend Henry Dowling, Tasmania's pioneer pastor, then serving the York Street Baptist Church in Launceston.

In 1843 she married William Gibson, a faithful Presbyterian, then introduced him to her favorite author, and together they became active financial supporters of the London Tabernacle ministries. When William Gibson died at seventy-three in 1892, he was acknowledged as the single most dynamic factor in the facilitation of Baptist church life in Tasmania. For many years he served as honorary treasurer of the infant Baptist association of churches. His stewardship became directly responsible for the formation and establishment of many Baptist causes, and for the staffing of the majority of them with graduates of C. H. Spurgeon's Pastors' College. With his own personal funds he built chapels and manses, paid the fares of outcoming pastors, and generally bolstered the entire evangelical life of the infant denomination.[11]

Hearing that C. H. Spurgeon's son was in Australia, the Gibsons invited him to visit with them for an extended period. When first married, the Gibsons had journeyed once a month to the York Street Baptist Church in Launceston (where Reverend Henry Dowling, Mary's uncle still pastored) for some Baptist fellowship. But for most of the time they gleaned their spiritual nourishment at home through the reading of Spurgeon's sermons, since no evangelical church existed then in Perth, the town closest to their Native Point sheep property.

David Gibson, government stock inspector from Hobart, settled in the area in 1809. Being from Perthshire, he named the town Perth, and, in 1828 secured a government grant of 7,300 acres along fifteen miles of the River Esk. There he bred merino sheep and soon became one of the leading farmers of the colony. He raised eleven sons and established a family active in Tasmanian politics for many generations. William Gibson, Sr., was the fourth child. He settled at Native Point, two miles upriver from his father. By 1856 he occupied a typical sheep farmer's homestead of local brick set among shade trees by the riverbank.

Continuing the selective breeding techniques pioneered by his father, William Gibson quickly gained a reputation all over the South Pacific for his production of stud rams with slim bodies and an amazing thirty-five pounds of wool clip yield from a single animal. His prize merinos sold often for 1,000 guineas each, or more. Every year Gibson raised at least one champion to be sold so that the proceeds would build a new Baptist church, or otherwise help in some capital need for the Lord's work. After his death Mrs. Gibson continued this dramatic support. She lived to be ninety-seven, still affirming, in 1903, that she had read *all* of C. H. Spurgeon's over 3,000 sermons, and continued to read them, without glasses, even at that advanced age!

Originally known as Van Diemen's Land, the island of Tasmania was settled in 1804 as a dependency of the penal colony of New South Wales. For many years it continued under the direction of the authorities of Sydney, but was opened to free settlement in 1853. The capital city, Hobart, beautifully situated where the river Derwent meets the sea, quickly developed as a large shipping and commercial center.

J. Edgar arrived from Somerset as the Hobart town surveyor in 1837. An active Baptist, he often wrote to the Baptist Missionary Society, and to others in England, encouraging them to send out a Baptist missionary to link together the few Baptists in the colony, and to foster the growth of churches.

Eventually Henry Dowling arrived in Tasmania as the pioneer Baptist pastor. Born in Somerset in 1780, he had served a church at Colchester for twenty years. He came under his own charges, and mainly to visit a son who had emigrated to Launceston four years earlier. Dowling found a small group of Baptists in Hobart, including Edgar, and met with them for several weeks before journeying north. He arrived December 2, 1834 in Hobart, and held his first Baptist services in Launceston, in the local courthouse, on the last Sunday of that month. Dowling returned to Hobart in 1835 to assist in the formation of Harrington Street Church, and tried to visit with them once a quarter for encouragement in their early years. The Hobart Baptist Tabernacle eventually grew out of this fellowship. Dowling's work centered in Launceston. There he built what was known as the York Street Baptist Church in 1840. His son, Henry Dowling Jr., became a leading Launceston citizen, served as mayor, edited the *Launceston*

Advertiser, and founded the Launceston Bank for Savings.

Henry Dowling Sr., a short stocky man, filled with abundant energy, traveled all over the island, preaching the gospel from house to house, and baptizing converts in many of its rivers. The government appointed him chaplain to the convict chain gangs, and to be a special missionary to the poor in Launceston, voting him 150 pounds a year and forage for his horse in return for his counsel in these areas. He died in 1869 in Launceston in his eight-ninth year. This earnest, able servant of God was honored by many as an effective pastor, and for his caring representation of the poor.[12]

Something of Dowling's fervor and commitment, reproduced in his niece, overflowed into the life of William Gibson. He built a chapel in Perth, and gathered workers from the various properties and residents of the town into Baptist services in 1862. Eventually a Baptist church, the only one outside of Hobart and Launceston, was formed in 1870. By 1889 a commodious tabernacle, octagonal in shape, with a large dome, had been erected. A visiting missionary designed it to resemble an Indian mosque. Services still continue there today.

Tom's visits in 1878, and again in 1880, were directly responsible for the erection of the Perth Tabernacle, and for the increased sense of stewardship exercised by the Gibsons. They resolved to bring to the young colony a number of men trained in C. H. Spurgeon's Pastors' College, to build homes in which they could live, and assist in the erection of Baptist chapels where they could preach. The churches still flourishing—Latrobe, Longford, Deloraine, and Sheffield, as well as Perth, remain as contemporary testimonials of their generosity. It is estimated that they gave over 70,000 pounds to Baptist work in Tasmania, the equivalent of many millions of dollars today.[13]

During his 1878 visit, Tom greatly enjoyed the restful life at Native Point. There he found himself deeply challenged by fellow-guest Henry Varley, his father's old friend from London. Varley had trained at the Pastors' College, and established a great evangelical work among the poor at Notting Hill, called the West London Tabernacle. After twenty years of service there, he entered full-time evangelism. Part Plymouth Brother and part Baptist, very much like George Muller, another close friend of the elder Spurgeon, Varley was then conducting evangelistic meetings in northern Tasmania. Tom felt challenged by his dedication, and commented to his father:

> When I see Mr. Varley preaching every day, I almost wish I could do the same, and thus devote my life. Perhaps the time will come when this shall be my proper course (evangelizing), and if these quiet months spell be the preparation for it, who shall call it wasted time?[14]

The restful time with the Gibsons passed all too quickly, with boating on the river, horseback riding, and in helpful converse with Varley and others. One highlight of the period was a visit to Henry Reed, of Wesley Vale. Reed had led a profligate life almost from his arrival in the colony in 1826. Returning to England for a visit in 1831, he experienced a remarkable conversion, and upon his reestablishment in Launceston led in the foundation of a city mission outreach where he labored for many years. His city rescue work became known internationally. The Henry Reed Memorial Church still operates today, now housing a Baptist congregation.[15]

After a brief period in Sydney in July, Tom set out for Brisbane and a series of services in the state of Queensland. He had just completed a week of meetings held in the Sydney YMCA hall and planned to travel north by ship. Very few Baptist ministers have been ordained by the Australian Steam Navigation Company, but Thomas Spurgeon always claimed that this was his distinction! He tells us that, when booking his passage to Brisbane from Sydney, the clerk, after quoting the fare, said, "You ought to wear a white tie." When asked the reason, he told him that clergymen were entitled to reduced rates. After some argument, the clerk asked if he were willing to sign his name "Reverend." This, evidently, was the first time Tom had faced the matter practically. He answered that he *would* do so *if it came cheaper*. Debate continued in the office until someone declared that he had journeyed a considerable distance the evening before to hear Mr. Spurgeon and had been crowded out:

> This was pretty proof positive that I did preach, and it was decided to carry the important matter to the manager for settlement. He pronounced in my favour, and from this day forth, and even for evermore, a man can be a minister in the eyes of the Australian Steam Navigation Co. without wearing a white tie![16]

This seems to be the only ordination ever given him!

Tom enjoyed the brief sea journey, the fifteen-mile trip up the river to Brisbane, and the warm welcome offered by many friends gathered to greet him. The School of Arts was filled at Ipswich. The sign said "Standing Room Only" at the Baptist chapel in south Brisbane. He gathered audiences of 1,000 and more in week-night meetings in the city. Other large crowds heard the gospel at Warwick, Toowoomba, and in the Brisbane town hall.[17] At Ipswich he met his father's old coachman George Coulson, and enjoyed his surprise in the discovery that Thomas was the one preaching in Australia, and not his brother Charles.[18] At Warwick, on August 26, a cablegram telling of his mother's severe illness summoned him unexpectedly home,[19] but not before he had preached a fine sermon on the seashore at Sandgate with his congregation seated on the sloping cliffs.[20] Reverend J. J. Voller, whose exciting shipwreck story Tom had read so often with such interest, was the Sandgate pastor then, active with an energy well beyond his years.[21]

Gideon Rutherford came to Melbourne to bid Tom farewell on September 12, when he sailed on the *Lusitania*.[22] Bad weather so delayed the ship's journey that he failed to arrive in Adelaide for the Sunday evening service he was scheduled to address on September 15. Instead he spoke to crowded congregations there on the Monday and Tuesday evenings.[23]

Mrs. Spurgeon had unexpectedly recovered from her critical indisposition before her son had reached England, but on Sunday November 10, 1878, Tom suddenly was called to preach the Metropolitan Tabernacle services in his father's place. Tom aquitted himself so well that he was asked to return for two Sundays following.[24] C. H. Spurgeon's illness came with such fierceness that he was forced to leave the Tabernacle pulpit entirely for three months. Father and son journeyed to the town of Mentone, on the French coast, where the elder Spurgeon rested his painful arthritis and gout, and supervised Tom's theological studies in preparation for an accelerated entry into the Pastors' College when they returned. Together they worked through Hodge's *Outlines of Theology,* while his father directed Tom's wider reading in politics, history, and literature. While there they met George Muller and Hudson Taylor, who both visited the recovering patient. Tom refused an invitation received while he was at Mentone to travel to America for further preaching opportunities. He desired most of all to remain in England and work alongside his father.[25]

By April of 1879 they were both back in London. C. H. Spurgeon had recovered sufficiently to preach again and Tom eagerly enrolled in the college theological course work. From his own experiences of Australian ministry the young student now evaluated his father's service with a greater understanding and fresh admiration.

The elder Spurgeon continues to be acknowledged by authorities as the mightiest preacher since the apostle Paul.[26] A 1934 comment states:

> A careful estimate (quoted by Dr. Carlisle) shows that Spurgeon preached to at least 10,000,000 people. He received into his church between ten and twelve thousand converts. His sermons were read by at least 40,000,000 people. The best of them (for they are not all equally good) have been translated into 23 languages. In all 3563 of the sermons were printed. Four hundred ministers from his college are on the list of accredited Baptist ministers in Britain. All the colonies (and especially our own) and every mission field have been enriched by men who owed their souls and their skill to this man.[27]

By 1934 some 130,000 copies of his seven-volume commentary on Psalms, the *Treasury of David,* were in circulation. Three hundred thousand volumes of his *John Ploughman's Pictures* and 50,000 of his *Lectures to My Students* had also been distributed. In the almost fifty years since that date Spurgeon's works have been reprinted again and again. Pilgrim Publications of Texas has republished the entire set of sixty-three volumes of the *New Park Street Pulpit,* and the *Metropolitan Tabernacle Pulpit.* Today C. H. Spurgeon still has more titles in print, among more publishers, than any other theological writer of the past or present,[28] and the demand continues.

Many factors enter into Spurgeon's greatness. Although a typical nonconformist of the lower middle class in society, C. H. Spurgeon undoubtedly possessed a keen intellect. He supported this by very wide reading, and a mastery of the works of the great Puritan divines. His own personal library totaled 12,000 volumes. He mastered Latin, Greek, and French, and carried off prizes in most subjects while in Maidstone and Newmarket schools. Spurgeon's extensive literary knowledge is reflected again and again in his sermons, and matched only by his extraordinary illustrative skill. His style reflected an independence of thought, an outspokenness, and a refreshing humor. In an age of flowery pulpit eloquence, when many preachers read dry-as-dust theological essays in the pulpit, Spurgeon dared to speak to the common man in a common tongue. He reached all classes and conditions of men because his approach was concrete, colloquial, and biblically simple. He worked extraordinarily hard, often putting in an eighteen-hour day. Conscious of the rhetorical abstractions so common to Victorian preaching, he openly attacked "tame phrases, hackneyed expressions, and dreary monotones."[29]

Spurgeon worked hard on the practice of vocal projection making his enunciation and articulation superb enough to be heard by many thousands without amplification. The Tabernacle services gathered up to 6,000 on most Sundays, in the mornings and again in the evenings. Two or three thousand others would also be often gathered for the two prayer services he directed during most weeks at the Tabernacle. His Thursday evening addresses delivered to them were every bit as thorough, and memorable, as his Sunday sermons.

The London pastor nurtured his rhetoric on Christian hymns and the old Puritan writers. He became a master of the English tongue who observed, collected, and created imaginative forms of expression. Many sermons show a clear understanding of sense appeal images. Above all his own faith was real, vital, challenging, and contagious.

To his wide reading and retentive memory, trained over years of continuing study, he brought a poetic and genial nature, winsome, hearty, sincere, and strong. He found his spiritual strength in the bedrock doctrines of grace and delighted most of all in the exposition of the truth of substitutionary atonement. The variety and abundance of his thought can easily be demonstrated simply by glancing through any volume of his sermons. The breadth and diversity of his sermons appear so overwhelming that any serious student will find their amplitude almost incredible.

C. H. Spurgeon began service as a country pastor thrust into the ministry while still the assistant teacher at a Cambridge school. Even at age eighteen, he proved his ability to handle ticklish and difficult situations by a wise use of Scripture and common sense. Called to preach at London's New Park Street Chapel in 1854 he came with a reluctant humility, declining a six-month invitation. He committed himself finally to the congregation for a three-month trial period. Long before the three months were over the church had filled from the 200 with which he began, to crowded services overflowing the 1,200 seats. Prayer meetings revived and membership applications flooded in. New Park Street Chapel huddled beside breweries and tanneries, behind the broader city streets, amid a metropolis totaling some four million. After that time, London was a bewildering labyrinth of busy streets, curved narrow lanes and alleys, and great poverty among its citizens.

The empty chapel filled so quickly that it immediately needed enlargement. While this was being accomplished, the congregation migrated to Exeter Hall, where the interest engendered in spiritual matters became so intense that both St. Paul's Cathedral and Westminster Abbey were also induced to begin regular Sunday evening services for the masses. Spurgeon commonly preached from ten to twelve times per week in his early years, touring the home counties, and going as far afield in Britain as Scotland and Ireland. Thousands heard him preach in Paris, Geneva, Belgium, and Holland. He addressed huge open-air congregations at Cambridge, Bristol, Birmingham, Liverpool, Bradford, Halifax, and in several centers in Wales. On June 11, 1858, he preached to many thousands from the grandstand at Epsom racecourse. On Clapham Common, ten thousand gathered to hear his address on July 10, 1859. Finally the Surrey Gardens Music Hall was the only London building sufficient to hold the regular crowds who wished to attend his Sunday services.

At first the popular press caricatured him, offering vulgar cartoons and fabricating all sorts of spurious and inappropriate sayings and actions as reports from his services. Gradually he came to be appreciated for his sincerity, character, and abilities. The great Metropolitan Tabernacle opened debt free in 1861. It seated 6,000, with a lecture hall holding 900 others, and with room for a children's Sunday School of 1,000. Spurgeon continued serving there for over thirty years with ever increasing crowds and ever broadening popularity. Prime Minister William Gladstone attended services. Members of the royal family slipped into back pews incognito. John Ruskin was a frequent visitor to his home. Through his ministry and students, Spurgeon founded more than 200 churches in and around London.[30]

The great preacher's ministry rode to great strength on the rising tide of a genuine spiritual awakening. Between 1860 and 1870, Baptist churches increased in London by 60 percent. Of 250,000 members recorded in 1865, almost half had been added as the fruits of the revival.[31] Something of the intensity of this period can be gauged from reports published in the Tabernacle news magazine *Sword and Trowel*. The congregation gathered for a week of intense prayer in 1865, described as a time of "deep, thrilling power, when all hearts and spirits were bowed down in deep repentance."[32] An appeal to the unconverted resulted in a number of Christians retiring "into a room below with many anxious ones, several of whom received peace with God,"[33] (note Spurgeon's use of an inquiry room).

He arranged for his deacons to organize and lead three weeks of special services in 1866, with detailed outreach plans, prayer meetings, and opportunities for those seeking salvation to receive counsel. A day of fasting and prayer recorded that 120 ministers and students met for "a time of melting penitence and earnest wrestling with God," which gathering had great effect upon the subsequent meeting of the London Baptist Association which Spurgeon fostered and thoroughly encouraged.[34]

In 1866 Spurgeon declared:

> We have had a continual stream of revival. The cries of sinners have sounded in our ears—every day we have seen souls converted—I was about to say almost every hour of the week, and that by the space of these twelve years, and of late, we have had a double portion.[35]

Six years later he reaffirmed this testimony saying:

> As a church we have lived in revivals for nearly twenty years; there has never been a time, that I can remember, when there have not been souls converted in our midst. I do not know that there has ever been a Sabbath without a conversion in this place; I do not think there has been a sermon without a conversion.[36]

Fifty years after the 1859 movement, Reverend Archibald G. Brown recalled those days as ones of special outpouring:

> As a church here we ought never to forget the gracious outpourings commemorated this week in the Metropolitan Tabernacle. . . . let it be remembered that C. H. Spurgeon was living in that revival age . . . when was this building reared? . . . when the flames of revival were sweeping through all London.[37]

C. H. Spurgeon recorded his own memories of the earliest days, saying:

> Shall we ever forget Park Street, those prayer meetings when I felt compelled to let you go without a word from my lips, because the spirit of God was so awfully present that we felt bowed to the dust. And what listening there was at Park Street, where we scarcely had air enough to breathe! The Holy Spirit came down like showers which saturate the soil till the clods are ready for the

breaking; and then it was not long before we heard on the right hand and on the left the cry, "What must we do to be saved?"[38]

The government held all national universities closed to all but members of the established Anglican Church when Spurgeon's Pastors' College opened in 1856. He began with the assurance that the providence of God would draw those around him who were called to preach, and set his curriculum to improve their lack of general education as well as of theology. In just ten years his students, going into British districts where mainly no Free Churches existed, baptized some 20,000 converts. Others served in places as far away and apart as South Africa, Spain, Naples, the Congo, North Africa, Falkland Islands, the Bahamas, Jamaica, India, and Japan. They filled pulpits literally from Rio to Canada, from New England to the United States West Coast and from the American South to New Zealand, Tasmania, and the Australian mainland, as well as all over England, Ireland, Scotland, and Wales.

Reverend George Rogers, pastor of the Camberwell Congregational Church, served as the College's first faculty member. Spurgeon retained him until his eightieth year, an evidence of the breadth of his fellowship. Entrance was not limited to Baptists but open to approximately 100 new students each year. On Friday afternoons "the Guv'nor" (as his students affectionately termed him) came himself to lecture on practical issues in the ministry. His several volumes of *Lectures to My Students* came from these classes. On these occasions he talked about literature, authors, poets, and reformers. Spurgeon counseled them on what books to buy, and selected readings which he delivered to them. He modeled interpretation for them through his elocution and delivery. Many of these lectures covered aspects of preaching and pastoral ministry so relevant that they are still enjoyed by the theological students of today.

Spurgeon's irrepressible humor breaks out continually:

> Put plenty into your sermons, gentlemen. After hearing some discourses I have been reminded of the request of the farmer's boy to his missus when eating his broth "Missus, I wish you would let that chicken run through this broth once more."[39]
>
> Don't go creeping into your subject, first to the ankles and then to the knees, as some preachers do, but plunge into it at once over head and ears; that is the easy way to get the attention of the people. Don't spar at them, but hit out boldly, straight from the shoulder.[40]

He was not above ridiculing some of the latest fads in eschatology either:

> Don't be so absorbed, like some brethren, with the doctrine of the Second Coming that you neglect to preach the first. I should like to say to some I know, "Ye men of Plymouth, why stand ye gazing up into heaven? Go on with your work."[41]

William Williams, a former student, recall that his talk was as enchanting as it was various:

> . . . talk charged with wit and humor, repartee and raillery, anecdote and illustration. Mimicry and genuine bursts of oratory, and which filled many an hour with merriment, and sometimes with even boistrous *abandon*; yet with such merriment and abandon that a closing prayer which carried all spirits into the presence of the Eternal seemed the most harmonious and fitting end to the afternoon's instruction and delight.[42]

When someone asked him once, "Who can possibly take your place when you are gone?" he replied, "I never trouble myself as to who shall marry my wife after I am dead."[43] "Here is a riddle for you," he once stated. "If Paul is the least of all saints, what size are you?"[44] Affirming that long prayers injure prayer meetings he exclaimed, "Fancy a man praying for twenty minutes, and then asking God to forgive his shortcomings!"[45] He delighted to tell any story that showed up supercilious piety:

> A member once said to his minister who wanted a little more salary as his family increased, "I did not know you preached for money." "No, I don't," said the minister. "I thought you preached for souls!" "So I do; but my family can't live on souls, and if they could it would take a good many the size of yours to make a meal."[46]

In counseling his students to avoid a small church, if possible, he said that such is "not unlike a rowboat which a man is in danger of upsetting if he moves about." He advised there was less danger of upsetting an ocean liner.[47]

An occasional hearer who made a fortune through shady transactions kept after Spurgeon to name a home he had built for retirement. He warded off the continuous inquiries but finally suggested—"What shall I name your villa? Why, *if I was you,* I should name it 'Dun Robbin.'" *(Done Robbing.)* This ended the correspondence.[48]

Tom succeeded well in his courses at the college. He achieved good grades and greatly enjoyed the classes. But returning ill health caused him to miss many days. A multitude of chimney pots continually belched out the black smoke of the London winter fires. Damp pea soup fogs and the rancid London air tore at his throat and attacked his weak chest so alarmingly that finally he was forced to resign. He began to make plans for a temporary return to the sunny South Pacific climate for the immediate future. More bothersome was the growing weakness he detected in his father's health. Occasionally C. H. Spurgeon would sit heavily on a chair to preach, leaning hard on his stick, and sometimes drawing each breath with pain. Tom had seen him preaching with one hand on the back of a chair and one knee resting on its cushions to obtain relief. In September of 1879 C. H. Spurgeon wrote responding to an Australian invitation:

. . . No, dear sir, there is no trip to Australia for me. How can I leave these great works, which flag if I am even a little absent? The care of them would follow me, would torment me, if I left them and work me far more harm than any amount of labour. When the Lord permits me to make the journey, He will give me the means both in men and money of leaving all the institutions in good trim. At present, however, ill I might be, I could not feel it right to go further than a few hours' journey, where matters of difficulty and need could be brought before me. I hope I have no overestimate of my own necessity to the work, but the fact is too clear to me that the leader must keep his post even with the best of people, when a work is so varied, so peculiar, and so clear of mechanical routine.

Alas, I have another matter to mention. I hoped that my dear son Thomas, would remain with me, to be my comfort and help. He is inexpressibly dear to me, and I am more grieved than I can tell to find that a cough and great delicacy of the lungs render his stay with us in England very inadvisable. I must, therefore, send him off to you again, and he now intends leaving London by the Sobraon, on the 26th September.

Though this is almost death to me, I hope it may prove to be the life of many in the Colonies. If you will again receive him as you did before, I shall be deeply grateful. He will probably remain for a considerable time, and possibly may settle in one of the Colonies. The Lord's will be done.[49]

A letter from Thomas to an Australian friend published at the same time, tells the story of his own disappointments clearly:

What with continued moisture and weak lungs, I have been compelled to give up preaching and to take shipping once more. Australia sunbeams must have another try to put me to rights, and I believe they will succeed under certain conditions (to be stated hereafter).

. . . It is my heart's desire to work for the Master *somewhere*; and if I can't do it in humid England, I must make hay *where the sun shines*. Whether or not He means me to labour at the Antipodes altogether, I do not know; but He will make it plain. For some time I must be dreadfully lazy. I fear I shall find it hard work to do nothing, but the friends must aid me—and then when I am quite robust I will be theirs to serve with all my powers.

I am purposing to go as direct as possible to Tasmania. I shall thus avoid the great heat and shall be out of the way of temptation to over-exertion. My chief reason, however, for wishing to get to Mr. Gibson's quickly lies in the fact that brethren McCullough and Harrison, who accompany me, are going to work there; and as they are from the Pastor's College and I have had a deal of anxious labour in securing two men, I am naturally anxious to introduce them and to help in putting them in working order.

They are real good fellows. Oh, that they might flash the truth in that charming isle, and even help to spread it among you! We are sailing in the *Sobraon* (27th September). Expecting thus to stay only a few days in Melbourne. I want to say that if by a sojourn in Tasmania my health is restored, I shall hope to be able to do a little preaching in Victoria; but I cannot think of settling down, as I want to visit Sydney and New Zealand, both of which places had promises last time, which I was not able to perform.

. . . The bitterness of leaving home is immensely relieved by the joyful expectation of reunion with some of my best friends. I trust the Lord will guide my course and make it plain (after He has made me strong) as to which side of the globe I am to work for Him. I fain would leave it all to Jesus! Best of blessings be with you and with the whole Israel of God!—Yours in hearty Christian love.[50]

Tom secured R. McCullough and J. S. Harrison, two graduates of the Pastors' College, at William Gibson's request, for the furtherance of the Baptist cause in Tasmania. The Gibsons agreed to pay their fares, help them erect new chapels, and provide for their initial support. The Gibsons' generosity was prompted by their affection for Tom and for his father:

They loved C. H. Spurgeon, whom they had never seen, and loved his son as if he had been their own. They consulted him about their plans for erecting places of worship, and he had an important part in the founding of the denomination on this beautiful island.[51]

Twenty-three years before, C. H. Spurgeon had spent a whole night in prayer. A disastrous cry of "fire" in the Surrey Gardens Music Hall resulted in a panic in which many were injured and some killed by the stampeding crowds. The young preacher almost lost his reason in the light of unjust criticisms of his part in the tragedy, but finally won through to peace over the long night of agony before God.[52] When Tom sailed on October 2, 1879 his father was equally saddened. He had joyously built high hopes of Tom serving at his side, especially in the light of his own illness. Again, he wrestled through a long weary night of similar agony. Again, he won the victory.[53]

By the time the three arrived in Tasmania at the end of 1879, Tom, too, had recovered from the bitterness of that forced separation. He had not coughed once on the journey,[54] and the welcome from the Gibsons at Native Point made up partly for his bitter disappointment about the Rutherfords: upon arrival in Melbourne at Christmas he had inquired about them, and learned that the whole family had moved to New Zealand![55]

From January through June of 1880 Tom fulfilled his own prescription of rest and relaxation. The sunny skies and clear air of northern Tasmania made him feel a new man again within a few weeks. Riding excursions into the woods to gaze at gigantic rocky mountains and 150-feet-tall eucalyptus trees, and hunting and fishing trips along the River Esk helped as well.

And then there were the "Tasmanian Tabernacles."[56] He set foundation stones for the churches at Deloraine and Longford, and worked with McCullough and Harrison at the task of organizing congregations to fill these chapels which Gibson built. The Gibsons' enthusiasm was contagious. They planned to nourish the infant Baptist causes on the island to the best of their ability. Tom agreed to be their agent in working with the London College graduates, assisting their placement under the Gibsons' enthusiastic patronage.[57]

Australian Baptist life on the mainland developed some important strengths in the 1880s. As the decade began South Australia boasted thirty-eight Baptist churches and Victoria, thirty-three.[58] Tom loved preaching to the shearers, and by early July his health had so improved that he gladly accepted an invitation to revisit the sheep station Warambeen where he had ministered in 1878. This time he found a flourishing church established where none had been before.[59]

Victoria's gold rush had centered on the city of Ballarat thirty years before. Tom enjoyed the railroad journey to the gold country and the natural beauties of the bush. In the forests beside him circled sheets of bark had flaked away from the giant eucalyptuses, while clusters of gum oozed from their high armpits, and beautiful red and yellow gum leaves, tipped with red and orange, gave the whole an iridescent hue. Here and there a family of five or six bush wallabies could be seen hopping quickly away from the shriek of the locomotive's whistle. Sheep seemed to be everywhere. Great horned rams lifted belligerent heads at the passing iron horse. Contemplative ewes chewed their cuds in the shade of the willows by the creek banks, as gamboling wool-haired moppets bunted and pranced.

Small cabins half-hidden in the bush slipped rapidly by, matched here and there by little villages which presented neat sidings, often crowded by a gang of children, all sans shoes. Their excited eyes plainly told that the visit of the train was the event of the day. Gangers [foremen of work gangs] on the permanent way hollered for a newspaper as he passed. Billboards touted the virtues of certain brands of sheep dip, or the services of stock and station agents. The color and variety of it all so contrasted with the ordered neatness of his English domicile that Tom wished that he had packed drawing materials so that he could have recorded these scenes for the future.

Earlier he had passed through quiet country towns dozing in the hot sun. Ringed by rows of double-storied shops and hotels, their timber and iron-lace verandas rested against each other with lopsided fatigue, the blandness of their main streets only relieved by a stark white flagpole or a pretentious clock tower. But Ballarat was different, a bustling city, only seventy miles from the sea and still bearing evidence of its gold-prosperous beginnings.

Ballarat began in the 1850s from the streets of canvas tents which mushroomed at the diggings. Men moved into the district at the rate of 500 per day. The boggy roads were choked with bullock wagons and hundreds on foot, as laborers left tools and others abandoned homes or businesses at reports of gold nuggets the size of emu eggs. Many lost what little they had; others found incredible wealth. By the days of company mining in the 1860s stores and luxuries abounded. Live theater and opera entertained a cosmopolitan community of 40,000 inhabitants. There were eighty-four miles of man-made streets, eleven banks, and fifty-six churches.

Thirteen breweries supplied 477 pubs and hotels, a record in Australia for any one city, and perhaps for the world. At the time of Thomas's 1880 visit Ballarat was still the most productive goldfield in the world. The Sovereign Hill camp area employed many Chinese laborers in their mines. Thirty thousand Chinese had scattered through the Australian colonies, most of them living on the goldfields. Generally they kept to themselves, following their own traditions from ancestor worship and joss houses to opium smoking, often gambling with abandon. The local Chinese quarter was also the red-light district. Many Chinese, however, were industrious and high-principled farmers. They developed geometrically perfect market gardens and hawked their vegetables in the town from door to door.

Self-reliant shearers who had not struck it rich also developed their own trades. Tom saw several with their carts full of freshly killed bush rabbits. These they skinned and gutted for the housewives who hurried out when they heard the cries of "Rabbitoh, Rabbitoh!" After his first Ballarat meal, Tom agreed that this "underground chicken," when slowly baked in a wood oven, tasted indeed as succulent as poultry.

Reverend W. Clark pastored the Ballarat Baptist congregation and invited Tom to preach the fourth anniversary services of his infant cause. Sunday July 11, 1880 brought the largest audience Tom had faced in the colonies to date. Clark had wisely taken the massive Ballarat Academy of Music for the occasion, and no less than 2,300 were present, eager to hear the young preacher with the famous name. The sermon was heard with "rapt attention" and was described as "forcible and homely" (meaning unpretentious). The service included the singing of some of the Sankey hymns which were Tom's favorites.[60]

Bearing his father's name was something of a handicap as well as a privilege. If Tom had not been destined to preach he was almost certain to try, and, in trying, to be compared unfavorably with his father. He wrote from Australia, saying:

> I do not think that I am being lionized or idolized in the true sense of the
> term. The attention paid to me and the interest taken by the great majority is

out of pure Christian love to the honoured name of Spurgeon and the honoured man who bears it.[61]

On July 29th and 30th, Tom ministered at the Parramatta Baptist Church, just outside Sydney, with great success.[62] But by September he was well into another northern itineration in the state of Queensland. German Baptists and others heard him at Ipswich.[63] John MacPherson, a London Pastors' College graduate, gathered good crowds for him in Toowoomba, and at Highfields.[64] Invited to ride in the engine cab of the Brisbane to Toowoomba train by the driver who had heard his father preach in London, Tom saw in the journey an analogy with many spiritual parallels. The difficulties of climbing, running without brakes, keeping the fire stoked, getting steam up, and following the laid-out track, were all developed by him as vehicles for spiritual truth with his usual imaginative and expressive skills.[65]

Returning for some weeks of Sydney ministry Tom enjoyed the beauty of the spacious harbor, fed by the Paramatta and Lane Cove rivers, whose ragged points and sweeping curves spread like a huge oak leaf. Houses were snuggled in coves among wattle and gum trees. Freestone mansions stood on the northern hills, while the metropolis sprawled toward the south. He found Sydney to be many times larger than he had expected, an English city with many colonial and American architectural influences. The bright botanical gardens surrounding the state governor's residence soon became a favorite spot for sunny afternoon strolls.

October 19, 1880 was a typical hot spring Sunday in Sydney, yet the Theatre Royal was filled at three in the afternoon. Many hundreds gathered to hear the twenty-four-year-old preacher who bore the illustrious name of Spurgeon. Some time previously Thomas Spurgeon had addressed 2,300 in the Academy of Music at Ballarat. This audience was not as large as that, but they had come for a special purpose.

Frederick Hibberd, later to be known as the "father of the New South Wales Baptist Union," had suggested that Tom hold this unusual meeting. The plan was to collect funds for C. H. Spurgeon's great London orphanage. Tom also seized this opportunity to publish the gospel message.

His text was "in thee the fatherless findeth mercy," (Hos. 14:3), and he drew a parallel between "the orphanage of my heavenly Father and that of my earthly parent," showing that "the qualification for admission to each is destitution, and the reception is gracious."[66]

He found the interdenominational audience so moved by his sermon, and motivated by the memories of good received from his father's preached and printed words, they donated fifty pounds—a very large sum for that time—for the London needs.

In sending the bank draft to his father, Tom also remarked:

> Thousands here are deeply interested in you and in your glorious work. They
> have eagerly seized this opportunity of manifesting their esteem and love.[67]

Earlier Thomas had received a cordial assurance of welcome and support for
evangelistic services in various districts, issued from the 1880 September
meetings of the Baptist Union of New Zealand.[68] Many graduates of his father's
college already served in that nation. He set off, therefore, with considerable
delight for the southern city of Dunedin, to fulfill a six-month interim pastoral
arrangement at the Hanover Street Baptist Church. Gideon Rutherford, now
active in that fellowship, had suggested his name for the vacant pastorate. Tom
was unsure of the potential for permanence there, but he hungered for a more
stable ministry, and the attraction of the Rutherfords' presence suggested this to
be at least a live possibility. He planned to serve their current interim need, and to
undertake some evangelism in the surrounding areas. If health and other matters
allowed he would seek God's mind for permanent service there.

The separate nation of New Zealand, situated about a three-day sail east of
Sydney, consisted of two large islands. The North Island fostered the growing
cities of Auckland and Wellington, Christchurch and Dunedin being the two
major centers in the South Island. Dunedin, the largest at the time, led the nation
with a quality university symbolic of the pious and industrious Scottish settlers
who began there in 1848. A Scottish Presbyterian stronghold, Dunedin was an
orderly city of stern Victorian facades softened with green hills and laced with
lush gardens. The pioneering days of the colony were by now almost over. Rail
tracks and roads crisscrossed the country and, as in Australia, prosperity rode
highest on the sheep's back.

Many of Gideon Rutherford's Scottish relatives farmed around the Dunedin
hills. He had lost his squatter's lease at Quambatook because of the government
division of surrounding areas into small farming lots for new settlers. Consequently, it seemed natural for him to transfer his business interests. Mark Twain
once described Dunedin saying: . . . The people are Scotch. They stopped there
on their way from home to heaven—thinking they had arrived.[69]

Tom certainly felt at home. He was royally entertained from January through
June 1881 at the Rutherfords' lovely home, "Dalmore," overlooking the town and
harbor. But the church also delighted him. A gracious old building, well
supported by some 300 members, it seemed to be a promising opportunity for
settled pastoral leadership.

Much blessing attended his ministries while there. The *New Zealand Baptist*
suggested that his work in Dunedin was "creating quite a stir in our midst. Great
numbers gather wherever he preaches."[70] The report continues recording that 700

to 800 had crowded out the chapel in seven services, with many remaining for after meetings and for counsel as new converts. One gathering reached 2,000 in the YMCA hall, and another overflowed the Queen's Theatre.[71]

But well before the six months concluded, Tom knew he could not stay. The Dunedin climate was too severe.[72] His coughing and breathing problems returned with the first touch of autumn. He determined to work his way towards the sunnier North Island via a series of evangelistic services among the Baptist churches which were now inundating him with requests. Perhaps there might be a place there where God would have him settle in a maturing work? He had heard that the city of Auckland had entered a strong growth cycle. Perhaps there was room for something in that area. Certainly he would talk with Reverend Alan Webb of the Auckland Wellesley Street Church about the possibilities.

When his final night came in Dunedin, Tom sat quietly with the Rutherford family around the kitchen fire. Lila huddled over the hearth just across from him, sharing the hot pot of cocoa they had brewed together, after the others retired. In the flickering firelight he inspected her freckled face with its high-colored cheeks, tracing her Scottish ancestry in the light, fair skin, while she gazed pensively into the flames. He had found her to be much more grown-up than the twelve-year-old he had known on the Quambatook sheep station. Now she was fifteen, and already showing signs of blossoming into a serene and poised maturity like her mother's. Seated in her dressing robe, ready for the night's sleep, with her long hair unbraided, before the fire, she had laughed with him and teased him. He was undoubtedly her favorite English "uncle."

After she retired, Tom sat dreamily before the fire for another hour. He had been somewhat shaken by her beauty. Again the thoughts which had pursued him three years before came to mind. But the whole idea was preposterous! *He* now twenty-four, and *she* barely fifteen. His mother would be scandalized. *Besides,* he thought, *his own health and lack of permanent ministry meant that such matters should be postponed for some time yet. Perhaps, in a few years. . . . Maybe when she was at least twenty or so? Ah, well, he would leave it all in the good Lord's hands, believing that what was to be would be, and that the Lord's time would be the best of all times.*

But that night his quiet bedroom was filled with strange dreams and probing questions, some of which arose from the sight of a bright-red toffee tin on the windowsill. This was Lila's room, surrendered to the visitor while she doubled up with one of the younger children. He knew that he had no right to do so, but curiosity forced him to lift its lid and examine the interior.

Yes, this was the tin he had sent to Quambatook to the Rutherford children, from Kerang, three years before. And, there in a corner lay an obviously saved toffee, its end-twist fastened with a pin to that same card he had written so long ago.

Tom didn't try to interpret the meaning of the saved card; nevertheless he was somehow comforted. At that time he had no idea that seven long years would yet lie between this night and the night when he would fully understand. Nor did he realize that the knowledge would come from a new wife, smiling with honeymoon embarrassment at the secret Tom had discovered, but not understood, long before she actually had defined it for herself.

*   *   *

With the discovery of gold in the Otago area in 1862, Dunedin's 12,000 hand-picked Scottish settlers found themselves suddenly swamped by an onrush of miners and adventurers. Gold finds in the North Island, particularly at Thames, had similar effects on other centers. The European population of New Zealand jumped from 30,000 to 170,000 within a few years, as cities mushroomed and shanty towns sprang up across the young nation. By the 1870s the generally reduced prosperity, falling wool prices, and economic disillusionment, sent many of the less hardy settlers off to Australia or to other lands where it was reputed that fortunes were more easily made.

But the British, American, Spanish, German, French, Italian, and Chinese settlers who remained developed such aggressive, independent communities that a vigorous young nation was quickly born.

The whalers and adventurers who had first settled the islands had been largely attracted by its complete freedom of restraint from law. They had settled alongside the Maori, natives who had themselves come from other Polynesian cultures many centuries before. But prosperity brought many new settlers and, as the cities developed, so did civilization.

Auckland, 1,200 miles by sea from Sydney, was a colony first constituted in 1853, with a strong local government. The Thames goldfields affected their growth as they had that of Dunedin. By 1881, when Thomas arrived, the population of Auckland was 16,664. Within the next ten years those figures doubled.

The city boasted a beautiful harbor with inlets and gullies creeping up into craters and hills that were almost miniature mountains. From One Tree Hill, the visitor could view ocean on both sides of the mainland. The harbor presented a magnificent panorama of sails and ships. The wharf area was a virtual forest of masts, and a string of piers and unloading docks. The streets of the city stretched almost from the landing areas right into a thriving metropolis thronged with cosmopolitan crowds and ringed by green hills.

By 1874 only four Baptist churches existed in the entire nation, one possessing a full-time pastor. In the next eight years, this number doubled, due to the enthusiasm of the Canterbury Baptist District Association. The periodical which began as the *Canterbury Evangelist,* renamed the *New Zealand Baptist* in 1880, lived up to the promise of its masthead, stating that the infant New Zealand Baptist Union then boasted of 2,281 members with churches in Nelson, Dunedin, Wellington, Christchurch, Auckland, and numerous other centers.

The church to which Thomas came for evangelistic services had begun under the ministry of Reverend James Thornton of Wales in the 1850s. By 1862 numbers had grown to such a dimension that the fine timber Wellesley Street Baptist Chapel had to be erected to house the growing Auckland congregation. After a ministry from Reverend P. H. Cornford, former missionary to Jamaica, they called Reverend Alan Webb, who had served for a time in India and then in pastorates at Maitland, New South Wales, and Harris Street, Sydney, to serve their needs. In 1881 Webb paid a two-month visit to Adelaide. He invited Tom to interim for him at Auckland during his absence, and to lead the church in some evangelistic outreach.

The original Wellesley Street Chapel held 300, and was enlarged in 1864 to hold 500. But after many members had been dismissed to form the new church at the Thames goldfields the chapel was seldom crowded.

Tom arrived in Auckland in July 1881. Under his earnest evangelistic emphases, the chapel was soon filled again. The newspapers of the period noted his oratorical skills, graphic imagery, and narrative power. The denominational magazine remarked, it seems somewhat with surprise, that he appeared to be well gifted for one so young:

> When first in the pulpit Mr. Spurgeon seems quite juvenile; but from the moment he commences his service his juvenility is gone, and we listen to one who knows what he uttereth. The gifts peculiar to a fluent speaker Mr. Spurgeon possesses in no small degree, whilst we feel persuaded he is possessed of the essential graces.[73]

Tom's characteristic good humor won him an instant liking from the colonial congregation. When introduced by the chairman at the twenty-sixth anniversary of the Auckland Church in September with the statement that they would now listen to Mr. Spurgeon—"a chip off the old block," he replied:

> I want to know why the chairman called my father an "old block"! He may call me anything he likes, but don't call my father names![74]

By November the relationship developed to the point that, having been advised by Alan Webb that he had accepted the North Adelaide Baptist Church and would not be returning to Auckland, the congregation unanimously invited Thomas to accept the permanent pastorate.

On November 11 he agreed to their invitation, subject to three conditions; if his health remained strong, if the Lord blessed the word, and if his parents offered no decided objections.[75] His father's reply affirmed that he too saw the opportunity as a sphere full of promise for the young preacher, and would support him in whatever decision he made. C. H. Spurgeon said:

> Do not come home. I would dearly love to see you, but how could we part with you again? Stay away there until there is a call to come home. When the Lord wills it, it will be safer and will be better for us all. To come home in 1882 would be a journey for which there is no demand at a time when you are needed elsewhere.[76]

In August 1881 Tom already had written J. S. Harrison, who had journeyed with him to Tasmania, asking him to come to help in special outreach services planned at Auckland for the new year. By the time Harrison arrived in January 1882, Tom's commitment to permanent service had been established, and the two set out to lead the church in a bold advance.

The young evangelists hired the commodious Choral Hall in lower Symonds Street, Auckland for regular services. Such blessings ensued that the arrangement continued for over three years, with Thomas himself directing all services after the initial January team outreach was completed. Ultimately he gathered the largest regular Free Church congregation in the Southern Hemisphere in Auckland with 650 active members and almost as many regular hearers and adherents for most services. This expansion developed while he was still a twenty-five-year-old bachelor. It seems to be almost as remarkable for that location and time, as the better-known ministry of his famous father in London which had begun twenty years before.

3 Showers of Blessing (1881-1892)

Ye fearful saints, fresh courage take;
The clouds ye so much dread
Are big with mercy, and shall break
In blessings on your head.

he Auckland *Star* regularly funded a census of church attendance in the city by sending reporters to every service on a given Sunday and publishing the survey results. Although Baptists only appeared as 3.63 percent of the early 1882 figures[1] they scored far higher proportionately in Auckland than did most of their sister denominations. The figures are largely explained by the Wellesley Street Baptist numbers. Thomas's congregation was listed as having

> . . . the largest congregation both morning and evening of any church in Auckland, 547 in the morning and over 600 in the evening. The *Star* put a footnote to our record saying that hundreds were turned away.[2]

Others reserved the Choral Hall for that particular Sunday, so Tom's people had been forced to return to the old church building for all services.[3] By this time J. S. Harrison had returned to Tasmania but Tom kept the evangelistic spirit of the January outreach meetings alive, packing out the Choral Hall with Sunday evening services of this character for three years.

Ten months later the blessings could be cataloged with more specificity:

> . . . The position now is—our Church membership has increased 107 during Mr. Spurgeon's pastorate, the chapel on Sabbath mornings—and utilizing seats in the aisles at *every* service—is often uncomfortably crowded, and we are aware that our inadequate accommodation hinders the growth of the congregation. The Sabbath evening services are held in the Choral Hall, where, notwithstanding the inconveniences consequent to holding services in a room not designed therefore, and at a distance from our centre of operations, a congregation gathers which would nearly or quite twice fill our own chapel, and we have evidence it would continue to increase were we in our own permanent home.[4]

The same report asserts that Sunday school services are embarrassingly full and that week-night prayer meetings had crowded out the schoolroom.[5]

Thomas's ministry was the catalyst for this expansion. His people recorded that they praised God for a pastor "whose soul is on fire of love, and whose talents are so fully consecrated to telling 'the old story.'"[6] When Tom first came his

61

congregation believed that the name of Spurgeon was "an earnest of the spirit and grace which are in him,"[7] but they also quickly noted his own abilities and the significance of these in his success:

> The illustrious name he bore, and the manifold gifts he possessed, gained for him a warm welcome, and the Church entered upon a new era of prosperity and blessing. His melodious voice, his poetic phrases, his scintillating humour, and his enthusiasm for the Gospel, gathered crowds around him, and a larger and worthier building than Wellesley Street became imperative.[8]

On May 7 of that year Tom had been able to write:

> I have had Friday meetings with converts: Schoolroom quite full and such nice times; about seventy have returned (decision) cards, over fifty wishing to join Wellesley Street. . . . Last Sunday night, although the meeting was not advertised, the Choral Hall was crammed full, and we had a glorious time.[9]

All this meant that by March 16, 1882, less than five months after he began, the decision to relocate and build a new worship center had been enthusiastically taken. They secured an acre of land in the heart of the city. Like his father before him, Tom resolved to open his Auckland Tabernacle free of debt, and, with the promise of some special help from the Metropolitan Tabernacle friends, the congregation prepared for a special fund-raising effort in December of 1882.[10]

They scheduled the program and publicized it as a "Grand Bazaar in aid of The Auckland Baptist New Church (now worshipping at Wellesley Street) Building Fund, to be held during the last week in December, 1882."[11] From 2 PM until 10 PM Monday through Saturday the local Army Drill Hall overflowed with stalls stocked by the Ladies Sewing Society, and rang with evening concerts and other festive occasions. Children's clothing, dresses, suits, fringes, ribbons, sewing novelties, knitted goods, millinery, groceries, hardware and produce goods, fruit, poultry, potted plants, books, jewelry, fancy goods, and toys were only some of the items placed on sale. Ten thousand persons attended the events over the week, and 1,062 pounds, 15 shillings, resulted from all efforts for the new building fund.

The church ladies carefully planned their efforts to catch the Christmas shopping crowds. They also served hot tea, scones, and cakes, and other light refreshments, all for cash for the Tabernacle cause. Satin banner screens and timber tables reproduced natural forest fern designs from the surrounding hills. A series of concerts and evening entertainments included a special presentation by Thomas himself. He showed "limelight views" (lantern slides) of his father's famous volume *John Ploughman's Pictures* in which homely epigrams, whimsical sayings, and amusing illustrations were blended to present an evening of memorable mirth and moral instruction.

Tom found the competition between stall holders valid, stating "a spirit of rivalry has provoked one another to good works."[12] A four-page paper, the *Baptist Builder,* was printed daily on the spot using presses operated by staff from the *Herald* and the *Star*. The local postmaster displayed the latest invention direct from the U.S.A., a telephone! W. T. Adcock offered his appeal for support in a twenty-eight-line poem which summarized the church growth, teeming crowds, and urgent need for a new church, and ended:

> Kind neighbours and friends, relations and all,
>> This is the time for your kindness and aid;
> Come up with your cash at sympathy's call,
>> That building may be no further delayed.
> Rest well assured that our object is right,
>> Funds we won't waste in spire or steeple;
> Help then to raise (though you give but a mite),
>> Tabernacle and schools for the people.[13]

On Sunday December 17, Tom spoke on "The First Tabernacle Bazaar." Basing his remarks on Exodus 35, he affirmed that he was not there to defend bazaars as they were usually conducted. He believed that when they were freed of the abuses which sometimes characterized them, he saw them as a legitimate means of raising funds. He said that they enabled those who could not give to work to provide goods for sale. He reminded them that some of the materials he would sell had come from the homes for elderly folks in London operated by his father. He claimed that the modern gift program was only an adaptation of the biblical one:

> The materials given in the olden time went directly into the construction of the Tabernacle, and the personal ornaments of gold and silver were melted down to make the sacred vessels of the sanctuary; but in modern times it was impossible to do this sort of thing. They could not construct their Tabernacle of antimacassars and babies' socks etc., consequently they had to be "melted down" so to speak, and the proceeds invested in bricks and mortar.[14]

The Baptist Builder carried a woodcut of the proposed design for the new Tabernacle together with the information that land and buildings would cost some 8,000 pounds, less whatever was obtained for the sale of the Wellesley Street property.

C. H. Spurgeon paid the outgoing fares of a missionary to serve among Maori nationals under the Auckland Church's direction. In April, 1833 missionary Fairbrother, a schoolmaster, settled in the Rotomahana district. There he conducted and administered simple medical aid and rudimentary education to the natives.[15] This Taupo Maori Mission appears to be one of the earliest Baptist outreach movements in New Zealand. The Auckland church also rapidly established strong fellowships at Ponsbory (Thames), and Cambridge.

The artist Charles Blomfield, an active member of the new church building committee, became Tom's closest friend. Child of a Baptist family previously associated with the London Tabernacle congregation, he had arrived in the colony as a lad of fourteen in 1862. Charles had served as volunteer Sunday School superintendent and in other leadership at the Wellesley Street Church. His training of the children's choir for the annual anniversary celebrations marked him as an expert musician. He later served as music instructor for the government school system in the North Island but his prowess as a landscape painter early earmarked him as a young man destined for fame.[16]

Charles Blomfield's self-taught ability to interpret the beauty of the New Zealand forests grew as an adjunct to the house painting and paperhanging business he operated in Auckland. He worked in every aspect of commercial sign painting and the application of gold leaf to store windows. He made custom picture frames and designed interior decor for some of the wealthier mansions in town. But his heart always remained amid the trees, ferns, and mountains of the Auckland hills. His style—sensitive, reminiscent of Turner, soon attracted much attention with its greatly detailed attention to the virgin beauty of the unspoiled forest and the various colors of its primeval splendor. He traveled widely and exhibited the results of his labors for sixty years, from 1862 exploring the countryside on his own. Often he tramped long distances and camped out in primitive conditions. His work and reputation remain today among the highest of all the painters New Zealand has produced.[17]

Blomfield's self-education included wide reading in the areas of poetry and literature. For many years he published articles in the literary columns of the Auckland newspapers expressing his perspectives on art, music, and the modern sciences with clarity and precision.[18]

Tom found him to be an ideal companion. In December of 1883 the two traveled by boat to Tauranga, then for two days by coach, and finally by boat across Lake Tarawera, to within miles of their goal, the famous Pink and White Terraces of the thermal area.[19]

The three-week trek took them to visit missionary Fairbrother en route.[20] On the way Tom gathered leaves and ferns to be later transferred into patterns and designs to decorate small timber tables he and other young men of the church liked to produce. Their route led through the tall kauri forests, thick with gigantic tree ferns and nikau palms. When they finally arrived in the hot springs district, it was with considerable awe that they approached the famous Terraces, known among New Zealanders as "the eighth wonder of the world."

Each mountainous outcrop sat in a shallow pool so sulphurous that a sixpence dropped in its waters turned immediately jet black. The White Terrace, 300 feet wide and 200 feet high, presented an ascending tier of shell-like stone pools, each semicircular, rising from the one below it like an ascending stair. The inside textures felt as smooth as alabaster, but the outside rims hung in varigated shapes which nature had carved with cornices and frescoes, beadings, and pointed droplets. Some pools possessed curved lips thicker than a man's arm, other walls were worn so thin one could almost see the sunlight shining through them.

The whole fabric, composed over centuries by silican deposits from the ever-cascading thermal waters, stood like a huge staircase coated with crystal: "Over all the steps a film of water, as soft to the touch as satin, glides incessantly, and trickles into the lake till it give[s] its name, Totamahna—the Warm lake."[21]

One geyser at the crest shot a twenty- to thirty-foot spray intermittently. Sometimes two of the three in the upper pool would shoot simultaneously, or so close together that the whole area would be wreathed in steam and the heavy sulphurous smell would reach an almost choking intensity. The White Terrace transfixed every traveler who came upon it with its immensity and grandeur.

> From the summit downwards it spread itself, in shape like an enormous fan, in build like a vast flight of alabaster steps rising to a throne. . . . where the throne should stand was a hissing cauldron, and the scorching vapour hid the ruling majesty from sight.[22]

Each ascending pool rose in temperature higher than that below it:

> What a staircase of loveliness! How wonderfully white were the porcelain cups, carved and fitted more exquisitely than any carver on earth could chase them; and what a sweet cerulean blue was the water they contained. . . . We were in the land of steam, certainly. Surely this is the engine-room of our planet! Everything seemed boiling. Boiling mud, through which the pent-up steam struggled, making a curious bladder-bursting sound of satisfaction when it did get out; boiling oil, at least the greasy water looked like it, and boiling water in any quantities, supplied quite free, as at our picnics.[23]

The Pink Terrace pools, by contrast, remained quite cool, and were delightful for bathing, right to the uppermost levels. In these the water took on a turquoise hue and the bottoms of the pools were smooth and sandlike. The formation rose in a smaller series of semicircular stages with no two of the same height, each having a small raised margin from which hung miniature stalactites:

> The terraces, at a distance, appear the colour of ashes and roses, but near at hand show a metallic grey, with pink and yellow margins of the utmost delicacy. Being constantly wet the colours are brilliant beyond description. Sloping gently from the crater in successive terraces they form little bathing pools, with margins of silica the colour of silver.[24]

Tom wrote that the chief charm of the smaller terrace was its color:

> Pink, they call it, but in places it is salmon colour with a sheen that makes it

look like the finest plush. . . . We were loath to leave these scenes of marvel which I have not half described. Never in a single day—I might say in a whole week, have I seen such sights or heard such sounds.[25]

Tom was so moved by the experience that he firmly advised his companion that here lay a potential which would make his name as an artist. He insisted, "You should come here and paint some real good pictures of these exquisite scenes; you would do very well with them."[26]

Charles took Thomas at his word. In January 1844, free from the tasks now associated with his appointment as a singing inspector in the schools,[27] he returned for six weeks to complete the task. Large supplies of camping gear and artist's materials had to be hand carried to the site. The natives (who regarded the terraces as their private property) had to be paid to allow him to stay close by the pools. Charles took his daughter Mary with him, who, though only eight years old, found the holiday with her father delightful, and the surroundings and the natives not at all frightening.[28]

Charles Blomfield's sketches, and the series of final oils which resulted, brought him both national and international fame. He kept the originals but made and sold hundreds of copies. Returning to Auckland from the Terrace district, Blomfield held an exhibition in early 1855. His reputation was established once and for all. Evaluators described his work in glowing terms: "The tender atmospheric effects, the delicate blush of spring, and, above all, the 'glimpse of the Beyond' conveyed by his canvases is only given to the true artistic soul."[29]

Tom's prophecy that Blomfield "would do very well" from the sale of terrace paintings proved true, but in a manner in which neither of them dreamed. On June 10, 1855, about eighteen months after the trip Charles had taken to record the natural wonders, his work became more valuable, though through a tragedy: overnight his oils became not only the first color records of the terrace beauties, but the only ones which ever would be painted.

Auckland residents awoke to a series of explosions some thought were gunfire. These proved to come from a volcanic eruption of gigantic proportions, which decimated much of the thermal area, killed many natives, and totally destroyed both the White and Pink Terraces. Several photographers had pictured their beauty in black and white but Charles Blomfield's oils still remain today as the only true record of their spendor. Tom later declared that he believed Charles had been chosen by God to record their magnificence for posterity. New Zealand recognizes Blomfield as its greatest painter of natural scenes in that era, and his fame is built largely upon the quality of the original terrace oils he created at Tom's suggestion, and the many hundreds of copies he made of them for others.[30]

From his earliest years Tom had expressed his own artistic temperament in sketching. He also wrote verse, as C. H. Spurgeon did. With a native talent for

rhyme improved by earnest effort, his work finally resulted in many poems in the
Sword and Trowel, his father's newsmagazine about the Metropolitan Tabernacle
ministries. In 1892 most of Tom's poetic work was collected into a 100-page
volume on evangelical themes. Many of his poems were created for children. A
large number of these, written especially for the children who belonged to the
temperance movement of the day, became quite popular as recitations for church
socials and other ancilliary evangelical meetings. A blue ribbon in the lapel was
the sign those days that the wearer had "signed the pledge," and was enlisted as a
temperance advocate. Hence Thomas's major book of poems, fifty-five in all,
was published by Passmore and Alabaster in London in 1892 as *Scarlet Threads
and Bits of Blue* as befitted its major themes of atonement and temperance. Tom
composed most of these poems during the Auckland ministry, and some reveal
the depths of his own devotional life over that period. The original of "Looking
Unto Jesus,"[31] also lists twenty-eight scriptural cross-references, one for each
two-line theme:

> "Looking unto Jesus,"
>   God's beloved Son,
> As my only model,
>   Perfect paragon;
> Striving to be like Him,
>   Seeking more to know,
> "Looking" till in all things
>   Into Him I grow.
> Acting as He acted,
>   Thinking as He thought,
> Speaking as He spake,
>   And teaching as he taught,
> Bearing in my body
>   Brandmarks of my Lord,
> "Looking unto Jesus"—
>   Spotless "Lamb of God."
>
> "Looking unto Jesus"
>   For encouragement;
> By a single vision
>   Rendered confident,
> Nerved for sacred service,
>   Fired for holy war,
> Considering our *Captain*—
>   Glorious Conqueror!
> He the shame despised,
>   He the cross endured;
> Joy was set before Him,

> Now the throne's secured;
> Chief among ten thousand!
> Let me ever be
> "Looking unto Jesus,"
> Sure of victory.
>
> "Looking unto Jesus"—
> Bowing to His rule,
> He my gracious Teacher,
> I a child at school.
> Waiting at His door-posts,
> Sitting at His feet,
> Ready for His service,
> For His use made meet.
> "Looking" for direction
> in Life's winding maze;
> To His faultless wisdom
> Leaving all my ways;
> Drinking of His fulness,
> Guided by His eye,
> "Looking unto Jesus"
> Till the shadows fly.[32]

Although some constructions lack polish, one cannot miss the devotional spirit of the young twenty-six-year-old preacher, nor his deep desire to follow God's will.

Other poems were suggested by pastoral situations in which Tom found himself at Auckland. He spent many happy hours as a guest in Charles Blomfield's home. One experience caused him to write a rhyme about Mary, Charles and Ellen Blomfield's eight-year-old daughter. It appears that this was written just after the time when Charles had taken her to the Terraces. After they returned the child was asked about her love for her mother with the following result:

> *Right Up to the Top*
> For children, and those of child-like spirit.
>
> "Does my little Mary love mamma?
> I would very much like to know."
> "Oh, yes, mamma, to be sure I do;
> Yes—I love you—oh—ever so!"
>
> "Do you love me *so much*?" asked mamma—
> Her hand held a foot from the floor.
> "Yes, of course I do," the fond child said;
> "Why, *I love you a great deal more!*"

"As much as this, then?"—the table's height—
Yes, and more, my own mother dear;"
The hand goes higher—she still cries "More,"
Till as high as the chandelier.

"How much do you love me, then, my child?"
Mary pauses—(her eyelids drop)—
Then cries, her gaze on the ceiling fixed,
"*I love you* RIGHT UP TO THE TOP!"

*   *   *

Would God that I loved my Saviour so,
And with Peter could say, "Yea, Lord,
Thou knowest all things. Thou knowest I love
Thyself, and Thy work, and Thy Word!"

I'd lean, like John, on my Lord alone,
Never using one earthly prop;
Trusting in life, and praising in death,
And loving "RIGHT UP TO THE TOP."

Forbid, dear Lord, that as Judas, I
(Though *he* dipped his hand in Thy sop),
Should prize the silver above *the Pearl,*
Not loving Thee "up to the top."

Like Thomas, I'd cry, "My Lord, my God,
Though *my* faith for seeing can't stop;
They are blest who've not seen, yet believe,
And love Thee 'right up to the top.' "[33]

On April 10, 1885 Tom dedicated the little poem to his much-appreciated friend and volunteer music director, writing on the original these words:

> . . . in the hope that it might prove a reminder of a (Sunday) school anniversary the great success of which was in no small measure due to the aforesaid C.(harles) B.(lomfield).[34]

Later Charles returned acknowledgment of the friendship by naming his newborn son *Tom.*[35]

The quality of Thomas' preaching over this period is reflected directly in sermons published in 1884. His father introduced the volume *The Gospel of the Grace of God*[36] as those sermons his son preached while he paid a brief visit to London in that year. They appear to be culled from his previously preached materials at Auckland. C. H. Spurgeon comments:

Friends, here stands among you another witness for Christ, upon whom the Spirit of God is resting. He has been up and down in the colonies for years, but on this occasion he speaks from London. We present to you certain of the messages which he has delivered for his Master—messages full of present power, and bright with prophecies of future usefulness if life be spared. Pray for our son, that his ministry, so happily commenced, may equal anything that has preceded it, so that, when the present generation shall have passed away, the younger stock may bear to the front the old, old banner of free-grace and dying love. . . . but when the first frost and fogs of winter surround our misty isle he must be gone, like the swallows, to a sunnier clime. He will leave us this little volume as a *souvenir*, and he will send us papers for *The Sword and the Trowel* as forget-me-nots; meantime, we will entreat the Lord God of his fathers to be with him, and to make him on the other side of the world a wise Master-builder, a workman that needeth not to be ashamed, rightly dividing the word of truth.[37]

Much of Thomas's sensitivity, insight, and imaginative power can be seen in the following:

I wonder which you think the best chapter in the Bible? My own mind is not made up yet. If I may have a choice it would light on any chapter that tells me about the sufferings of Christ. A joyful sorrow fills our hearts whenever we read the old, old story of Jesus and his love. But putting those chapters aside, and giving them pre-eminence, I think—well, there is the 14th of John, and the 3rd of John, and 23rd Psalm, and the 53rd of Isaiah—but I must not think of any more, yet I cannot forget the 11th of Hebrews, that wondrous record of the deeds of faithful men and women. I like to read that chapter as if I were walking through some grand cathedral with painted windows of the saints on every hand, and with the tattered banners of brave regiments hanging down the nave, while the organ peals out some martial melody as if it told the story of never-to-be-forgotten heroisms. Throughout the chapter we see the portraits of the saints; there hang the flags of faith that braved the battle and the breeze, while the heavenly music proclaims, "these all died in faith."[38]

Wherever the Gospel is preached some will receive the truth in the love of it and bind it to their hearts. We would not cease to preach the Gospel even if encouraging results did not follow; but we are the more ready to labour on when we are assured that our labour is not in vain in the Lord. Some one asked if the people of New Zealand would listen to the Gospel. Did he think that we wanted a different sort of Gospel for the ends of the earth—an article specially manufactured for the Colonies? My experience is that wherever the old truths are clearly and earnestly preached, there are ears to hear them and hearts to understand. Until a better Gospel is given to us, which can never be, our intention is to go on preaching the atonement and substitution of our Lord Jesus Christ, persuaded that God's word shall not return unto him void, but that it shall accomplish his purpose, and prosper in the thing whereto he sent it forth.[39]

Oh, it is a blessed thing for any man when his self-satisfaction is shivered to a thousand fragments, and he begins to see himself as God sees him—a sinner, helpless, hopeless, and unsaved. The mariners, as they cross the sea, have a custom of putting a man on the very bows of the vessel to keep a smart look-out, and through the night, as the bells ring the hours, he shouts out how things are going on. Oftentimes in the stilly night, when sleep was wanting, we have waited for the tidings as if we enquired, "Watchman, what of the night?" and have rejoiced to hear the assuring cry, "All's well, all's well." 'Tis no small comfort, either, to hear those welcome words above the roar of the hurricane, and the clatter of the storm, "All's well, all's well." But there are some men who keep on saying "All's well" when it is anything but that. The storm does not affright them, and the dangers are not perceived. They cry peace, peace, when there is no peace. Better a thousand times would it be for them if in agony of soul they shrieked out, "Breakers ahead!" than that they should soothe themselves to slumber with "All's well" when really all's ill, for it must be ill with them until they exchange their self-righteousness for the better righteousness of the sinner's Saviour. It happened with some of us, that as soon as we found that we were wrong, we tried to set matters right ourselves, as if, forsooth, we could do without a Saviour. We soon discovered our folly; for the more we tried, the greater and more frequent were our failures. We found that there were rocks ahead, and so, as the sailors have it, we put the helm "hard over," in order to avoid them,—in other words, we effected a certain sort of reformation in our lives, changed our course a point or two, and it was well for us we did; but we soon discovered that there were rocks all round us, and that it was not in man to direct his way. We were hedged in round and about, and above and beneath, by the multitude of our transgressions. Then we also began to pray, for it was with us as with the mariners in the hundred and seventh psalm. When all their wisdom was swallowed up, then they cried unto the Lord in their trouble. Blessed is he who, having got to his wit's end, has still wit enough to look to the strong for strength, and to him who only can deliver. In answer to our earnest cry, we saw, dancing over the dreaded breakers, the twinkling light of the pilot's boat, and presently we hailed him aboard our storm-tossed barque. Then we cried aloud for very joy, "We have found him, we have found him." Since then he has been a pilot to our souls. He has guided us where we could not steer ourselves, and will yet bring us to the desired heaven of everlasting peace.[40]

It appears that in these third and fourth years of his Auckland ministry Tom began to hit his full stride as a powerful preacher. He early mastered the gift of using analogies and illustrations from experiences about him. Always a lover of the sea, he eventually published one collection of imaginative sermons built around the analogies of sea travel entitled *Down to the Sea*.[41] Some consider this work to be his best.

Plans for the new Auckland church proceeded slowly. Of course it would be a Tabernacle like the London one, but scaled to fit the colonial need and climate. Not as large, naturally, but big enough in concept and design to befit the upsurge now filling Wellesley Street and the Choral Hall with regular overflows each Sunday. On April 19, 1884, the Monday which followed Easter Sunday being a public holiday, some 2,000 persons gathered to set a foundation stone for the new church. At 3 PM, in brilliant sunshine, 400 children from the Sunday School opened the proceedings with musical praise directed by Charles Blomfield, and Tom declared:

> I verily believe we have had a manifestation of God's providence in the progress of this cause. I need not to tell you that we were driven by pressure of numbers to erect this place of worship. And the numbers are not lessening but increasing every week.[42]

The annual report of the Wellesley Street Church, a Bible, the church constitution and bylaws, copies of current Auckland newspapers, a complete set of the *Baptist Builder* (as published the week of the previous December bazaar), and a copy of the Easter Sunday order of worship used in services the day before, were all collated and buried with the foundation stone. A declaration that the stone was laid as a foundation for the Auckland Tabernacle, which was to be "For the Worship of Almighty God, and for the Proclamation of the Gospel" was also included along with a complete listing of the members of the building committee and the church office bearers. A dozen ministers from sister denominations joined with Baptist leaders to bring fraternal greetings.[43]

In the evening, 650 gathered in St. James Hall to hear further congratulatory speeches. Mr. Reid, the Wesleyan minister, alluded to the fact that the new building would bring Baptists closer to the Methodists, and he hoped that he would love them none the less when they came nearer to each other.[44] In fact, the buildings were almost behind each other, facing different streets. Tom responded from the chair by saying that the buildings did not face each other and adding "though we shall be fighting, it will be back to back, shoulder to shoulder, and with a common enemy."[45]

Tom laid his own check for thirty-five pounds on the foundation stone that afternoon. The greater proportion of it, he confessed, had been saved from marriage fees he received as pastor at Wellesley Street. He announced his intention to open the Auckland Tabernacle free of debt, just as his father had opened his in London over twenty years before. The offering that day totaled 500 pounds.[46]

Two days later Tom called a meeting of the deacons and asked for six months release from the pastorate. He affirmed his clear intention of returning, but felt that, after three years and some months of unremitting effort in Auckland, his health was such that he needed a long vacation. He indicated his desire to return to England and to gather extra funds from his father's congregation and from others to assist in the erection of the Auckland building. The church was in fine condition, the Sunday School and Maori mission in great strength. His father would arrange for an effective substitute interim pastor to come out to serve while he was absent, and there was every reason to believe that God's hand upon the whole church would continue in blessing. Reluctantly, they agreed.

In early May, 1884 the Wellesley Street Chapel filled again to overflowing to bid farewell to their beloved young pastor, temporarily. In his address Tom spoke of the assurance of his return. The English winters were so cold, he affirmed, that there was no possibility his health would allow him to remain in London. Even in Auckland his recurring weaknesses had precluded him from fulfilling the pastoral visitation tasks he desired. But here he had still been able to do ten times more labor than in his fatherland, and thrice as much in Auckland as elsewhere. He urged them to continue in their labors to gather funds for the new church building. He had prepared a lecture on New Zealand, entitling it "Brighter Britain" (because of the sunshine and the English immigrants), and hoped to deliver it in many places in the old country. He would take a model of the Auckland Tabernacle foundation stone and invite his friends to deposit their offerings upon it for the building needs.[47]

The Auckland membership stood at 500, and he had baptized sixteen new members the Sunday before he left.[48] The congregation, disappointed at the thought of losing their popular pastor, albeit only temporarily, realized that he needed the rest, and that the practical needs of the building program made the departure a valuable plan. His popularity was not limited to those among his own people. An Auckland resident, not a Baptist, reported visits to hear the young man, suggesting that although he was only twenty-six, he promised to equal and perhaps surpass his famous father: "It is not so much what he says that constitutes the attraction, as his thorough earnestness and perfect elocution. I do not think I missed one syllable in the discourses I have heard from him."[49]

Tom's plans included an extended call at the Gibsons' Launceston property in Tasmania on his way back to England. His journey there took him first via Sydney, where, after some renewed fellowship with Frederick Hibberd, he attended a rally addressed by his friend R. T. Booth, the Gospel Temperance Missioner. He was delighted with the old campaigner's resourcefulness when he turned from speaking to leading the assembly in a song, as torrential rains thundered down onto the iron-roofed Temperance Hall, virtually drowning his words. "I have never spoken against *water*," Booth thundered, "and I do not intend to do so tonight!"[50]

The long train journey to Melbourne was followed by an unexpected visit to the Baptist Home Mission Tea Meeting in the company of Mr. Bunning of Geelong. The town hall crowd swelled from 1,500 to 2,000 when it was publicized that Tom would attend. His greeting was brief. After apologizing for the "famine" he had caused by attracting so many unexpected guests, Tom spoke glowingly of the fine reports he had heard of the Baptist bush missionaries, and of his affection for Kerang and Quambatook, areas in which he had seen the pioneering efforts of the now healthy work begun seven years previously. He punned that he was now engaged in similar work as they for he was presently involved in a "mission" to visit his "home," and encouraged them to press on with their effective programs to reach the country areas.[51]

Prior to the formation of the Baptist Union of Tasmania (which coincided with Thomas's 1884 visit), only Harrington Street, Hobart, and York Street, Launceston, had been established as official Baptist churches. Gibson began the Perth Baptist services in 1862 but a church was not formed there until 1870, and the Perth Tabernacle not erected until 1889. The Hobart and Launceston churches, nurtured by Henry Dowling, were of the Strict Baptist variety. After Dowling's death in 1869 York Street became virtually defunct. William Gibson bridged the gap between the old and new Baptist life of the colony, his Perth church being organized along more open lines in the Spurgeon tradition, a move initiated by his wife's enthusiasm for Spurgeonic perspectives. Tom first came in 1878, then again in 1880. This time when he arrived, it was to conduct opening services for the new Launceston Baptist Tabernacle erected in Cimitiere Street.[52] Mr. Gibson and his son had built and furnished the new Launceston church with a gift of some 10,000 pounds.[53] They firmly believed that Thomas would respond to their call to be its first pastor.

Reverend A. Bird from the Isle of Wight had been C. H. Spurgeon's nomination for the Launceston task which Thomas had already refused a year prior to the building dedication. The commodious new Tabernacle seated some 1,500, having two flights of stairs leading to a large balcony and an inclined floor, the whole erected of solid local bluestone. Tom's morning sermon, "long and impressive," was on 1 Kings 8:30, and his evening one on the parable of the prodigal son. Crowded congregations flocked to the opening celebrations and to the Monday evening tea meeting. The local press reported that although he was only a young man "his deliverance was good, the tone of his voice clear and musical, resounding like a bell through the large building. His language was simple, yet eloquent."[54]

By now the churches at Deloraine and Longford, staffed by J. S. Harrison and

R. McCullough, who had traveled out with Thomas in 1880 at Gibson's invitation, were functioning effectively. At Gibson's suggestion McCullough had removed to Hobart where the Harrington Street Church had failed. He began services in the exhibition building there in 1883 with some from the older fellowship. Soon the Hobart Tabernacle opened, Gibson donating 900 pounds towards its establishment. Pastors Grant, Clark, Wood, Blaikie, and others came to serve the developing Baptist causes. The Gibsons erected a standard Baptist tabernacle, $70' \times 30' \times 30'$ in a number of centers; those still standing today at Deloraine, Longford, Sheffield, and Latrobe remain as effective centers of ministry. The Gibsons fostered other work by giving practical support at Devonport, Burnie, and similar centers.

Through his friendship with the Gibsons, Tom was largely responsible for these developments. On Tuesday May 27, 1884 he met with graduates of the London Pastors' College now serving in Tasmania to form the Baptist Union. With William Gibson, senior, as president, his son as treasurer, Dr. Benjafield of Hobart as secretary, the five Spurgeon men, and several others, the churches of Perth, Longford, Deloraine, Constitution Hill, Hobart, and York Street, Launceston joined with the new Launceston Tabernacle fellowship to begin a partnership of fellowship in the gospel. Later the "entire Baptist Union" walked with him to the wharf to bid him farewell on the *Iberia!*[55]

By the time he sailed he had already gathered some 275 pounds from the Gibsons and other friends towards the Auckland project. But on board his thoughts were only of family, home, and the beloved Metropolitan Tabernacle. Just that year another biography of his father had appeared, including in it a description of the Tabernacle service its author attended in 1876. As Tom read it, his heart ached to be once again where he had been blessed so often before:

> There was no accompaniment to the singing. A man beside him on the platform stepped forward and "raised the tune." The preacher (you could see by his movement) joined heartily in the singing. All had books. The whole congregation rose. Some twenty-five hundred voices sent up their wave of song from the body of the building. This was met by another wave from two thousand voices in the first gallery where I stood, and from the upper gallery a thousand voices met these billows of song till all mingled and rolled in an oceantide of melody uplifting and sublime. I could not sing, the whole scene was overwhelming. I sat down and wiped away my tears. . . . Then followed a prayer, deeply devotional, tender, plaintive, beseeching, in power and pathos beyond anything I have ever read in his sermons. The impressions left by that prayer are fresh in my mind and heart today.[56]

At Paddington station Tom was met by his brother Charles and rode in triumph, first to the Tabernacle for his father's greetings, and then to Westwood. His first experiences were reflected in a letter to New Zealand friends:

Sunday at the Tabernacle was almost too good. Such sermons! Such singing! Such a communion service! Such hearty welcomes! Dear father announced that I would preach on Sunday week with collections for the Auckland Tabernacle, and the people are delighted at the prospect of hearing me and helping us.[57]

C. H. S. distributed handbills to that Sunday's congregation summarizing the progress of the Auckland work to date and including a statement of anticipated costs. At the foot of the bill he added his own encouragements—"Dear friends, read this statement and let my dear son have the help which I am sure he deserves." The press reported Tom's appearance as very frail, and not at all like that of his robust twin brother, Charles:

> In the matter of preaching, he has certainly improved, and the New Zealanders should consider themselves fortunate in securing as their pastor, not only of a son of the great preacher, but one who so well represents his father in that remote corner of Great Britain. There was a large congregation at the Metropolitan Tabernacle on Sunday morning, notwithstanding the tropical downpour which visited London, and despite the fact that everybody is supposed to be out of town just now. During his prayer, Mr. Thomas Spurgeon besought a blessing upon his congregation beyond the sea, "whose Sabbath is almost done," although, with us it had little more than begun. Might the sun which was just then setting in that land "bring brightness and blessedness to the homes of each of them" "Have mercy upon me, O Lord! for I am weak"—Psalm vi. 2—formed the basis of his subsequent sermon, which will be found in this week's *Christian World Pulpit*, and in which he set himself to show that weakness of body was very nearly analogous to spiritual incapacity. He first of all gave us what he termed the description of the complaint of soul-sickness or spiritual disease, and closed with a prescription for the same. Some people, he proceeded, said they had got sluggish livers, but surely they were themselves sluggish livers, for they lived at a slow and dying rate. They seemed to be ever bearing about burdens and had not strength enough to feel their weakness. It was worse with those who were in a similar condition respecting their souls—sleepy Christians. You cannot get a sermon to suit them, for they pick holes alike in the discourse and the preacher. These timorous ones, though they have believed, are afraid to be baptized. We were not all born Samsons, and, personally, he was well aware of that fact, and a frail constitution might sometimes account for weakness of soul. An unhealthy climate often occasioned weakness of body. He could not see how those who lived in a tainted atmosphere could expect to be strong; and he for one should not be surprised some day to see nearly the whole of London coming out to New Zealand just to get a breath of fresh air. Many Christians who lived in the vitiated atmosphere of unhallowed associations would be far more healthy spiritually if they got away to the hill-tops, and lived more in the light of God's countenance. A

robust man could not live on sweetmeats and pastry, nor could the spiritual life be fed upon three-volume novels. The prescription for the spiritual disease was to be found in the words of the text, "Have mercy upon me, O Lord!" God's mercy is the antidote for our misery; God's strength alone can counteract our weakness. Mr. Thomas Spurgeon also occupied his father's pulpit in the evening, and on both occasions produced a most favourable impression. The day's collection amounted to 165 pounds, which must be regarded as liberal, seeing that the Tabernacle friends had previously contributed 500 pounds towards Mr. Thomas Spurgeon's work in New Zealand.[58]

Before he had left Auckland Thomas had a copy of the Auckland Tabernacle foundation stone made with the object of taking it with him and inviting his friends to place their contributions upon it. The facsimile proved to be too heavy for portability. However, Mr. W. Lambourne made a quarter-sized replica and a tripod which allowed the smaller stone to be screwed up into a suspended state and to be "laid" when an appropriate coin was placed on it. Tom wrote back that the model created great interest.[59] A special welcome given to him at the orphanage fête proved most productive. He fitted up a stall with a display of objects from Australia and New Zealand, including some of Charles Blomfield's paintings, and some fern and seaweed pictures of his own. But the little working model of the Auckland Tabernacle foundation stone sustained the most attention:

> I explained that it worked best for gold, but that it was obliging when any coin was placed thereupon, with the handle turned. Down went the stone, and then came orthodox taps with the mallet. The little contrivance quite took the fancy of the crowd and the stone has been well and truly laid by scores of interested persons.[60]

Tom said he had also become quite used to having someone thrust a sovereign into his hand for the Auckland funds while walking through the Glasgow or London streets.[61]

C. H. Spurgeon cultivated his natural gift of extemporaneous speech with original phrasing and outstanding communication of orthodox doctrines in sermons possessing an astonishing breadth of variety. He was a man of shrewd common sense with absolute confidence in his message, who applied what he said to the needs of his hearers with immense earnestness of purpose. He demonstrated a power of naturalness, freshness, and vitality of thought. Spurgeon followed George Whitefield as his pulpit model, and worked very hard to discipline his energies and talents towards excellence in preaching.

Spurgeon never advertised a subject, introduced few novel ideas, and preached no sensational sermons tuned to contemporary ears. But he knew how to use humor, how to phrase a point or sermon division succinctly, and how to illustrate his truths using appeals to sight, smell, hearing, taste, and touch. He refused 10,000 pounds offered to undertake a lecture and preaching circuit in New York in 1859, giving himself solely to his London ministries. In 1876, when only 727 of his ultimate 3,500 published sermons had appeared in print, a contemporary wrote of him with amazement:

> . . . Never, in any period of the Christian Church, did any man rise and hold in sustained attention and active Christian useful labour a weekly congregation, certainly not numbering less than from five to six thousand persons, with no popular prestige, no music to aid, no robes to give effect, no ceremonial of service—plain, simple, and unadorned.[62]

He continued unspoiled by his popularity and unprovoked by the many abuses heaped upon him by some who did not understand his genius or his commitment. If he did not preach *great sermons* he certainly was a *great preacher of sermons*.

Above all Spurgeon possessed a voice that could "roar like the ocean breakers and coo like a mother dove."[63] Joseph Parker declared: "It was the mightiest voice I ever heard; a voice that could give orders in a tempest, and find its way across a torrent as through a silent aisle. Very gentle, too, it could be sweet and tender, and full of healing pity."[64] Thomas found it to be "so varied in its tones and so full in its compass that it was in itself a whole orchestra."[65] He said that in the thousands at the Tabernacle Spurgeon's voice seemed so restful it put everyone at ease. The trams and buses of the streets could not drown its flow. In manner his voice was dignified and conversational, not at all the delivery of a fiery orator:

> Vast as was the auditorium, the faintest tone could be distinctly heard by the attentive throng; and when the power of the mighty instrument was used, the place seemed to tremble with its sonorous thunder.[66]

Hood, who affirmed that Spurgeon's voice was his *least* attribute, attests to its power also in superlatives:

> . . . a voice like the man and the matter, independent of most nervous impressions, all nervous agitations. It is a clarion of a voice; other voices of orators have pierced us more, have possessed more accent, have been able to whisper better, but we never knew, nor conceived a voice with such thunderous faculty. I have called it a trumpet, and better still, a bell; its tones roll on, there is no exhaustion; . . . they are full and sweeping, and they give the idea of a great, fully-informed, and immensely capacious will and nature.[67]

But the man was so much more than professional skill and natural ability. He knew men. He knew God. He knew the Bible. Alive to everything around him, he was quick to seize a notable event to give the gospel prominence. The sinking of the *Princess Alice*, the Indian Mutiny, and other political and national elements in his society were eagerly used to illustrate spiritual truths. His bright humor and empathy with suffering humanity saved his Calvinistic belief in divine sovereignty and his Puritan passion for righteousness from harshness. The sermons he published and the books he wrote and edited are estimated to contain some twenty-three million words, the equivalent of the twenty-seven volumes of the ninth edition of the *Encyclopaedia Britannica*.[68]

To all these attributes of greatness another element must be added. His doctrine stood as foundation and core to all that he was and did. Spurgeon followed an orthodox system built strongly from the Calvinistic heritage of his day, but his biblicism was not of the narrow, rigid, exclusivist type. On the contrary, he found a way to weld the ribs of biblical revelation into support for a free and joyous faith which spanned the gulf between the first-century world and his own world with a bridge as beautiful as it was functional. His hearers traveled this road of faith with delight, but they walked on solid foundations.

When he preached on the second advent of Christ, Spurgeon always did this with reserve and balance. He derided those who looked for times and seasons. He saw Christ's coming again as a personal revelation, and to be visible, final, and imminent. He expected a personal reign of Christ from Jerusalem. One of his former students described his position as one not at all excessive:

> . . . he did not flaunt any theory in the matter. Not long before death, he, with some other Evangelical Baptists, signed a statement of doctrine which closed with an affirmation of the pre-millennial Advent. But if he had drawn it up himself I very much doubt if he would have inserted that sentence. He said, "I care nothing about petty speculation about prophecy." . . . He devoted himself to the comfort and strengthening of the saints.[69]

His ability to bring comfort and strength to those in need arose largely from his understandings of the doctrines of grace.

The Baptist Union, to which Spurgeon belonged, provided a common meeting ground for the two streams of Particular and General Baptists who had characterized the English scene. Some of the early Baptists had paralyzed evangelism through an overly rigid adherence to extreme views of election and double predestination. The eclectic perspectives advocated by Robert Hall, and later applied by William Carey and Andrew Fuller set the stage for the ultimate fusion between those who viewed the atonement as limited in scope and those who saw it as universal propitiation for all the sins of all men. The point of adjustment came as many moved to see that an atonement potential for all could still be ruled as ultimately effective only for those who respond by faith.

Individual congregations also often retained their traditional practices of strict admittance to communion. Spurgeon, and others, viewed the table as open to any believer, but saw in such fellowship the right to approach the unbaptized with the charge that the fulfillment of the one ordinance laid upon them the obligation also to fulfill the other. While many differing shades of practice ranged across the English scene among Baptists, the vast majority followed Spurgeon's openness, and at the same time retained his commitment to the foundational doctrines popularly known as "Calvinistic."[70]

A master of Puritan literature while still in his teens, Spurgeon held a view of the majesty and sovereignty of God which pervaded all of his life and experience. A singular prophecy that he would preach to multitudes in London pronounced upon him as a child by a well-known evangelist received literal fulfillment as to specific situation and occasion. This "coincidence" strengthened his grasp of such doctrines and faith in the providence of God.[71] When the Metropolitan Tabernacle was dedicated in 1861 the afternoon and evening meetings were given over to expositions of the doctrines of grace (election, human depravity, particular redemption, effectual calling, and final perseverance).[72]

But for all his commitment to such foundational concepts, he possessed little patience with those whose theology was bound and limited by them. In a letter written after his first Sunday in London Spurgeon asserts:

> The London people are rather higher in Calvinism than myself, but I have succeeded in bringing one church to my own views and will trust with Divine assistance to do the same with another. I am a Calvinist, I love what some call "glorious Calvinism," but Hyperism is too hot spiced for my palate.[73]

He discussed the tension between election and the man's free will by saying:

> . . . the fact is that the whole of truth is neither here nor there, neither in this system nor in that, neither with this man nor that. Be it ours to know what is scriptural in all systems and to receive it.[74]

By his own testimony, he felt that when he was coming to Christ it was a work he was doing himself. While he sought the Lord earnestly, he had no idea that the Lord was actually seeking him.[75]

In claiming that it was impossible to preach the gospel without holding to justification by faith without works, the sovereignty of God, the omnipotent conquering love of his electing grace, the special redemption of his elect, and the security of their atonement effected by Christ, he stood firmly in the Calvinistic heritage. But in denying that these doctrines impinged upon the free will of men, he followed the Fuller-Carey tradition and allied himself with evangelicals of a wide range:

> As for our faith, as a church, you have heard about that already. We believe in the five great points commonly known as Calvinistic; but *we do not regard those five points as being barbed shafts which we are to thrust between the*

ribs of our fellow-Christians. We look upon them as being five great lamps which help to irradiate the cross; or, rather, five bright emanations springing from the glorious covenant of our Triune God, and illustrating the great doctrine of Jesus crucified. Against all comers, especially against all lovers of Arminianism, we defend and maintain pure gospel truth.

At the same time, I can make this public declaration, that I am no Antinomian. I belong not to the sect of those who are afraid to invite the sinner to Christ. I warn him, I invite him, I exhort him. Hence then I have contumely on either hand. Inconsistency is charged against me by some people, as if anything that God commanded could be inconsistent; I will glory in such inconsistency even to the end. I bind myself precisely to no form of doctrine. I love those five points as being the angles of the gospel, but then I love the centre between the angles better still. Moreover, we are Baptists, and we cannot swerve from this matter of discipline, nor can we make our church half-and-half in that matter. The witness of our church must be one and indivisible. We must have one Lord, one faith, and one baptism. And yet dear to our hearts is that great article of the Apostles' Creed, "I believe in the communion of saints." I believe not in the communion of Episcopalians alone; *I do not believe in the communion of Baptists only, I dare not sit with them exclusively.* I think I should be almost strict-communionist enough not to sit with them at all, because I should say, "This is not the communion of saints, it is the communion of Baptists." Whosoever loves the Lord Jesus Christ in verity and truth hath a hearty welcome, and is not only permitted, but invited to communion with the Church of Christ.

However, we can say, with all our hearts, that difference has never lost us one good friend yet. I see around me our Independent brethren; they certainly have been to Aenon today, for there has been "much water" here; and I see round about me dear strict-communion brethren, and one of them is about to address you. He is not so strict a communionist but what he really in his own heart communes with all the people of God. I can number among my choicest friends many members of the Church of England, and some of every denomination; I glory in that fact. *However sternly a man may hold the right of private judgment, he yet can give his right hand with as tight a grip to everyone who loves the Lord Jesus Christ.*[76]

"In theology," said Spurgeon, "I stand where I did when I began preaching, and I stand almost alone. If I ever did such a thing, I could preach my earliest sermons now without change so far as the essential doctrines are concerned. *I stand almost exactly where Calvin stood in his maturer years; not where he stood in his Institutes, which he wrote when quite a young man, but in his later works*; that position is taken by few. Even those who occupy Baptist pulpits do not preach exactly the same truths that I preach. They see things differently; and, of course, they preach in their own way. Although few will deny the wonderful power of the truth as it has been preached at the Tabernacle, it is not according to their method; yet it is the Calvinistic way of looking at things which causes my sermons to have such acceptance in Scotland, in Holland, and even in the Transvaal, where a recent traveller expressed his astonishment at finding translations of them lying beside the family Bible in a great many of the farmsteads of the country. I am aware that my preaching repels many; that I cannot help. If, for instance, a man does not believe in the inspiration of the Bible, he may come, and hear me once; and if he comes no more, that is his responsibility, and not mine. My doctrine has no attraction for that man; but I cannot change my doctrine to suit him."[77]

Spurgeon's sermon on "Compel Them to Come In" reflects his intense zeal for the conversion of his hearers. He was criticized by the stricter Calvinists for his evangelical passion but replied that he could not reconcile how one could give an open, pressing invitation to Christ and throw the responsibility of acceptance or rejection upon the hearer. He merely said that he believed this is what the Bible taught him to do and that in doing it he was obeying God. He urged them on another occasion to obey the biblical command to proclaim the gospel and leave the results to God:

> Remember, though you imagine, perhaps, from what I have been saying, that the Gospel is restricted, that the Gospel is freely preached to all. *The decree is limited but the good news is as wide as the world.* The good news is as wide as the universe. *I tell it to every creature under heaven because I am told to do so.* The secret of God which is to deal with the application, that is to be proclaimed to all nations.[78]

The extent of the atonement seems not to have been the problem for Calvin that it became for some of his later followers. In his comments on 1 John 2:2 Calvin expresses his agreement with the idea that Christ suffered sufficiently for the whole world, but effectively only for the elect.[79] Spurgeon agreed. He was criticized by general atonement advocates because of his exclusivist theology, and by the strict and particular advocates for his openness. The greatest majority of Baptists today appear to hold to the position Spurgeon first popularly advocated. Many of the broader inclusivists having since moved into Universalist and Unitarian fellowship.

Spurgeon often declared that he saw God's will and man's will as simply two sides of the one question of salvation and that human nature was only able to view salvation from either one perspective or the other at the one time. Just as a man can only view one corner or other of a house, or at the most two, and never four at one time, so man walks around salvation understanding it from the perspective of election and predestination, or from that of free will and human responsibility. But he can never see the whole house, with all its sides at once. But that does not mean that the various views are irreconcilable, merely that from our plane of vision we cannot view them together as one might poised above the house. A favorite text for Spurgeon was John 6:37 in which he found election in the first half balanced by the promise that those who freely come will be accepted in the second half. He stedfastly resisted the attempt to confine him in either a Universalist or a Calvinistic prison:

> I know there are some who think it necessary to their system of theology to limit the merit of the blood of Jesus: if my theological system needed such a limitation, I would cast it to the winds. I cannot, I dare not, allow the thought to find a lodging in my mind, it seems near akin to blasphemy. *In Christ's finished work I see an ocean of merit*; my plummet finds no bottom, my eye discovers no shore. *There must be sufficient efficacy in the* blood of Christ, if God had so willed it, to have saved not only *all in this world, but all in ten thousand worlds*, had they transgressed their Maker's law. Once admit infinity into the matter, and limit is out of the question. Having a Divine Person for an offering, it is not consistent to conceive of limited value; bound and measure are terms inapplicable to the Divine sacrifice. *The intent of the Divine purpose fixes the APPLICATION of the infinite offering, but does not change it into a finite work.* Think of the countless hosts in Heaven: if thou wert introduced there today, thou wouldst find it as easy to tell the stars, or the sand of the sea, as to count the multitudes that are before the throne even now. They have come from the East, and from the West, from the North, and from the South, and they are sitting down with Abraham and with Isaac, and with Jacob in the Kingdom of God; and beside those in heaven, think of the saved ones on earth. Blessed be God, His elect on earth are to be counted by millions, I believe; and the days are coming, brighter days than these, when there shall be multitudes upon multitudes brought to know the Saviour, and to rejoice in Him. The Father's love is not for a few only, but for an exceeding great company. "A great multitude, which no man could number," will be found in Heaven. A man can reckon up to very high figures; set to work your Newtons, your mightiest calculators, and they can count great numbers; but God and God alone can tell the multitude of His redeemed.[80]

Some people love the doctrine of universal atonement because they say, "It is so beautiful. It is a lovely idea that Christ should die for all men; it commends itself," they say, "to the instincts of humanity; there is something in it full of joy and beauty." I admit there is; but beauty may be often associated with falsehood. There is much which I might admire in the theory of *universal redemption*, but I will just show what the supposition necessarily involves. If Christ on His cross intended to save every man, then He intended to save those who were lost before He died. *If the doctrine be true, that He died for all men, then He died for some who were in hell before He came into this world,* for doubtless there were even then myriads there who had been cast away because of their sins. Once again, if it was Christ's intention to save *all* men, how deplorably has He been disappointed, for we have His own testimony that there is a lake which burneth with fire and brimstone, and into that pit of woe have been cast some of the very persons who, according to the theory of universal redemption, were bought with His blood. That seems to me a conception a thousand times more repulsive than any of those consequences which are said to be associated with the Calvinistic and Christian doctrine of special and particular redemption. *To think that my Saviour died for men who were or are in hell, seems a supposition too horrible for me to entertain.* To imagine for a moment that He was the Substitute for all the sons, and that God, having first punished the Substitute, afterwards punished the sinners themselves, seems to conflict with all my ideas of Divine justice. *That Christ should offer an atonement and satisfaction for the sins of all men, and that afterwards some of those very men should be punished for the sins for which Christ had already atoned, appears to me to be the most monstrous iniquity that could ever have been imputed to Saturn, to Janua, to the goddess of the Thugs, or to the most diabolical heathen deities. God forbid that we should ever think thus of Jehovah, the just and wise and good!*

There is no soul who holds more firmly to the doctrines of grace than I do, and *if any man asks me whether I am ashamed to be called a Calvinist, I answer,—I wish to be called nothing but a Christian; but if you ask me, do I hold the doctrinal views which were held by John Calvin, I reply I do in the main hold them, and rejoice to avow it.* But far be it from me even to imagine that Zion contains none but Calvinistic Christians within her walls, or that there are none saved who do not hold our views. *Most atrocious things have been spoken about the character and spiritual condition of John Wesley, the modern prince of Arminians. I can only say concerning him that, while I detest many of the doctrines which he preached, yet for the man himself I have a reverence second to no Wesleyan.* The character of John Wesley stands beyond all imputation for self-sacrifice, zeal, holiness, and communion with God; he lived far above the ordinary level of common Christians, and was one "of whom the world was not worthy." *I believe there are multitudes of men who cannot see these truths, or, at least, cannot see them in the way in which we put them, who nevertheless have received Christ as their Saviour, and are as dear to the heart of the God of grace as the soundest Calvinist in or out of Heaven.*[81]

On January 15, 1859, Spurgeon delivered a masterly sermon on Romans 9:13—"Jacob have I loved, but Esau have I hated." He affirmed the truth that God's love for Jacob was unearned and unmerited and solely from his grace by referring to Romans 9:11. He also illustrated Jacob's total unworthiness from Jacob's dealings with God and with Esau. Coming to face the question as to why God "hated" Esau, after declaring that it was only by grace that he loved Jacob, the preacher asserted:

Now the next question is a different one: *Why did God hate Esau?* I am not going to mix this question up with the other, they are entirely distinct, and I intend to keep them so, one answer will not do for two questions, they must be taken separately, and then can be answered satisfactorily. Why does God hate any man? I defy anyone to give any answer but this, because that man deserves it; no reply but that can ever be true. There are some who answer, divine sovereignty; but I challenge them to look that doctrine in the face. Do you believe that God created man and arbitrarily, sovereignly—it is the same thing—created that man, with no other intention, than that of damning him? Made him, and yet, for no other reason than that of destroying him for ever? Well, if you can believe it, I pity you, that is all I can say: you deserve pity, that you should think so meanly of God, whose mercy endureth for ever. You are quite right when you say the reason why God loves a man, is because God does do so; there is no reason in the man. But do not give the same answer as to why God hates a man. If God deals with any man severely, it is because that man deserves all he gets. In hell there will not be a solitary soul that will say to God, Lord, thou hast treated me worse than I deserve! But every lost spirit will be made to feel that he has got his deserts, that his destruction lies at his own door and not at the door of God; that God had nothing to do with his condemnation, except as the Judge condemns the criminal, but that he himself brought damnation upon his own head, as the result of his own evil works. Justice is that which damns a man; it is mercy, it is free grace, that saves; sovereignty holds the scale of love; it is justice holds the other scale. Who can put that into the hand of sovereignty? That were to libel God and to dishonour him.

. . . If any of you want to know what I preach every day, and any stranger should say, "Give me a summary of his doctrine," say this, "He preaches salvation all of grace, and damnation all of sin. He gives God all the glory for every soul that is saved, but he won't have it that God is to blame for any man that is damned." That teaching I cannot understand. My soul revolts at the idea of a doctrine that lays the blood of man's soul at God's door. I cannot conceive how any human mind, at least any Christian mind, can hold any such blasphemy as that. I delight to preach this blessed truth—salvation of God, from first to last—the Alpha and the Omega; but when I come to preach damnation, I say, damnation of man, not of God; and if you perish, at your own hands must your blood be required. There is another passage. At the last great day, when all the world shall come before Jesus to be judged, have you noticed, when the righteous go on the right side, Jesus says, "Come ye blessed of my father,"—("of my father," mark)—"inherit the kingdom prepared"—(mark the next word)—"for you, from before the foundation of the world." What does he say to those on the left? "Depart, ye cursed." He does not say, "ye cursed of my father," but, "ye cursed." And what else does he say? "into everlasting fire, prepared"—(not for you, but)—"for the devil and his angels." Do you see how it is guarded? Here is the salvation side of the question. It is all of God. "Come, ye blessed of my father." It is a kingdom prepared for them. There you have election, free grace in all its length and breadth. But, on the other hand, you have nothing said about the father—nothing about that at all. "Depart, ye cursed." Even the flames are said not to be prepared for sinners, but for the devil and his angels. There is no language that I can possibly conceive that could more forcibly express this idea, supposing it to be the mind of the Holy Spirit, that the glory should be to God, and that the blame should be laid at man's door.

Now, have I not answered these two questions honestly? I have endeav-oured to give a scriptural reason for the dealings of God with man. He saves man by grace, and if men perish they perish justly by their own fault. "How," says some one, "do you reconcile *these two doctrines*?" My dear brethren, I never reconcile two friends, never. These two doctrines are friends with one another; for they are both in God's Word, and I shall not attempt to reconcile them. If you show me that they are enemies, then I will reconcile them. "But," says one, "there is a great deal of difficulty about them." Will you tell me what truth there is that has not difficulty about it? "But," he says, "I do not see it." Well, I do not ask you to see it; I ask you to believe it. There are many things in God's Word that are difficult, and that I cannot see, but they are there, and I believe them. I cannot see how God can be omnipotent and man be free; but it is so, and I believe it. "Well," says one, "I cannot understand it." My answer is, I am bound to make it as plain as I can, but if you have any understanding, I cannot give you any; there I must leave it. But then, again, it is not a matter of understanding; it is a matter of faith. These two things are true; I do not see that they at all differ. However, if they did, I should say, if they appear to contradict one another, they do not really do so, because God never contradicts himself. And I should think in this I exhibited the power of my faith in God, that I could believe him, even when his word seemed to be contradictory. That is faith.[82]

Thomas shared this same perspective. After his period in England was complete, one of his last services was the opportunity to preach for his brother Charles at the South Greenwich Baptist Church. Appropriately, the congregation there planned to donate a large clock for the new Tabernacle at Auckland.[83] Tom chose this theme of divine choice and human responsibility with which to conclude his English ministry:

I imagine that some one in this congregation would like to say to me, "But how do you reconcile those two things? Here is Christ saying, 'Let anybody come and I will receive him'; and yet in the same breath he declares that only those can come whom the Father draws, and who have been already given to the Son." My dear friends, I do not see the need to reconcile them. God's word is true. "Let God be true, and every man a liar"; and, if they do seem to contradict each other, let them seem to contradict, though, indeed, to me it is not so. I do not see that they are at variance the one with the other. I am sure that I have been given to the Son, because I have come; and I was most certainly drawn, for I should not have come else. And you who have not come can be sure that you have been given only by coming. That is God's way of proving the fact to you. You want to find it out by some other plan. You want to go round by the back way and see into the secrets; but the Lord says, "Knock at the front door, and you shall be let in." He has every right to put it so, and to claim from us our faith in the Lord Jesus Christ without any further promise than that the faith shall be honoured and the sinner saved.

Man's responsibility and the sovereignty of God's choice are not at variance one with the other. They are distinct and separate, I grant you. They do not coincide, but there is no collision. Keep them separate—render to God the things that are God's, to man the things that are man's, and you will come to believe if you cannot fully understand that he who has compassion on those on whom he will have compassion, is perfectly honest and gloriously consistent when he cries aloud to all the world, saying, "Him that cometh to me I will in no wise cast out."

The natives of Australia were very much surprised the first time they saw a man on horseback. They had seen a horse before, and they had seen a man before, but they had never seen a man and a horse together before. They fancied that some unheard-of monster was coming upon them, which in the distance looked like a gigantic emu. But when the apparition drew near, and they perceived that the creature resolved itself into man and horse, their fears were allayed. The reason why the doctrines of Divine sovereignty and human responsibility appear so inconsistent to some is, that they are not regarded as quite distinct: the one being as far above the other as man is superior to the horse. They were made to go together, though they can never be one. No one would think of reconciling steed and rider. Seek not to reconcile these doctrines. Give each its proper position, and grace and wisdom appear, instead of inconsistency and partiality. Assign to God the honour that is due to his name, and the right to choose and to refuse, and at the same time feel that thou thyself art answerable for all that thou dost or dost not do. Then, and only then, the mystery is solved. "He doeth according to his will in the army of heaven, and among the inhabitants of the earth: and none can stay his hand or say unto him, What doeth thou?" At the same time, every man is intelligently responsible, and, since faith in Christ is the ordained way of life, it is for each to come to Christ and trust in him, thereby proving that they are ordained unto everlasting life.[84]

From the sharing of such perspectives both Spurgeons gained their spiritual power and doctrinal strength. Their emphasis was a fresh one for the centuries in which they served, offering some relief from the oppressive biblicism of previous times. It became an area for which Spurgeon's college graduates were widely known and largely explains the attendant blessings of conversion which permeate their ministries in those revival days. During that same period, Tom continually referred to the experience of his own conversion based upon a simple acceptance of the substitutionary atonement of Christ in his behalf:

> How well do I remember the happy days when my brother and I used to learn from our precious mother (God ever bless her), the way to heaven. On Sabbath evenings we stood beside her at the piano and sang the songs of Zion. Amongst the best of them was,—
>
> > "There is a fountain filled with blood,
> > Drawn from Immanuel's veins";
>
> and when we came to that beautiful chorus "I do believe" and so on, Mother used to say, "Now do not sing this if it is not really so with you. Do not let it be mere song on your part. Let me sing it alone unless you really mean it." And oh, how our little hearts used to break with longing for the day when each could sing for himself,
>
> > "I do believe, I will believe,
> > That Jesus died for me."
>
> The day came at last to both of us—the happiest day that ever dawned on either him or me—and we have been able to sing ever since, despite our many faults and failings,
>
> > "I do believe, I will believe,
> > That Jesus died for me,
> > That on the cross he shed his blood
> > From sin to set me free."[85]

Tom did not leave England easily. His health made it imperative that he should return, as did the promise and potential at Auckland. But he had noted an increasing indisposition in his father, far more marked than in his previous visit five years earlier. C. H. Spurgeon could be hopeful and buoyant one hour and writhing with arthritic pain in the next. Often in the mornings his hands and feet swelled so that he had to remain seated most of the day and even handle papers very laboriously. His right hand would lock so that he would have to work on it sometimes for an hour, loosening its action joint by joint, finger by finger. He did not complain, but Thomas realized that he often preached in the most acute agony and shuffled more than he walked.

The letters Tom sent to Auckland were full of good news:

> There was a large attendance at the Wellesley Street Baptist Church last evening to hear the reading of some pastoral letters received by the mail from Mr. Thos. Spurgeon. From these communications we gather that in addition

to the 1000 pounds obtained for the new Tabernacle through the influence and exertions of his father, Mr. Thomas Spurgeon expects to bring to Auckland with him 1500 pounds as the result of his lecturing tour in England and the colonies. Among other gifts he is bringing with him are a new pulpit Bible for the Tabernacle, the gift of Mr. C. H. Spurgeon; a clock for the same building, the gift of Mr. Charles Spurgeon's congregation at Green-wich; and a communion service from the deacons of the Metropolitan Temple. Mr. Spurgeon expresses a confident hope that the Tabernacle will be opened free of debt, relying on the self-sacrificing spirit of his people, and the liberality hitherto evinced towards the cause by the Auckland public. He warns his congregation that even in such an event their exertions must be continued for another year, so that the Church agencies may be thoroughly equipped, the Sunday-school and infant class rooms fitted up with all conveniences, and stabling accommodation provided on the block for the use of members attending the services from the suburbs or country.[86]

On December 12, 1885 Thomas sailed on the *Liguria* along with a Pastors' College student H. H. Driver, returning to New Zealand, and J. R. Cooper and his bride en route to the Perth church in Tasmania. The Auckland people welcomed him, delighted at the 2,500 pounds he brought with him for the building fund. A 'soiree' (the Victorian name for a tea meeting) hosted by the combined ladies in the congregation was matched by a huge welcome banner painted by Charles Blomfield in the Choral Hall for the first Sunday. The church now possessed 650 members, the building progress had begun, and Tom's health had been improved by the long sea voyages.[87]

The Auckland Tabernacle architect Edmund Bell and the builder, James Holland, had made the best of the commanding church site at the top of Upper Queen Street. Already the uncompleted building stood out as a landmark; one whole side visible from the harbor, its massive proportions stood out high above nearby buildings. Cost estimates had now escalated to 13,000 pounds, with an extra acre of land beside the new building also to be purchased and added. The final erection cost 14,628 pounds, and by the opening day, Tuesday May 12, 1885, the final 1000 pounds had been made up to within the last 100 pounds. This final 100 came in just in time to open the building debt free and, upon being informed of this, the assembly sang the doxology for the second time.

The building committee had planned a solid, elegant, and commodious house of worship, using ideas from British sources and blending these with others utilized in the Auckland Theatre Royal and the Opera House. An imposing exterior facade of Corinthian pillars led to a portico up a flight of six steps. The pediment supported by the pillars had molded capitals and pedestals. Lavish windows outlined by striated moldings and ornamented with pediments set off a high-pitched slated roof.

The large Tabernacle interior seated 1,200 comfortably but 1,700 jammed in for the May 17 services, and 1,500 was a common crowd in the years which followed. The auditorium featured an inclined floor with chairs radiating from the center. A gallery, carried on iron girders with an open ornamental iron balustrade, looked up to a multiformed ceiling divided into rectangular areas by mouldings and angles to assure good acoustics. No auditor was placed more than 50 feet from the preacher. Charles Blomfield decorated the interior, painting the high ceiling beams in lustrous pastels and gold-edged decor lines which retain their beauty to this day. Later he added a pulpit alcove and the text "Praise Ye the Lord." In 1898 a larger pulpit rail was also added.

The pulpit table was a facsimile of the one in London. The Bible, suitably inscribed, was that originally used in the New Park Street Pulpit by C. H. Spurgeon. A patented ventilation system allowed for congregational comfort and handsome gasoliers diffused ample light for the evening services. The church became the largest Free congregation regularly meeting in the Australian colonies, aided by the ample worship facilities afforded by the new building.

Sunday May 10 concluded the services in the Choral Hall. The following Sunday evening, May 17, saw the spacious new building filled, with every corridor, aisle, and vestry packed with worshipers. The steps to the rostrum and the area behind the preacher were also crowded. Many hundreds had to be turned away.[88]

The crowds continued to come and Thomas's ministry went on from strength to strength from 1885 for another four years. He went camping with Blomfield and found many ideas for sermons in his observations of nature.[89] He celebrated Queen Victoria's Jubilee with thanksgiving services in 1887, and gained a reputation similar to his father's for sermon delivery of a superior standard. The headmaster of the Auckland High School regularly took scholars to the Tabernacle to hear Thomas read the Scriptures and learn elocutionary values from his enunciation.[90] Henry C. Dane of the U.S.A., who visited Auckland in 1887, found the Tabernacle to be the largest and most active church there, and wrote that the pastor seemed to be:

> . . . a plain, unaffected, strong preacher, often when deep in his subject, much like his father in manner and style. There is that same deep ernestness, that same yearning of soul, that same sweetness of spirit, that same simplicity, and devoutness of manner which captivates and captures his hearers, and that same boldness of utterance which commands the respect of all.[91]

Dane described a baptismal service in which Thomas immersed five regular applicants, four Episcopalians, and two Methodists, and others who desired to remain with their own churches, but to be immersed as believers.[92]

Thomas was also one of five Baptist leaders who met in 1887 to set in motion plans for the training of students which ultimately resulted in the founding of the New Zealand Baptist Theological College in 1925.

It was around this period that he realized that his father had taken an unpopular theological stand in London which had brought him under much criticism. C. H. Spurgeon gently refused to identify the evangelical faith with the rather watered-down version being offered by Henry Ward Beecher. Dr. Joseph Parker had taken him to task for his apparent individualism. He did this through an "open letter" published in the press, in which he attacked C. H. Spurgeon's narrowness. He demanded that Spurgeon

> . . . widen the circle of which you are the centre. You are surrounded by offerers of incence. They flatter your weakness, they laugh at your jokes, they feed you with compliments. My dear Spurgeon you are too big a man for this. Take in more fresh air. Open your windows . . . scatter your ecclesiastical harem.[93]

Parker lived to regret his thoughtless censure and to apologize for it (although not to Spurgeon). He rendered a generous tribute to him when Spurgeon died.[94]

The period produced such a variety of less-than-orthodox interpretations of faith that these pressures mounted to the point that where Spurgeon felt that he had to do more than to gently negate the increasing secularism and apostasy around him. Biblical criticism openly advocated an evolutionary hypothesis as the basis for interpreting biblical literature. New liberal theologies sprang up in abundance overnight, systematically eliminating all supernatural elements from Scripture and attacking its inspiration.[95] Finally Spurgeon gave his approval to an article for the *Sword and Trowel* which asserted, in part:

> The atonement is doubted, the inspiration of Scripture is derided, the Holy Spirit is degraded into an influence, the punishment of sin is turned into a fiction, and the resurrection into a myth, and yet these enemies of our faith expect us to call them brethren.[96]

Despite his earlier assurances of openness in fellowship with all true believers, some immediately thought that his protest was against the abandonment of Calvinistic views. He emphatically denied that this was the issue.[97] He complained that progressive theology taught that "men *can* escape if they neglect the great salvation."[98] Of particular import in this area was the doctrine of postmortem salvation advocated by the Universalists who objected to the orthodox views of judgment and eternal punishment. In a letter to Mr. Auslane he affirmed:

> The Restoration theory carries with it so much of the same evils as the Romish Purgatory, and is accompanied with as many other errors, that

personally I cannot be in communion with any one holding it; but you must use your own discretion.[99]

Regrettably his concerns brought him into severe conflict with the Baptist Union. He wanted them to accept an elaborate doctrinal statement of the order of the Evangelical Alliance, but the prevailing view of the Union was anticredal. Spurgeon's deep concern was for many within the Union who were openly denying the orthodox truths. A comedy of errors ensued (amply documented elsewhere[100]) which resulted in Spurgeon's being censured and virtually forced to resign from the Union. It appears that some who could have clarified matters refused to do in public what they in private had promised to do. Spurgeon's principles would have been compromised had he stayed.[101]

Yet in all this he refused to try to unduly influence others. He specifically rejected the idea of forming a new denomination, although his ability to lead so many Baptists was undeniable had he chosen to exercise it.

Spurgeon had waited a long time before voicing his protests. He hesitated to speak until he was absolutely sure. As one reads the correspondence and its results, sadness at the many misunderstood communications is matched by wonder at the enigmatic behaviors of leaders who perhaps ought to have acted differently. Dr. James A. Spurgeon did *not* withdraw from the Union with his brother, yet said he supported him. Secretary W. A. Booth, who agreed with Spurgeon in private, refused to support him in the Union council meetings. Spurgeon had letters and other documentation to support all his charges, but refused to name individuals and chose to withdraw rather than to split the Union.

Above all else, C. H. Spurgeon appears to have attempted to act honestly and with sensitivity. Others were unwilling to follow his lead, although ultimately the Union did adopt a more specifically evangelical statement of faith. Immediately upon his withdrawal, Spurgeon joined the Surrey and Middlesex Baptist Association, whose members were of a more sympathetic order. Four years after the break, he invited the Union president to participate in College conference meetings. He was not antidenominational, and his quarrel was not with persons but over slackness in some ideals.

Such a stand is not to be interpreted as a spiritual versus social gospel fight. Twenty-one missions halls associated with the Tabernacle involved over 2,000 in the poorer parts of the city, ministering to every need imaginable. Their volunteer and supported workers helped with poverty, unemployment, family needs, and educational lacks among the masses. In some districts these were the only charitable agencies at work. Recent studies have documented that his concern for the poor and outcast of London far outweighed that of his contemporaries.[102] He began an evening school for the uneducated poor long before London's city evening schools were founded. The city fathers used his work as a model for their own.[103]

After serving as a pastor for twenty-five years, he was presented with 6,476 pounds, which he immediately gave back to the church as an endowment for almshouses operated for the elderly and indigent of the area. He led fights for social reform in the districts where his missions served, operated a large orphanage, and used his sermons to plead for the poor weavers, to speak against slavery, and to tackle other social questions of the day. He took offerings for the Free Hospitals of London, and lashed out at factory sweatshops and greedy owners. His own generosity and large-heartedness was proverbial. Spurgeon gave away his earnings from publication to poor students, funding passages for them from his own pocket to missionary appointments, and supplying books for preachers' libraries. He often paid the utility bills for the vast enterprises he founded from his own pockets. As Thielicke has commented, we still stand today "in need of the simple way in which Spurgeon dares to say that what really and ultimately counts is to save sinners . . . anything else is watered-down social gospel . . . twaddle."[104]

Thomas followed the Downgrade controversy in the press reports and through letters back and forth, empathizing with his father, and supporting him as best he could. Twenty years later he would recall these months when he took a similar stand—one which initiated similar consequences.[105] But for now, his mind and heart were on other matters.

The town gossips had tried their hand at matchmaking many times over the years. But Tom told them nothing of his heart. After several years of correspondence, he announced his engagement to Lila in 1886, and they were finally married on February 10, 1888. The Hanover Street Baptist Chapel in Dunedin was crowded to capacity with many well-wishers for a ceremony conducted by Reverend A. North, assisted by Tom's father's friend George Muller, who was visiting the colonies at that time. They set up housekeeping at Remuera, about three miles from the Tabernacle and lived there very happily, delighted especially with the arrival of little Daisy, born in late December 1888.

But that gift of joy lived only three months. The baby's unexpected death reduced Lila to a depression that seemed constant and incurable. Tom never quite forgave himself for his involvement with the church which had taken him away so much from his wife and child. The months had sped away and the shock of the child's passing seemed to underscore the strain of his Auckland service. Some years later he wrote:

> Have some of my readers lost their little ones? Then hear me, for I too have walked that Via Dolorosa. A certain well-loved text hung on my study-wall, illuminated by my own hand. I little thought, as I drew the letters and gilded the capitals, that the words would have a very literal fulfillment. But I knew it ere the blossom fell. She had been sick a little while, and none could tell how it might end. As I hoped, and feared, the truth leapt from the wall right

into my heart, in the twinkling of an eye: "Suffer the little children to come unto Me." Soon after that my firstborn was with the angels. Then, once more "was there a voice heard, lamentation and weeping, and great mourning." Did we do wrong to grieve? Is weeping sin? Nay, nay; for "Jesus wept." But we did not sorrow as those without hope; we did not refuse to be comforted. I own no foot of land save a little plot in an Auckland cemetery, and there, beneath a drooping acacia, is a little shell-strewn mound, and a simple stone with this inscription—

DAISY SPURGEON,
AGED 3 MONTHS.

"Even so, Father . . . "[106]

The death of Daisy brought to focus the inordinant amount of work Tom was undertaking each week. An 1877 visitor to the Tabernacle noted that he had inquired as to the pastor's schedule from a deacon and found that Thomas had:

> . . . attended two ministers' meetings, two Gospel temperance committee meetings, spoke at an annual meeting in a Methodist church, visited several sick members, preached at an outstation 9 miles from Auckland and conducted the ordinance of the Lord's Supper.[107]

And all this in one week, as well as preaching three church services. In the same week he had also participated in nine church business and prayer committees, and interviewed several applicants for church membership in extended counseling sessions.[108]

The Auckland church supervised three outlying branch churches, all with multiplied agencies and organizations such as the Tabernacle itself possessed. Tom felt that not only was the work suffering because he had lost some freshness, but also that his own health had now deteriorated to the point that he was unable to give them his best again. The added strain of Daisy's passing and his wife's distress led him to the conviction that he should resign and seek a place of service with a lighter load. Accordingly, on June 10, 1889 his resignation was accepted with great regret by the church. They appreciated his promise that he would remain with them until the end of the year to give some time to help find a replacement.[109]

The official church letter replying to his resignation included many expressions of thankfulness and concern. His people expressed a "heartfelt sorrow and regret at the continuance of physical weakness and ill-health" which precluded him from continuing. They rendered him an "affectionate sympathy in this and his other troubles, and in the bereavement he has lately suffered." The congregation gave thanks to God and him for the manner in which the church had been strengthened, for the large numbers won to Christ, and they earnestly thanked the pastor for his "untiring devotion to the limit of his strength." They spoke glowingly of his preaching of "the Gospel of the Grace of God in all its fullness and freeness," and assured him of their thorough support in the months remaining together, and their prayer for future ministries.[110]

In his eight years of Auckland service, Thomas baptized 330 persons, welcomed 587 into membership and preached to ever-increasing numbers. For his farewell meeting every available seat was filled. The *Leader* asserted that no doubt existed that his "blameless life, elocutionary power, clear enunciation, good memory, and above all his clear and fearless preaching of the old Gospel story of man the sinner and Christ the Saviour account for Mr. Spurgeon's hold on such vast numbers."[111]

His father's summary note defined the situation with some precision. He wrote a brief paragraph asking readers of the *Sword and Trowel* to undergird Thomas in prayer, and saying:

> The Lord, by his means, raised the Baptist Church in Auckland, New Zealand, to such prosperity that it overgrew his strength. He became ill, depressed in spirit, and therefore, compelled to retire from the arduous post. . . . He is true as steel to the old faith, and full of a deep longing for conversions.[112]

Tom attended the Baptist Union meetings in Dunedin, unsure of his future sphere of service. There his fellow pastors invited him to work as an evangelist serving all the churches. He saw this as God's hand and agreed to begin the following June after a vacation in Tasmania, again with the Gibsons. After resting there most of February he preached at Launceston, Longford, and Hobart in March, led several Baptist Union rallies, visited Latrobe and Devonport for other ministry, and returned to his itinerant New Zealand tasks by June.

In his first year of New Zealand evangelistic service, Tom visited nineteen centers, conducting 236 gospel meetings, and delivered lectures in the interest of home and foreign missions. The reports tell of abundant blessings in towns scattered over both the North and South Islands. In three years of such service, he missioned in every church in the Islands but one. Within the first year, fourteen where he served had reapplied for further meetings. During these three years he kept a personal record of almost 800 inquirers who found Christ and were led to professions of faith through his evangelism.[113]

Sometimes Lila traveled with him, a faithful and encouraging companion. But with the birth of their son Harold on July 2, 1891 she divided most of her time between their home in Auckland and her family home in Dunedin.

*　　*　　*

Thomas longed for a settled work again. He had refused several overtures in New Zealand, including a call to return to Auckland, and felt that evangelizing, although obviously God's call for the present, was not to be his permanent service. An unexpected telegram from his mother changed the whole course of his thinking and of his future ministry. C. H. Spurgeon, ill at Mentone for three months, had passed to his reward quite suddenly on January 31, 1892.

4 Grace Sufficient (1891-1894)

Judge not the Lord by feeble sense
But trust Him for His grace;
Behind a frowning providence
He hides a smiling face.

In the early weeks of May 1891, C. H. Spurgeon's illness worsened. Years of struggle against arthritic gout had left him so pain-wracked and weary that he was able to preach at the Tabernacle only occasionally, appearing in that pulpit for the last time in early June. The affliction induced what was later described as a severe "congestion of the kidneys" immobilizing him with crippling headaches for hours.

The popular and religious press reported weekly (some times daily) bulletins of the patient's condition. Over this period ten thousand condolences had arrived by mail at his Westwood residence. By November he had recovered enough to travel to a favorite sunny vacation spot in the south of France. There, at Mentone, he worked quietly, when he was able, on what he purposed to be a commentary on the entire New Testament, assisted by his wife and by his private secretary, J. W. Harrald. But at 11:05 PM on January 31, 1892, after a day of great pain, and some hours of coma, the beloved pastor entered into his rest. He died when only fifty-seven years of age.

Visiting brethren cared for the Tabernacle pulpit over the long months of his illness. W. Y. Fullerton prepared a weekly sermon for issuance from the large stockpile of unpublished materials accumulated by the publisher. Plans for memorial services included talk of a Westminster Abbey tomb. But the church officers chose interment at Norwood Cemetery among the common people of South London.

After a brief service at Mentone, the remains, in a plain, olive wood casket, shipped across France, received at Victoria Station, lodged at the Pastor's College, were finally placed in state in the Tabernacle where they lay February 9 through 11. One hundred thousand visitors paid their last respects beside the palm-lined coffin on the Tuesday and Wednesday, members of Parliament jostled alongside the poor costermongers from the South London slums. Mourners trooped past the casket from 6:30 AM through 7 PM. Many returned to crowd the consecutive memorial services on the second day.

Five hundred of the orphanage children joined Tabernacle members, and with the workers associated with the forty mission centers sponsored in London by the great church for the first memorial service of the morning. The 2 PM service was limited to ministers and theological students. At 7 PM general Christian workers held their services of honor and homage. So many pressed at the front doors at 5 PM, seeking early entrance for the 7 PM service, that the afternoon attendants were released through the rear doors in order to exit safely. Fullerton and Smith, the church-sponsored evangelistic team, conducted a final 10:30 PM watch night service, also crowded.

But none of these compared in attendance or interest to the official Thursday funeral. The press reported this great gathering as "simple yet solemn, unpretentious, yet impressive."[1] It proceeded "amid such public manifestations of sorrow as rarely occur in the metropolis."[2] Sixty individuals, each representing a separate mission, religious association, or society, sat in special pews reserved that they might honor Spurgeon. Representatives of some foreign governments sat alongside of city dignitaries and local officials, while hosts of Londoners packed the Tabernacle galleries and crowded into the aisles.

To the thousands squeezed into the church itself had to be added the throngs crowding the nearby streets and lining the sidewalks of the funeral procession route. All traffic had to be suspended in the area for some hours while the cortage of broughams, landaus, clarences, and other carriages progressed to Norwood Cemetery. The procession took twenty-five minutes to pass a given point. The six-mile journey took two and one half hours to complete.

"Many shops on the route were closed, every house had the blinds drawn, the streets were crowded with thousands of reverent mourners, and all men were uncovered as the coffin passed."[3] The eight hundred-plus policemen recruited from suburbs round about directed the huge crowds with great difficulty. Transferred by special train later to a station near the cemetery these officials controlled access there via a ticket system. One of their leaders affirmed that the whole affair was the "biggest since the Duke of Wellington's funeral."[4]

Not far from the site missions pioneer James Moffat lay buried, close to the family vaults of the Olneys and the Higgses from his own church, the pastor's remains were installed in a special vault, which may still be seen today. His favorite hymn, "There Is a Fountain Filled with Blood," highlighted the fervor of the simple service attended by the immense assembly. Eulogies were offered by close associates, and the benediction was pronounced by a future Bishop of London.

The 12,000 at the cemetery that day remembered best the stirring words of Archibald Brown, pastor of the East London Baptist Tabernacle, graduate of Spurgeon's College, and close confidant of the great preacher:

> Beloved President, Faithful Pastor, Prince of Preachers, Brother Beloved, Dear Spurgeon,—We bid thee not farewell, but only for a little while "Goodnight." Thou shalt rise soon at the first dawn of the Resurrection Day

of the redeemed. It is not the "Goodnight" ours to bid, but thine. It is we who linger in the darkness; thou art in God's own light. Our night, too, shall soon be past, and with it all our weeping. Then, with thine, our songs shall greet the morning of a day that knows no cloud nor close; for there is no night there. Hard worker in the field thy toil is ended. Straight has been the furrow thou hast ploughed. No looking back has marred thy course. Harvests have followed thy patient sowing, and heaven is already rich with thine ingathered sheaves, and shall be still enriched through years yet lying in eternity. Champion of God, thy battle long and nobly fought is over. The sword which clave to thy hand has dropped at last; the palm branch takes it place. No longer does the helmet press thy brow, or weary with its surging thoughts of battle; the victor's wreath from the Great Commander's hand has already proved thy full reward. Here for a little while shall rest thy precious dust. Then shall thy Well-beloved come, and at His voice thou shalt spring from thy couch on earth fashioned like unto His body in glory. Then spirit, soul and body shall magnify thy Lord's redemption. Until then, beloved, sleep. We praise God for thee, and by the blood of the everlasting covenant hope and expect to praise God with thee. Amen.[5]

Problems surface promptly when a church loses its pastor. The Metropolitan Tabernacle stood as the largest regular congregation of worshipers gathering in the Western World. When viewed as the central citadel of Evangelicalism, its influence crossed many national and denominational boundaries. C. H. Spurgeon had already published the largest collection of individual sermons ever distributed in history. Twenty-five thousand copies of each weekly issue circulated in Britain and the U.S.A. in English, and many in other parts of the world, some in a variety of languages. The loss of such a voice, eagerly heard by half the world, occasioned much speculation concerning the identity of a potential successor.

Internal discussions among the South London congregation brought four unofficial prospects immediately into view as having potential interest. *Dr. James A. Spurgeon,* the late pastor's brother, already held the courtesy title of Tabernacle copastor. Previously the church had elected him to superintend the business and administrative affairs of all the organizations intimately associated with the work. These included the orphanages, Pastors' College, the many city missions, and the almshouses for the elderly.

A well-trained preacher, James had organized an active congregation for the Baptists meeting at Croydon, in southwest London. He also held the title of pastor there, because of his regular Sunday ministry among them. However, the call to exercise his special gifts alongside his brother at the Tabernacle during the weekday tasks had specifically excluded any right to that pulpit succession. His pulpit abilities were generally considered to be somewhat less than adequate for such a key preaching task. *Charles Spurgeon* and *Thomas Spurgeon,* the late pastor's twin sons, both were now known as effective Baptist pastors. Charles, then serving at Greenwich, was an acceptable preacher, although by no means an outstanding one. Thomas, being so long in the South Pacific, was known somewhat only by reputation. Only a few knew him well, and these from his brief visit to London in 1885.

Amid such uncertainties stood the obvious and effective service of *Dr. Arthur T. Pierson*. He served as the current Tabernacle pulpit supply, under an arrangement originally requested by C. H. Spurgeon himself during the days of his last illness. As a popular interdenominational missions enthusiast, and conference speaker, Pierson was recognized for his fidelity to the inspiration of Scripture. His experience as a pastor and evangelist of note was international. Although an American, whose ministerial accreditation, convictions, and associations were Presbyterian and not Baptist, he quickly secured an avid following from many in the Tabernacle congregation. He appeared to give initial encouragement to the idea of some permanent pastoral placement among them.

Pierson's evangelical message, sharp logic, and magnetic delivery blended well with the congregation's hearty singing. The rustle of their Bible leaves as they followed his expositions, and the attendant spiritual blessings, made both pastor and people initially feel that perhaps an ongoing association might be part of God's will.[6] Pierson's personal diary comment on the beginning experiences shows the depth of his feelings:

> Three months of uninterrupted health and happiness. Everybody cordial, sympathetic, and responsive. Fifty souls gathered in December, and many more enquiring. Immense after-meetings in the Tabernacle. Prayer meetings of the profoundest interest.[7]

At the request of the church officers Pierson continued to supply the vacant pulpit beyond his few months engagement through until June of 1892. His mature ministry to the sorrowing congregation marked him as a man of great grace, and many gifts. An ability to phrase truth in memorable imagery is evident in his message at C. H. Spurgeon's funeral. In this he likened the late pastor to a cedar fallen in Lebanon, commenting that its crash had shaken the whole world, leaving a vacancy vaster than any known during the past century:

> We have come together to bury our dead . . . The rich and the noble and the affluent might have made a pilgrimage to his tomb, but we thank God we are met to lay his sacred ashes in our own Norwood, where the common people who heard him gladly may wend their way to his place of burial. You have no occasion to build him a monument, for his monument is in the hearts of millions of people, more enduring than brass. You have no need to hire a gardener to keep his grave green, for the tears of widows and orphans will water the sod. You have no occasion to see that flowers are planted around his sepulchre, for there will be flowers blooming in all parts of the earth that

will be brought by pilgrim bands in remembrance of untold blessings that came from his lips, that will be brought from all quarters of the earth to be set alongside his place of rest. My brother we shall never see another like unto thee! Those eyes now closed in death . . . have lost their light for ever. The voice that spoke in tones so convincing and persuading is hushed in death, and the hand whose grasp uplifted many a fallen one, and gave new strength and encouragement to many a stricken one, will never again take ours within its grasp. . . . We are glad that heaven is richer although we may be made poorer; and by this bier we pledge ourselves that we will undertake by God's grace to follow thy blessed footsteps even as thou didst follow those of thy blessed Master.[8]

Pierson, trained at Union Seminary in New York, was best known for his fostering of the Student Volunteer Missions Movement, and his associations with D. L. Moody and others of prominence.[9] From experiences in the 1857 New York revival, he had gained insights into evangelism. He followed this with deep spiritual experiences through associations with Moody men P. P. Bliss and D. W. Whittle in Detroit in 1874[10] and also with George Muller.[11] His pastorates became noted for outreach programs and soul-winning zeal.[12] Detroit's Fort Street Presbyterian Church was finally rebuilt under his pastoral leadership. But he resigned in protest to their commitment to a stately edifice with rented pew instead of the free tabernacle, structured to reach the common people as he had envisaged.[13]

His introduction to Spurgeon came through reading of his sermons and a service he attended while visiting Britain August 19, 1866. He described the singing congregation then as offering "a great wave of praise," Spurgeon's prayer as "marvellous" and declared, " . . . nothing impressed me more than his entire freedom from all artificiality or affectation. . . . He is the most effective preacher of the century."[14]

When called unexpectedly to preach for Spurgeon in December 1890, an emergency occasioned by the beginning of Spurgeon's fatal illness, he spoke of the day, and of the congregational response rapturously, " . . . never did I feel such a divine uplifting. . . . I felt that nowhere on earth would I so gladly hold forth the Word of Life."[15]

After hearing about the recurrence of Spurgeon's illness in July 1891, Pierson gathered with others then attending the Niagara Bible Conference to pray for his recovery. He then wrote a letter of warm fellowship to tell Spurgeon of the support of his American brethren, and offered to help again, anytime he could. Perhaps he had in mind only an occasional service. But Spurgeon had his secretary write immediately by return with an invitation to conduct all services for several months from October. Pierson quickly confirmed his acceptance.[16]

The two met just as the pastor left for France. Pierson not only secured his blessing but also a thorough endorsement through Spurgeon's pastoral letters to the congregation:[17]

> He has come among you in humble but unwavering faith that the Lord is about to bare his arm in our midst. I hope he has come to reap where others have sown. I expect a great revival. I pray for it and I look for it.[18]

The last words offered by the pastor to W. Y. Fullerton expressed a wishful, but forlorn judgment. "There is no danger of him being thought of as my successor, since he is a Presbyterian!"[19]

Not only was this so, but Pierson clearly indicated he did not ever intend to become a Baptist.[20] Because he was open to believers' baptism rather than antagonistic towards it, he had built an immersion baptistry in his Detroit Presbyterian pastorate many years before. He immersed those who preferred this mode, while continuing infant christening as his regular practice.[21] Dr. James Spurgeon became so intimate with his new American friend that he immediately proposed a joint pastorate as the solution, with Dr. Pierson as preacher without any need for a change in his views.[22]

Under James's aggressive leadership, the church officers met with Pierson to explore the proposition. Characteristically the logical American recorded twenty-eight arguments which seemed to suggest the possibility of his continuance, and forty-eight reasons countering the idea. Accordingly, he advised them he would not extend further his associations with them. He counseled them to proceed with the settlement of some other permanent pastor.[23] He did, however, promise to return for another supply period, if they had not settled the matter by October 1892.[24]

Meanwhile James continued to lose credibility as a legitimate candidate himself. He had labored well under C. H. Spurgeon's leadership, but failed in what seems to have been an attempt to seize power upon the pastor's decease. C. H. Spurgeon functioned as a "purely unselfish and upright autocrat, supported by a diaconate and elderhood—the church had only a nominal voice,"[25] states "a member for 34 years" in the public press of the period. He nominated new church officers whose elections were formalized by vote of the church assembly:

> Loved, honored, and confided-in as Mr. Spurgeon was by all the members, there was no inclination to dispute his will in this or other things. Also, as it was known that the deacons and elders never acted against his wishes, a free hand was left to them, under him, and the church invariably agreed to all decisions come to by them, when informed of them.[26]

James, only three years his brother's junior, had trained for the ministry in Regent's Park College, but served his early pastorates in Union chapels rather than specifically Baptist causes. He was an advocate of open membership without immersion as a prerequisite:

> While I hold adult baptism to be necessary, and hope always at the proper time manfully to support my views, yet, if a person wished to come into this church, I should ask such to read and prayerfully study the Scriptures on the subject, and if any other conclusion was deliberately arrived at I should warmly receive them, leaving the minor point as between the person and the common Lord.[27]

His high handedness upset some Tabernacle members:

> . . . things are being done in the Tabernacle which are altogether foreign to the genius of Nonconformity and the principles of the free churches. The sooner autocracy receives a check the better it will be for the cause of truth and the peace and prosperity of the church. One cannot help asking from whence Dr. Spurgeon derives his commission to "lord it over God's heritage." Surely not from the Tabernacle church. Was it conferred with the degree recently received?[28]

Pierson and James Spurgeon treated each other with open admiration. The visitor began it with a clumsy attempt to impart unwarranted honor to James in memorial services for C. H. Spurgeon. His eulogy for the deceased likened his work, and that of James, to the evangelical team of John and Charles Wesley of the previous century. He lauded James as his brother's inspiration, affirming that men had not yet fully appreciated James's contribution to his brother's success, but would in the future. The press reported that Pierson said, "God bless James, and long may he survive, to give his wisdom, counsel, and energy to the work they jointly carried forward."[29]

While nothing in these statements was of itself unworthy, many found them inappropriate in a memorial address supposedly honoring his brother. Others found them offensive.

Pierson dedicated his *Lectures on Preaching,* published at this time, to James. After their delivery to Spurgeon's College students, he lauded James in its preface as one " . . . by whose constant and cordial cooperation and courteous consideration every burden was lightened during eight eventful months of mingled sorrow and joy at the Metropolitan Tabernacle."[30]

James reciprocated. He began openly to advocate Pierson's permanent return as pastor over the public protests of many members, and eventually of the man himself. A report of the farewell to Pierson (after his initial supply period) includes the statement by James that he knew that Dr. Pierson would return as he (James) " . . . had received an assurance from the Master, not the doctor, and was willing to leave the servant to the Master!"[31]

But Pierson had already publicly declared his ambivalence about returning even for supply. He felt compelled to reply, at the meeting, contradicting James's assurance, and stating that such a return was not practicable, and that he was willing for God to dispose of all matters as he would.[32]

W. Stubbs became so incensed at the aggression of James that he published a very bitter letter on August 20, 1892:

> Many of us think that in some respects Mr. James Spurgeon has mistaken his calling, as he appears to be more at home in commercial pursuits than in the pulpit, and as a private member, in common with many fellow-members, we scarcely know him except that we hear his voice for a few minutes at the Monday evening prayer meeting, occasionally at the baptismal service, and on the first Sunday evening in the month for a few minutes only. It is a long time since we heard a sermon from him, and I think, in common with other members, that he cannot be pastor of two churches, and that 500 pounds per annum for a few hours during the week is altogether out of place.[33]

The London correspondent for a Chicago paper wrote:

> Mr. James Spurgeon has been appointed pastor in succession to his brother (sic), and his power and influence are supreme. So long as that is the situation—and Mr. James Spurgeon is not the man to needlessly relinquish the reins of office, whoever comes to the pulpit will have to regard the present pastor as head and chief.[34]

Despite protesting petitions from members, James continued to push the officers in the authoritative style which his brother had perfected. But as James lacked his brother's sensitivity, as well as the pastoral rights C. H. Spurgeon had won over long years, the tensions increased. He apparently believed his aggressive leadership to be both needed and desired, but failed in judging its acceptance by the congregation. No one could slip into the beloved pastor's shoes and expect the loyalties and deference earned by him to transfer automatically. Editorial comment in the *Echo* highlighted the general embarrassment. It was headed "A Ticklish Position":

> Few men of mediocre talents have ever been placed in a more difficult and delicate position than Dr. James Spurgeon. Had he not been the brother of our most popular preacher of the day he would never have risen above the ordinary ruck of Baptist ministers. He is a good solid man, but has not a spark of his late brother's genius. This fact was fully recognised when he became his late brother's assistant. Accident has left him temporary master of the situation. And as he thus became a sort of Nonconformist pluralist, he has been criticised with no little asperity. . . . Such high-handed proceedings cannot but aggravate ill-feeling. Were I a Piersonite I should wish Dr. James Spurgeon on the other side of the Atlantic.[35]

Perhaps some criticisms of James's behavior, exacerbated by his arrogance, were unwarranted. But the editor of the denominational paper, apparently aware of more than he was publicly willing to report, complained in an editorial headed "Principle in Preachers" that it was:

> . . . Impossible to aquit either Dr. James Spurgeon or Dr. Pierson of serious
> blame, and even of inconsistent trifling. . . . the future pastor of the
> Tabernacle may or may not have appeared in sight, on that point we have no
> right to anticipate the ultimate judgement of the church; although Dr. James
> Spurgeon has hardly exhibited all the sweet sympathy and meekness, which,
> as the brother of the departed saint, was his rightful heritage.[36]

The editor likened James's authoritarianism to a Roman Catholic rather than a
Baptist tradition.[37]

The news of his father's passing came too quickly for Tom to attend London
memorial services. He planned to visit the family there as soon as he could
disengage himself from promised New Zealand evangelistic tasks. Known mostly
as the son whose health forbade extended ministry in England, Tom's potential as
his father's successor had never been seriously evaluated. When the officers
engaged him to preach for three months, while Dr. Pierson returned to the U.S.A.
for some responsibilities there, the possibility lay still unexplored. Tom, never a
self-seeker, had refused to lift a finger or write a word to anyone encouraging
their interest in him as a potential pastor, although the matter loomed large in his
prayers.

On the last Sunday of July 1892 Tom sat at Pierson's side in the Tabernacle
service, although he took no part in it. His pulpit ministry which began the next
week, however, caused such excitement that immediately he found himself to be
the center of attention. Tom's future then became a part of the violent maelstrom
that swirled around Pierson and his Uncle James Spurgeon.

Pierson left without any specific assurance that he would return later for more
pulpit supply. His missions conference tasks, Presbyterian convictions, and old
associations compelled him to hesitate. The contrast between the American
visitor's heavy doctrinal sermons and Tom's bright analogies from Scripture
caused one respondent to plead, after only two weeks of Tom's services, that the
gifted son should be persuaded to stay with them. The same correspondent
recalled listening week after week to Dr. Pierson's "learned discourses" until he
"felt like Ezekiel's 'dry bones.'"[38] Another affirmed that " . . . to have an
unbaptised pastor over the deceased great pastor's baptised church would be an
insult to our principles."[39]

While some objected to the public airing of the church tensions, and found
them inappropriate for discussion in the daily press, others vehemently defended
such activities, particularly in *The Baptist*. They believed the future of the church
to be intimately associated with the welfare of the entire denomination, and of the
general evangelical world.

A visitor to London at that time complained that the only way to visit the
church on Sunday morning was by cab. He reported that he found the morning
Sunday School in "full blast, occupying not only the basement of the building

but two large rooms of the Pastors' College (which adjoins) as well."[40] He described the huge crowds, packed galleries, and spirited singing, and said of Thomas that he " . . . is quite unlike his lamented father in appearance being short, and rather spare. But he preaches with true Spurgeonic fire and faith."[41]

Standing room only crowds continued. S. Chandler wrote to *The Baptist* expressing common sentiments. He contrasted Pierson and Thomas Spurgeon with the comment:

> Those who have heard the eloquence of the latter will need no words of mine to remind them of the spiritual stirring his discourses have caused; those who know of the noble work of this somewhat young life will not require me to emphasise that his zeal is second to that of nobody working in the Christian Church, and those who would make capital for their side of the argument out of the fact that he does not enjoy the most robust health will surely stand ashamed when they are confronted with the fact that on that account alone, which is dispensation of God Himself, they would debar him from the pleasure and the honour of serving his great Master in the highest capacity which is open to him, and would thrust into his father's place others less fitted to bear our deceased leader's mantle, because, however unworthily, they might stumble along with it for a longer period.[42]

The questions and concerns continued. If the matter were only one of physical stamina, surely Thomas could be persuaded to take an extended holiday in the severe London winters, as his father had done for many years. By late August the agitation had escalated to a proportion which brought a distinct rift in the congregation. Was the feeling one of sentiment which sought to welcome the father's son, and not one of a desire for superior preaching, as was a necessity for so strategic a pulpit?[43] A secular newspaper editor summed up the situation by stating that Thomas's limited ministry surprised everyone by its power. He reported the common feelings by stating:

> When it was found what sort of stuff was in him the feeling began to gather force and volume that it would be a pity that the church of the Tabernacle should lose the services of such a rising and gifted man. His delivery had steadily improved during the short time he had occupied the Tabernacle pulpit; but great as were the demands which such an immense building made upon the voice of a speaker, Mr. Thomas Spurgeon had in that respect proved himself capable of being heard in every corner of the edifice. . . . He has undoubtedly much of his late father's appearance while his voice is musical and far-reaching, and his bearing, if somewhat nervous at times, graceful and correct. He adopts what is known as the Evangelical style, and shows a strong desire to reach the hearts of the people. His delivery may be described as pleadingly passionate, and as partaking strongly of the emotional. He avoids preaching over the heads of his congregation, and evidently wishes to make both himself and them feel effectly at home.[44]

Tom's Monday prayer meetings were described as "equalling, numerically, any ever held in the Tabernacle's palmiest days,"[45] and every seat was occupied for the Sunday evening services.[46]

Despite such high interest in Thomas, the church could hardly go back on the previous invitation to Dr. Pierson to return for further supply after the current engagement. Such matters were brought to a head by a letter from Dr. James Spurgeon to be read at the September 17 service. In it he indicated that the American had given a final response to the return invitation. *The Baptist* reported this epistle along with "an anxious condition of feeling" among those who, even holding Dr. Pierson in high esteem, were hesitant to allow the late pastor's son to leave England's shores without at least the possibility of his ultimate succession being fully discussed. The officers were petitioned to do this, but found themselves embarrassed by the Pierson supply commitment. *The Baptist* of August 19 revealed one member's feelings well before Pierson had replied to the final supply invitation:

> I have personally spoken to a great many, and with all (not even one exception) it has been said how delighted they should be to welcome Mr. Thomas Spurgeon as pastor. It only remains for the deacons and elders to call a church meeting when they would doubtless be convinced of this matter. But this, I fear, they will not do, having virtually closed the pulpit for some time to come against a pastor by their appointment for a limited period of Mr. James Spurgeon, and their invitation to Dr. Pierson to return for nine months.[47]

The "terribly unsettled state" meant that "among the rank and file discontent reigns supreme" and "a considerable and growing majority are very desirous that Mr. Thomas Spurgeon should at least be *invited* to take the vacant pastorate."[48]

The Pierson letter, referred to in James Spurgeon's advice to the church September 17, indicated that the Presbyterian affirmed his unserving commitment to infant baptism, believed that a Baptist church should have a Baptist minister, and other facts that would preclude him from candidature for the permanent pastorate.[49] Apparently James suppressed this letter and caused even more bad feeling.[50] A specially-called church meeting in October failed to gain access to the letter. Such an uproar was occasioned by Dr. James Spurgeon's threat to resign if the church approached Thomas that the meeting could only be calmed by the officers' assurance that no future invitations, even for pulpit supply, would be extended without congregational concurrence.

Such matters were not usually congregational, but were the responsibility of the officers rather than of the people.[51] James Spurgeon wrote the church affirming that "no other than a Baptist can be chosen to the pastoral office according to the deed of trust."[52] But his opposition to any consideration of Thomas remained firm. Was James, himself, determined to be the pastor? Did

Pierson have in view becoming a Baptist, despite his protestations? Such questions appear unanswerable today. Pierson later confessed his neglect of sensitivity in many relationships,[53] and characterized much of his own behavior as less than desirable.[54]

An outspoken *Baptist* editorial summed up the situation, using the figure of a stout ship battered by storms and near to foundering. The Tabernacle seemed about to wreck because of:

> . . . a weakening of the confidence hitherto existing between the acting commander and the passengers. Meanwhile, indications have also not been wanting of a condition very near akin to mutiny on the part of the officers. It was not because the principal navigator was ignorant of the ship's proper course, but rather by reason of his idea of conceiving the idea of experimenting in the neighbourhood of reefs. . . . his resolve on so new and serious a departure has, it is idle to deny, precipitated a crisis which, but for the over-ruling hand of the Master Mariner of his Church, might prove disastrous beyond parallel. . . . To perform any act or utter any words which might reasonably bear the interpretation of hauling down the Baptist flag, obviously endangered the ship. . . . it is impossible to aquit either Dr. James Spurgeon or Dr. Pierson of serious blame, and even of inconsistent trifling.[55]

On October 9 a meeting was called on petition from a group of church members. Their announcement quoted a letter from Dr. Pierson to Mr. Brookman, in which the correspondant said " . . . the officers of the Tabernacle know that they are free to act in any manner pertaining to the Tabernacle without reference to me." In it Pierson also affirmed cooperation in a potential call to anyone they desired.[56] Even this failed to resolve matters. Much ground was apparently gained, however, by the Thomas party circulating a quotation from C. H. Spurgeon's sermon number 1,164 in which he stated:

> It may not be my honour to be succeeded in this pulpit by one of my own sons, greatly as I would rejoice it, it might be so; but, at least, I hope they will be here in this church to serve their father's God, and be regarded with affection by you for the sake of him who spent his life in your midst.[57]

This many regarded as near to an endorsement of an approach to Thomas as C. H. Spurgeon could make, in retrospect. *The Baptist* commented on the special meeting as dealing with "grave issues involved at a crisis." It reported the tension created by James Spurgeon's dissent from the officers' desire to invite Thomas for a further period of supply after Dr. Pierson had fulfilled the coming return engagement. Further discussion elicited the fact that the officers were also seriously divided over the resolution put to the meeting that all matters be left in their hands for the time being. Mr. Higgs affirmed that he strongly objected to Dr. James Spurgeon placing his veto on the proposal to approach Thomas over the desire of the officers. A final decision sustained the responsibility of the officers in future arrangements, but secured agreement for congregational approval for them. This also included a warm letter to Thomas in which the words that the church "hopes to see him again in the Tabernacle pulpit at the expiration of Dr. Pierson's term of service" were added with enthusiastic approval.

Thomas completed his pulpit supply tasks on October 9, 1892, after preaching a farewell sermon where some 7,000 persons crowded the Tabernacle "to excess."[58] He invited them to remain for a few moments afterwards while he expressed his thanks for the opportunity to visit with them and preach for them over the past three months. He asked them to "clear the decks for action." In a positive appeal for cooperative endeavour, he requested that all grudges be forgotten, all disappointments remitted to the past, and that no thought concerning the past or the future should interfere with the work ahead. He thanked them for attendance, support, and encouragements in his ministry, for the vote of thanks passed at the recent church meeting, and concluded:

> I came at your call, and, as I thought, and I still think, at the Master's call. I have tried to serve you under circumstances which, I confess, have been most trying, for I had hardly recovered from what was to me the shock of returning to stand here when sorrow of another sort possessed my heart. I seem to have been unwillingly in the midst of strife. Well, dear friends, I have tried to serve you, or perhaps I might say tried rather to serve my Master, and I am glad to know that many of the Lord's people have been helped by my poor words. I thought when I went away last that I might never come here again, for my dear father said to me, "Good-bye, son Tom, but you must not come back for I could not say 'good-bye' to you again for I shall never see you in the flesh," and so it was. The hope of seeing Jesus makes our hearts one. In my heart the flag flies half-mast high, but it is still the flag of the Master whom we all serve.[59]

Then followed what can only be described as "one of the most remarkable and affective scenes which ever occurred at the Metropolitan Tabernacle.":[60]

> Women were to be seen everywhere weeping and sobbing aloud, and even men were carried away by the influence of the moment. From the body of the hall and from the upper and lower galleries were heard loud cries of "God bless you," "Good-bye," and "Come back again."[61]

When departure arrangements were completed, so many friends desired to accompany him to the ship that the *Empress Frederick,* a vessel owned by the Victoria Steamboat Association, had to be especially chartered. Four hundred who arrived at Old Swan Pier near London Bridge traveled with him on the steamboat to Gravesend on Friday October 14. There he was to join his wife and young son, who had already journeyed by rail to join the New Zealand Shipping Company's *Kaikoura* for the journey home.[62]

Despite a cold, wet morning, so many gathered that Thomas had great difficulty boarding the Thames steamer at 9:45 AM. Those who crowded on board for the six-hour return journey were matched by a cheering, sympathizing crowd thronging the pier and parapets of London Bridge calling farewells. These were then echoed by the bargemen from their crafts and the warehousemen alongside the river all the way to the landing stage at Greenwich. There Tom's brother Charles stood with many from his church congregation to call greetings and wave handkerchiefs.[63]

Just before reaching Gravesend J. R. Thomas, secretary of the ad hoc group which sought to secure Thomas' further services at the Tabernacle, gathered with his twenty-six committee members to present an illuminated address.

The "tribute of affection and esteem" expressed their conviction that God would yet lead him back to be their pastor. They expressed concern that events had developed in such a complicated fashion that the immediate decision could not be made. Thomas tendered thanks to the committee, saying he had intended to comment about the Tabernacle pulpit but had felt it better to remain silent and to let others express their feelings as they pleased, calling them to continued prayer and patience.[64] The editor of *The Baptist* commented on the entire situation in Tom's favor:

> Mr. Tom Spurgeon's attitude and whole behaviour throughout the recent Tabernacle crisis seemed to be beyond all reproach. He made no single slip in his pulpit allusions, nor would he suffer himself to be drawn by intrusive Press interviewers. Such a demeanor during a season of so much personal trial, made so much heavier by the many indiscretions of well-meaning friends, naturally endeared him to the whole body of Tabernacle worshippers, and must still add to his multitude of friends the wide world over. In a conversation I had with him just before he sailed he was surprisingly buoyant in spirit.[65]

He was also quoted as having no unkind word for anyone and expressing his conviction that everything would come out right. His admirable attitude was further reflected in a special trip taken to say good-bye to Uncle James, who was indisposed at the time of his return.[66]

In leaving Dunedin, New Zealand, for the trip to London, Thomas had stated that he believed that all the steps that made history in a man's life were hinges on which destiny turned. He affirmed his conviction that God distinctly ordered all the details of his life.[67] Many times in the months which followed he had unfolded and folded again a precious letter, dated seven years before, written by his father. Each time he had done so, he had decided that it was not yet the time to share it with others. So he carried it carefully for a further eighteen months and then shared it publicly at a most dramatic moment, as we shall presently see. But for now its contents bolstered his faith in God's providence.

Although rumored that his return to New Zealand was to recover health and strength, the decision was actually to preach the month of January in the Dunedin pulpit for Reverend A. North. He then planned to resume his itinerant evangelistic labors in the colony.[68] In a letter dated March 10, 1893 he speaks of being " . . . earnestly and happily engaged in evangelistic work. Meetings in small towns and country places seem very different from the gatherings in the great Tabernacle; but the same gospel of the same Saviour is supplied by the same Spirit."[69]

The fruit of this evangelism remained strong for many years.[70]

Meanwhile James Spurgeon continued his opposition to the idea of Thomas's return so vehemently that the officers feared a split in the Tabernacle fellowship of even greater proportions. On January 2, 1893 Thomas Olney, one of the senior deacons, wrote to James expressing regret that for the first time in twenty years that a serious difference should exist between them.[71] Matters reached such a pitch that, at a special church meeting called for March 29, 1893, "the church emerged like a ship that had been through a hurricane, battered and torn, but still seaworthy."[72] They accepted James Spurgeon's resignation and voted to invite Thomas Spurgeon to accept pulpit supply for a period of twelve months from July 30, "with a view to the pastorate."[73]

A majority of 1,600 voted for this move and the 569 who did not vote were not against this approach, but merely expressed a preference that the matter be left in the hands of the officers.[74] Having prayed about the matter for many months, Thomas was able to reply his cabled acceptance immediately, coupled with the verse "Not that we are sufficient of ourselves to think anything as of ourselves, but our sufficiency is of God."[75]

An affectionate crowd gathered in Auckland, and mustered in larger numbers at the wharf to bid him farewell. Congregationalist and Wesleyan pastors joined with many others to wish him well in his service "in the largest church of Christendom." They expressed their conviction that "by your natural gifts, experience and training of past years God has been preparing you for this high and useful position."[76] The help he had rendered to pastors, the quickening of churches, and the numerous conversions resulting from his itinerant ministries were all noted by the New Zealand Baptist Union. His fellow Baptists rejoiced in the opening opportunities, but lamented the loss to their home missions needs.[77]

Traveling across the Pacific this time without his wife and child, Tom wandered into the Central Union Church during a brief stopover at Honolulu and, when his identity was discovered, was pressed into the conducting of a service that evening.[78] He arrived in San Francisco on June 9, 1893. He visited Salt Lake City, Denver, and Omaha, on his way to Chicago where D. L. Moody had invited him to join with others in a great evangelistic outreach scheduled at that time.

The World's Fair Gospel Campaign, engineered by Moody, is regarded by his biographer as the greatest evangelical enterprise of his career. Largely overlooked by other historians, this campaign reached the Chicagoans and the many visitors to their city who came for the four hundredth anniversary of the discovery of America. Called the Columbia Exposition of 1893, this celebration ran from May through October of that year. Moody dreamed of a bold attack and gathered a great band of prayer supporters, and enlisted many prominent Evangelicals from Great Britain and America to help him with a multitude of evangelistic services and meetings.

Moody's first thoughts about the campaign arose in direct connection with Spurgeon's death. He rejected the idea because of his own poor health, and revived it only when he was dramatically saved from a near-fatal shipwreck. Advertising cost over $500 per day. Meetings were scheduled in fifty-five churches, all the area YMCAs, eleven large assembly halls, the Central Music Hall, the Grand Opera House, seven other theaters. One central theater meeting in the Haymarket attracted 3,000 every Sunday. Up to seventy meeting places were in use in a single day for these efforts! One hundred twenty-five separate meetings were held some Sundays.[79]

On Sunday June 18, Thomas preached for Moody at the First Congregational Church of Chicago, and in the evening at Moody's own Chicago Avenue Church. He was intrigued by the vastness of the exhibition, the buildings, exhibits, and surroundings, but impressed most of all by the organizing genius of Moody who, with the Bible Institute as headquarters, reached out to blanket the city with evangelism. Thirty and forty thousand worshipers gathered on some Sundays and many other thousands were contacted through weekday services. A. C. Dixon, J. Wilbur Chapman, R. A. Torrey, J. H. Brookes, and many other American evangelists associated with Moody in the work. Other partners included John McNeill, Henry Varley, John G. Paton, and song leaders Ira D. Sankey and Charles M. Alexander.[80] Thomas delighted in this royal company, rejoicing at the power of the gospel in gathering so many into the kingdom through their united efforts.[81]

Although requested to stay and preach at the Northfield Conference by Moody, Thomas pressed on to Brooklyn. There he preached for A. C. Dixon at Hanson Place Baptist Church, and Dr. McArthur at Calvary Baptist Church in New York. Dixon later commented:

> It was the reputation of C. H. Spurgeon which, for the most part, drew the people; but after the sermon, all felt that there would be in future no need of another's reputation to attract the people of Brooklyn to hear Thomas Spurgeon preach. . . . I have rarely seen an audience more deeply moved. His humble unassuming manner, his heart-earnestness, his clear unfolding of the text, his homely and happy illustrations, his musical voice, his utter dependence on the Holy Spirit, and, above all, his exaltation of the Lord Jesus Christ as pre-eminent in all realms, made us realise we were listening to a truly great sermon by a truly great preacher.[82]

Brief visits followed, to Boston, Plymouth, and Martha's Vineyard. After a lecture at the Calvary church, he took ship to London, appearing unexpectedly at the Tabernacle prayer meeting on Friday July 28, 1893. The congregation recessed their service for a period to cheer and wave an exuberant welcome to him.[83]

On July 30 he spoke in the Tabernacle pulpit on the call of Peter and Andrew with a breadth of expression and strength of analysis that thrilled his listeners. At this first Tabernacle service, he acknowledged that the Lord's call to him, as to the first disciples, was a choice of "the weak things of the world to confound the mighty," concluding with the confession, " . . . We shall have our risks to run as these men had. Yes, and our bitter disappointments. But there will be a miraculous draught of fishes, too, as on the day of Pentecost."[84]

His listeners spoke joyfully of his delight in the doctrines of grace, direct boldness in prayer, authenticity of faith, and clarity of enunciation.[85] He received thirty-five new members on the first Sunday in September, and the Sunday and week-night congregations equaled those of the best times in the Tabernacle's past history.[86] Before he had returned, it was resolved that an extra Friday evening prayer meeting should be scheduled at the Tabernacle especially for blessings on his coming ministry. Hundreds attended, and the meetings continued well after his arrival.[87] A November report stated:

> Not-withstanding his very arduous duties he continues to enjoy excellent health and be thoroughly "at home" in his . . . work at the Tabernacle. The congregations are still very large, 49 new members were added to the church October 1; enquirers and candidates come forward in most cheering numbers; the spirit of love and unity is increasingly manifested; and the pockets as well as the hearts of the hearers have been reached.[88]

By January 1894, 200 persons had been baptized under his ministry,[89] and the conviction grew daily among the congregation that they should proceed with a final call. He had come to a fellowship still strong in heart. The annual report of March 1893 revealed 5,179 members, nineteen preaching stations, twenty-five branch Sunday schools with 491 teachers and 7,786 scholars, and missions halls providing for a total sitting of 3,480 persons.[90]

On March 21, 1894 Olney presented five reasons why Thomas should immediately be called to the permanent pastorate. These were:

1. He preached Christ crucified.
2. His sermons appealed, as they were so well illustrated.
3. His ministry had the seal of God upon it.
4. He had worked harmoniously with Dr. James Spurgeon in a difficult situation.
5. The various works such as the college and the orphanage were as prosperous under his leadership as was the church itself.[91]

The counting of the ballots of the almost 3,000 members who were present, occupied almost an hour. While the church trust deed provided that only a simple majority was sufficient for election of a pastor, the 2,127 who supported the motion represented almost 80 percent approval, as only 649 felt they could *not* approve the motion. Of the latter, many accepted the consensus with good grace, while others felt led to withdraw from the fellowship. The agreement that, "Thomas Spurgeon, having supplied the pulpit, with a view to the pastorate, for eight months, be elected pastor,"[92] was viewed by the press as settling the matter completely. The prestigious *British Weekly* commented that "if the minority was considerable, the majority was nevertheless decisive."[93]

*   *   *

Tom carefully unfolded the brittle pages of the letter which he had carried close to his heart for almost nine years. He read the words, so familiar, with that peculiar kind of special and subdued excitement which they always elicited. Though he knew each phrase by heart, somehow the bold black strokes of his father's handwriting never ceased to stir him.

The broad creases of the yellowed letter's worn folds, where he had bent them so long ago to fit the inner pocket of his wallet, had lain so long in their places that each page now almost divided itself into quadrants. With the epistle spread before him, he composed a careful letter of reply to the church:

> To the Members of the Baptised Church of Jesus Christ
> Worshiping at the Metropolitan Tabernacle
> BELOVED BROTHERS AND SISTERS
> I was in due course informed of the result of your meeting of last Wednesday week. I find that you did then confer on me, by a decided majority, the highest honour that could be afforded to a servant of Christ Jesus. You have, with no uncertain sound, proclaimed your desire that I shall become your permanent pastor. I can scarcely believe that this is really so— that I of all men am requested to follow such men as Keach, and Gill, and Rippon, and Angus, and, (more wondrous still!) to succeed my own beloved and illustrious Father. Yet, with these figures, and your Chairman's letter before me, I must believe what seems incredible.
>
> Since hearing of your choice, I have been wondering if your voice is indeed the voice of God, and I have seriously, and prayerfully considered the whole question in all its bearings.
>
> When I regard, gratefully, and with surprise, the steps which have led to his resolve of yours, and the way by which I myself have been conducted; when I find that I can conscientiously say that I have never sought the post, and that I do not now even personally desire it; when I think of the strength vouchshafed to me for the not altogether easy task of the past eight months,

and of the measure of blessing graciously granted; above all, when I remember the right hand of the most High, and His exceeding great and precious promises, I feel constrained to say, "I must not shrink from this evident duty, nor fail to enter this open door."

> In humble and absolute dependence upon Divine aid, and counting on the earnest and affectionate co-operation of officers, and members, and hoping for the prayers of not these only, but of Christians the world over, I do accept the position to which you have invited me, with its glorious privileges, its stupendous tasks, and its solemn responsibilities. It will be my joy to serve you for Christ's sake just so long as the Lord evidently would have me do so.[94]

His letter continued showing an empathy for those who "did not join in the invitation," inviting them to "sink personal opinion for the common good" and offering them respect and concern. In discussing future plans he assured them of continuity in present approaches:

> My manner of life from my youth know all the members. My articles of faith and methods of work you are all aware of. The ever-new old Gospel is all I have to preach, and I propose to carry on the work in the same spirit which has obtained hitherto, and, as far as possible, on the same lines, and with the helpers. O that we might have somewhat of the same success![95]

His letter concluded with many tributes of praise to God and an acknowledgement of his weaknesses and faith in Divine support.

In due course, the letter was printed and circulated to all, but read almost immediately to the congregation. Excitedly, the deacons called a special meeting for April 2. Though the only notice had been that given at the Sunday services the day before, a large number filled the main area of the auditorium and portions of the first gallery. Thomas Olney, church treasurer, began the meeting with a hymn and prayer, and then read from the church's trust deed showing that the calling of Thomas as pastor had been in accord with all legal requirements.[96]

After the storms and stresses of recent days, the newspaper reporters noted a special sense of peace and refreshment in the proceedings. Thomas's letter, read to the gathering by Mr. Olney, was affirmed by a spontaneous stamping of feet all over the assembly, and an almost continuous "Ah-h-h-mm" of assent, subdued but sustained throughout the reading of his words.[97] Halfway through the reading of the letter, Mr. Olney, emotionally overcome, asked his nephew to finish it, explaining that "he could not see." This resulted in the audible whisper in many places of, "No, poor fellow, his heart's too full."[98]

At the conclusion of the reading, the chairman expressed satisfaction that the interregnum between pastors was at last at an end. Again he became visibly moved when, amid the excitement and wild waving of handkerchiefs, he handed "our dear pastor" the chair. Three times the welcome applause to Thomas crescendoed, and only after it had finally subsided was he able to make himself heard.[99]

The new pastor carefully discussed each detailed paragraph in his acceptance letter, noting his gratitude and their confidence. He remarked that his comment that "I have never sought the post, and I do not now personally desire it" showed how his flesh shrank and his spirit trembled, from the enormity of the task, but that he nevertheless possessed confidence in the Lord's strength. He then expressed his love for those who had not voted affirmatively for his coming. He appealed again for their cooperation.[100]

Throughout his remarks, the jovial assembly often interrupted with sustained applause. Moved by what they recognized as authentic humility, they paid special attention as he declared his doctrinal commitments, the product of his own theological studies and of his father's influences:

> Mr. Olney said quite rightly that I am a Baptist,—I am, from the crown of my head to the sole of my foot,—if you are a Baptist you must be one altogether, for you have been immersed. I own also to being a Particular Baptist,—very particular in some things, and Particular in the theological sense, believing in Particular Redemption, though no one loves more than I do to preach of salvation free to all. I am a Calvinistic Baptist, too: though that term is not much in fashion nowadays, I am not ashamed of it, and I trust I never shall be. The cross of Christ is the central object of all our ministry; around that we weave our garlands, and on the Saviour we place all our crowns.[101]

Giving a further brief word about Lila and the children, still in New Zealand, and of his anticipated joy at the coming reunion after what would be eleven months of separation, he paused dramatically for a few moments. Then he smiled, and said with great solemnity:

> And now I have a little secret for you. I was going to keep it for that kind welcome meeting the officers have arranged to hold on the twelfth; but I have thought since it is too choice a morsel to fling first of all to the public. I shall give it *then*, God willing; but I am going to give you a taste of it first of all. It is only a piece of paper, but it is very precious to me, for my dear father's signature is on it.[102]

Taking that special letter from his pocket, and opening it slowly, with an obvious reverence for its well-worn pages, he paused again, while the interest intensified. Then, with something in his voice which made every listener attentive, he continued:

> This whole letter is of a tender and most loving sort. It is signed with my beloved father's name, and was written in 1885, just after I started back to

> Auckland. *I beg you to bear in mind that I have had this letter in my
> possession all that time*; but I have considered that the time had not yet
> arrived to make it public.[103]

At this point the deepening silence became absolute. Tom's voice, faltering a little at first, then strengthening in power and timbre, declared that he would read the letter's final words only. One brief sentence punched out its staccato phases: "Get very strong, and when I am older, and feebler, be ready to take my place!"[104]

The gathering sat as if stunned, the impact of those terse words settling slowly upon them. Then followed a burst of tumultous cheering. They had, then, done exactly as their revered C. H. Spurgeon had wished! As wave after wave of applause arose, their new pastor's voice was heard clear and strong:

> You see, *you* called me, and from the Glory came the voice of my father's
> God, *and there is the voice of my earthly father*. What wonder that I have said
> I *must* enter in this open door! Let us sing 'Praise God, from Whom All
> Blessings Flow'![106]

Then the doxology was sung with abandon and watered by many tears. After a vote of thanks to Thomas Olney for his tact and energy in holding the fellowship together during a period of exceptional difficulty, the meeting dispersed. So many crowded around the lower rostrum to clasp Thomas's hand that all could hardly be accommodated for the best part of thirty minutes.[107]

The official welcome on April 12, 1894 gathered two thousand for a preliminary tea and packed the Tabernacle for a 7 PM meeting from which thousands had to be turned away. The orphanage choir sang. There were greetings from F. B. Meyer, Charles Spurgeon, Jr., and many others. Even Dr. James Spurgeon, obviously awkward in the situation, spoke with grace from his position as the president of the orphanage and the Pastors' College. He stated his conviction that the Tabernacle would now be his nephew's lifework, and offered a brotherly bridge to past tensions by stating: "I bespeak for him a free hand. And if anybody quotes me against him, I shall not thank him for doing it. I beseech you give him all the help you can, for he certainly will need it."[108]

Thomas Olney concluded the evening with these words:

> I am glad to welcome him because he is very much like his father, because he
> is the son of his father, a home-made article . . . and because he is, I believe,
> the right man in the right place, thoroughly furnished for this good work. We
> are looking forward to good times, and wish to be left, without being
> troubled and bothered, to do the work that is before us. All I say is, "Give
> him fair play!"[109]

The effect of that week of high excitement was felt over many months. Tom was hardly back to reality by the time his family arrived and were welcomed at the Stockwell Orphanage on Friday July 19.[110] He had lain awake for many hours on the evening of the April 12 gathering, reliving it all.

Strange how God's providence wove together such a pattern, only now discernable, from the tangled threads which stretched down the years, he thought. Memory raced quickly over his health problems, the unexpected Australian blessings, the glorious work in Auckland, Daisy's death, and the dreadful pressures of the past two years. He had held himself aloof from all partisanship, endeavouring to practice a modesty and self-restraint in the tense Tabernacle atmosphere which would honor the Lord and validate his own ministry.[111] Had he chosen to reveal that 1885 letter of his father's at any time, its contents could have swept him overnight into the pastorate on a great wave of sentimental affection. He was glad now that he had trusted in God's sovereignty to take care of all things.

I wonder if I should have told them about D. L. Moody's word to me on the last Sunday when I was here in 1893? he thought. *He told me plainly in the Tabernacle vestry that day—"You are yet to come back to this place, and I am going to pray God here and now that it may be so."*[112] *No, I think father's letter was confirmation enough. The fact that he wrote it nine years ago seals the arrangement better than anything else ever can. How sad that Uncle James has not remained—it would have been a delight to work together, but it is not to be.*[113]

The insomnia of that night was now no rare experience for Tom. But this time he felt especially restless. Somewhere in a forgotten corner of his mind a thought lay suspended which he could not quite grasp. Its half-hidden presence seemed to suggest ideas as foreboding as they were attractive. Not until early morning did relief finally come as, with the insight which often triggers upon a momentary relief from concentration, a phrase jerked itself awkwardly into his consciousness—"behind a frowning providence He hides a smiling face."

Quickly Tom arose, fumbled for a candle, and opened the hymnal which lay beside his Bible on the bedside table. *A hymn! That is what it was!* Yes, part of the fourth stanza in that very same hymn of William Cowper's which had come to him on that far-off night in Victoria after he had first preached there in 1877, and had likewise been sleepless with excitement.

He read each line slowly, savouring every word, weighing each phrase:

> God moves in a mysterious way
>   His wonders to perform;
> He plants His footsteps in the sea,
>   And rides upon the storm.
>
> Deep in unfathomable mines
>   Of never-failing skill,
> He treasures up His bright designs,
>   And works His sov'reign will.

Ye fearful saints, fresh courage take;
  The clouds ye so much dread
Are big with mercy, and shall break
  In blessings on your head.

Judge not the Lord by feeble sense,
  But trust Him for His grace;
Behind a frowning providence
  He hides a smiling face.

His purposes will ripen fast
  Unfolding ev'ry hour;
The bud may have a bitter taste,
  But sweet will be the flow'r.

Blind unbelief is sure to err,
  And scan His work in vain;
God is His own interpreter,
  And He will make it plain.[114]

Tom closed the book, snuffed the candle, and settled back to sleep. Blessings had certainly come out of buffetings for him. God's sovereignty could never be mere doctrine again; it was confirmed experience. But what did that mean for the future? Were all the tensions over? He had first journeyed to the South Pacific to regain a lost health that would enable him to work alongside his father in London. Instead he had discovered a ministry out there which had precluded his return, and had experienced the dogged ill-health which, until now, had continued to position him away from the beloved Metropolitan Tabernacle.

That mysterious Divine will had exiled him all those long years from his English roots, and had permitted his health to breakdown at the peak of his college studies, in the midst of Auckland successes, and elsewhere. Now God had moved him full circle, not to help his father, but actually to succeed him!

*   *   *

With a quiet prayer for special grace on Lila and the children so far away, he settled at last to a rest intermittently, troubled by a series of shaking, nervous starts, each of which awoke him with fresh surprise. Altogether a night presenting a model, in embryo, of all that his fourteen years as pastor at the Metropolitan Tabernacle would bring.

LIST OF ILLUSTRATIONS

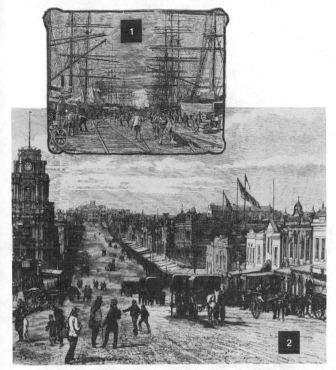

50

51

52

53

71

72

73

74

75

76

77

85

86

87

88

89

90

CHARLES BLOMFIELD

LANDSCAPE ARTIST IN OIL.

HOUSE, SIGN, AND DECORATIVE PAINTER,

WAKEFIELD STREET, AUCKLAND.

91

92

93

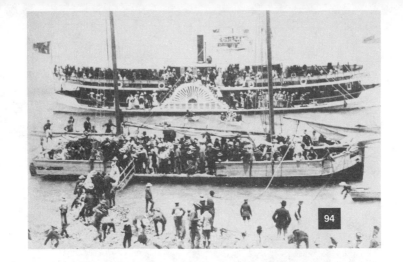

97

ᴛʜᴇ Bᴀᴘᴛɪs

Published at the Auckland Tabernacle Ba.

VOL. I.   AUCKLAND, DECE

98

THE PROPOSED NEW
(Corner of Queen Street and

Programme of Evening Entertainments,
To Commence at Eight o'Clock.

MONDAY, DEC. 18.—THE FINE ART GALLERY
will be open throughout the evening.
Valuable pictures have been kindly lent.
Title of picture and name of lender will
be attached to each. Admission, 6d.
and 3d.

TUESDAY.—MR. T. SPURGE
Ploughman's Pictures
solving views. Mr.
Street, has generously
pulate the lantern.
WEDNESDAY.—CONCERT, U
of Mr. HOOD, assiste
BARTLEY and other fri
THURSDAY.—POPULAR SCI
MR. JOSIAH MARTIN;
light views.

100

103

104

BUILDER.

Edited by Thomas Spurgeon

2.   Price 3d.

FRIDAY.—DISSOLVING VIEW ENTERTAIN
    by THOMAS SPURGEON and MR. DE
beautiful pictures of London. The con
    story of "Simon and the Pig" w
delight the children.

SATURDAY.—MUSICAL ENTERTAINMENT. Par-
    ticulars to be announced.

Admission each evening, 6d.; Children under
                twelve, 3d.
        From 8 till 9 o'clock

99

102

101

105

106

107

108

109

121

122

C. H. Spurgeon 1856

The lamp of my study. —
The light is bright as ever. 1861
O that mine eyes were more opened 1864
Being worn to pieces rebound 1870 The lantern
mended & the light as joyous to mine eyes as ever

123

124

125

126

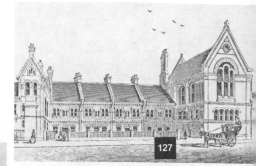

132

133

136

137

138

139

C.H. SPURGEON'S First Words at the Tabernacle

139

I WOULD PROPOSE THAT THE SUBJECT OF THE MINISTRY IN THIS HOUSE, AS LONG AS THIS PLATFORM SHALL STAND, & AS LONG AS THIS HOUSE SHALL BE FREQUENTED BY WORSHIPPERS, SHALL BE THE PERSON OF **JESUS CHRIST.** I AM NEVER ASHAMED TO AVOW MYSELF A CALVINIST; I DO NOT HESITATE TO TAKE THE NAME OF BAPTIST; BUT IF I AM ASKED WHAT IS MY CREED, I REPLY, "IT IS JESUS CHRIST." MY VENERATED PREDECESSOR, DR. GILL, HAS LEFT A BODY OF DIVINITY, ADMIRABLE & EXCELLENT IN ITS WAY; BUT THE BODY OF DIVINITY TO WHICH I WOULD PIN & BIND MYSELF FOR EVER, GOD HELPING ME, IS NOT HIS SYSTEM, OR ANY OTHER HUMAN TREATISE; BUT CHRIST JESUS, WHO IS THE SUM & SUBSTANCE OF THE GOSPEL, WHO IS IN HIMSELF ALL THEOLOGY, THE INCARNATION OF EVERY PRECIOUS TRUTH, THE ALL-GLORIOUS PERSONAL EMBODIMENT OF THE WAY, THE TRUTH, & THE LIFE

C.H. SPURGEON'S Last Words at the Tabernacle

140

If you wear the livery of Christ, you will find Him so meek and lowly of heart that you will find rest unto your souls. He is the most magnanimous of captains. There never was His like among the choicest of princes He is always to be found in the thickest part of the battle. When the wind blows cold He always takes the bleak side of the hill. The heaviest end of the cross lies ever on His shoulders. If He bids us carry a burden, He carries it also. If there is anything that is gracious, generous, kind, and tender, yea lavish and superabundant in love, you always find it in Him. His service is life, peace, joy. Oh, that you would enter on it at once! God help you to enlist under the banner of **JESUS CHRIST**!

141

142

143

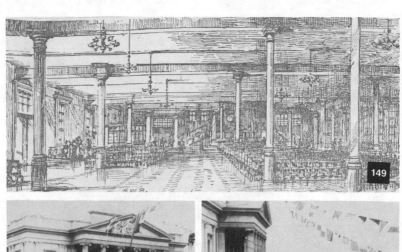

156

157

158

159

160

161

162

163

164

165

166

167

168

169

170

171

172

173

174

175

176

177

178

179

180

181

182

188

189

190

191

192

193

194

195

196

197

198

199

5 Bud and Flower
(1894-1908)

His purposes will ripen fast,
Unfolding ev'ry hour;
The bud may have a bitter taste
But sweet will be the flow'r.

At the March 14, 1894 meeting which called Thomas to the permanent pastorate the congregation heard that some 200 persons had been received into Tabernacle fellowship during his eight months of temporary service, and that forty of these attributed their conversion directly or indirectly to his ministry.[1] Four years of similar blessings followed. His February letter to Dr. Alfred Hall described a service characteristic of those days:

> At the close of the evening service I conducted an aftermeeting. Lecture hall filled. Many asked for prayer, and later quite a number audibly expressed their decision to accept Jesus as their Saviour. Later still the inquiry room was full of seekers and workers. I stayed until 9:15, and was then obliged to leave the struggling sheep. I doubt not the Good Shepherd came to their rescue. Praise ye Jehovah![2]

Two years later, one reporter described his visit to a service as quite the equal of former experiences there under C. H. Spurgeon's ministry. The "magnificent congregation," exceeding in numbers those of any other church in the metropolis, included many young men. Thomas's demeanor was natural, free from all affectation and mannerism, robust, clear and appealing in style, the visitor affirmed, adding:

> If there were any present who resisted his appeals, no one could fail to understand what he meant. . . . His illustrations,—he did not use them very freely—were homely and familiar, and very much to the point. There was no word-painting, and hardly a scenic phrase; but now and again his line of thought in exposition and preaching was lit up with a quiet gleam of humour, and there were aportions of the sermon in which there was a vein of real eloquence, not the eloquence of a man who is not trying to utter fine sentences but is profoundly anxious to reach the hearts of his hearers, to press the aims of Divine truth upon their consciences, and to win them to the acceptance of the Gospel. . . . The occasional hearer is not left in doubt as to the preacher's doctrinal position and beliefs. He stands in the old ways . . . he holds with a firm grip the great fundamental truths of revelation. Indeed, it may be said that the double truth of man's need as a sinner and God's mercy

in redemption through the atonement of Christ were as the warp and the woof
in the whole texture of the service.[3]

The sermon that evening dealt with self-righteousness based on Proverbs 16:2,
"all the ways of a man are clean in his own eyes, but the Lord weigheth the
spirits." The argument developed from the excuses and denials men make of sin
when they speak of it as a weakness and a failing of humanity rather than a
serious transgression of God's Law. The tendency to compare ourselves with
others rather than with God's standards, which he saw as leading to the final
result of a self-justification that cannot sustain us before God's judgment. This
powerful and convicting analysis ended with the proclamation of freedom from
the real guilt and power of sin through the merit of Christ as our ransom.[4]

One highlight of those years came when Tom dedicated a monument of his
father's ministry at the opening of a new building at the Stockwell Orphanage.
The artist represented C. H. Spurgeon in typical preaching attitude with one hand
raised, amid scenes of his ministry among the orphanage children and at the
Pastors' College. Thomas applauded the memorial as altogether suitable.[5]

Uncle James,however, continued as an annoying thorn in everybody's side.

Although he had resigned from all Tabernacle connections upon Thomas's
succession to the pastorate, James Spurgeon continued as president of the
Pastors' College, and in his management tasks at the orphanage. In January 1895,
just as Thomas was granted a seat on the college board of trustees, James
announced his intention of leading the college back to a position of direction
under the Baptist Union, from which it had asserted independence amid C. H.
Spurgeon's tensions over the Down Grade controversy. James saw the duty of the
college to be the cultivation of friendships with those authorities and denominational leaders who had serverely censured his late brother, and he refused to
withdraw from this position.[6] This gave Thomas another sleepless night, so
distressing that he confided to a friend his most bitter (albeit private) criticism of
his uncle in no uncertain terms:

> I told some of the brethren that it was enough to make my father turn in his
> grave—scarcely 3 years since and his rotter brother undoes his work and
> removes from his stand, and disgraces his dearest institution. Alas, alas![7]

By May of 1896, James had become so headstrong in these desires, not shared
by the other trustees, that he finally resigned all connections with the college in a
surprise statement at the annual college public meeting, protesting against its'
independence, and announcing his personal and full return to the Baptist Union
fold.[8] It was known that Thomas strongly supported the idea of the college
independence, while encouraging enlistment of students from the Union as well
as elsewhere. The sustained cheering which supported Thomas's presence clearly
indicated where the sympathies of the majority of college supporters lay.[9] He said

quietly, "Dear friends, I should be sorry if this meeting assumed the form of a demonstration—and I regret to have to use the words—on either side. I am not going to reply to the remarks that have been made."[10]

His tact was noted by the official denominational paper with this comment, " . . . And so, in one half-minute we had passed the quicksands."[11]

James's opposition had also exacerbated tensions just three months before through a different circumstance. Dr. A. T. Pierson had returned to England for a variety of ministries and submitted to baptismal immersion at the hands of Dr. Spurgeon, under circumstances which brought much ill-feeling among some Tabernacle members and others. The reaction of sections of the Christian press was one of incredulity and criticism.[12]

After meeting on Saturday for a dinner at James Spurgeon's home, Pierson went to James's church, the West Croydon Baptist Tabernacle, and, accompanied by fourteen of his deacons and close friends, James there immersed the American Presbyterian in a ceremony which surprised many of them with its immediacy. Pierson preached the Sunday services on the following day, and was honored with a reception in the school hall fostered by James Spurgeon on the following Monday. A very large company included many invited guests from the current Metropolitan Tabernacle membership. Pierson testified that his change of views arose from a restudy of Scripture and from the entry into a deeper life of grace which had been his in recent months. He closed with some comments concerning the difference that would be marked in the Metropolitan Tabernacle if pastor and people were to have the Holy Spirit upon them in fresh measure and power.[13]

Though Dr. Pierson's remarks may have been made in good faith, they were felt to have communicated a spirit of criticism for Thomas's current ministry, though Pierson expressly stated that this was not his perspective. The presence of a large segment of his previous supporters from the Tabernacle, especially invited, did little to cool feelings, and the whole privacy and seeming haste of his immersion left some feeling that he was simply making a play, again, for the Tabernacle pulpit.[14]

James tried to organize the college students to present a memorial address of appreciation to Dr. Pierson on the occasion, without the support of the college authorities. The students refused, although he himself offered to pay the costs of the illuminated manuscript proposed.[15]

The whole matter left a rather sordid impression upon all, and increased James's unpopularity at the Tabernacle.

In a letter describing the increased activity attendant upon evangelist John McNeill's January, 1898 campaign, Thomas commented that he had not seen his uncle for months and that James was "very angry" about the C. H. Spurgeon autobiography, edited by Mrs. C. H. Spurgeon, which had just been published, calling it a "tissue of lies." In fact, Thomas believed that the anger resulted from the fact that James himself had planned a biography of his brother, and that the current production had stolen potential sales for it.[16] The undercurrent of Pierson-related opposition was also in evidence at the February 19 meeting in 1896. Here a proposal for a suitable assistant to Thomas (Mr. Sawday) was carried over their protests. Tom saw this as a real victory for his leadership, and that of the church officers who supported him.[17]

His sermons, reported weekly in *Word and Work,* and in the *Christian Signal,* continued to be popular. His ministry flourished despite some environmental changes in South London around the Tabernacle, which made the reaching of numbers increasingly difficult during his pastorate.

The third week of April, 1898 brought Thomas a situation which was to be his greatest trial. A session of conference meetings for the Pastor's College was in full swing. Between four and five hundred ministers gathered in the assembly hall of the Pastors' College, then located at the rear of the Tabernacle building, to hear the annual conference report. They rejoiced in the news that 968 men had been educated for the ministry at the College over the forty-two years of its operation, and that 668 were currently Baptist pastors, missionaries, evangelists, or in other Christian service. Four hundred thirty-eight churches were currently connected with the College Conference, staffed by men who were its graduates, and some 4,182 persons had been baptized in these fellowships in 1898 alone.

James Stephens, a part-time tutor at the college, was presenting a paper. Suddenly Pastor Frank Nicolson, of Bedford, rushed down the aisle to whisper an urgent message in the chairman's ear. "I think," said Tom Spurgeon, interrupting the speaker, "that you should know that the Tabernacle is on fire!" A groan came from the assembly. "I do not see that we can do anything," continued the president. "We had better finish the session," and with perfect composure he resumed his seat.[18]

Mr. Stephens proceeded manfully, but in a few minutes the audience heard the crackling of burning wood, the heat became intense, and smoke found its way in curling wreaths into the hall. Although the gallery was crowded with ladies, no panic ensured. The conference assembly trooped downstairs and by the time they reached the open air, the Tabernacle was blazing. With a mighty crash, a major portion of the roof collapsed. Tom looked at the disintegrating structure, " . . . his features working, his body shaking with sobs. Then he turned away, as it seemed, a broken man."[19]

Some of the delegates hastened to the back of the building and rescued items from the vestries, including a fine set of communion plates, valuable oil paintings of the previous pastors who had served the congregation, the church records and minute books, and the famous study chair used by Dr. Rippon. A marble bust of C. H. Spurgeon, too heavy to be easily removed, was hastily covered with some carpet. It survived as a grimy and smoke-stained relic.

Apparently the fire had begun in an overheated basement flue. The dinner for 400 conference guests was in preparation. Some dry, exposed beams caught fire at the first floor and roof levels, and the flames attacked the timber portions of the stone structure without restraint.

One local reporter vividly described the scene:

> It was about half past twelve when the fire was first noticed, the discoverers being some workmen on a neighbouring building. They saw smoke coming through the roof of the chapel, and immediately afterwards noticed a red glow behind the windows. A few minutes afterwards the whole building burst into flames. Hundreds of workpeople rushed in alarm out of Messrs. Rabbit's boot and shoe factory which is separated from the Tabernacle by only a narrow passage. The bells of the establishment rang furiously at the same time. Just behind the Tabernacle is Temple Street, filled with the dwellings of poor people. Panic-stricken this colony threw their bedding and furniture into the road, breaking some of the windows in the operation.

> The first evidences of fire occurred in the south-east corner of the building, and the cause was officially assigned to "a defective flue." A good deal of cooking periodically proceeds in the basement, where social gatherings are held, and on Wednesday extensive preparations had been made for the provision of refreshments for visitors to the conference. The annual supper of the Pastors' College was announced to take place at night, the collection at which often amounts to 2,000 pounds. It is surmised that an extra strain upon the flues communicating with the kitchen—or the apartment that represented the kitchen—proved too much, and that some weak spot was the fatal means of communicating the fire to the roof . . .

> Along the apex of the roof, which ran from Newington Butts to a street in the rear, was a continuous range of immense Louvre ventilators, some 70 or 100 feet heigh. The fire quickly laid hold of these, and in a few minutes both slopes of the roof were stripped of their slates, while the rafters and ventilators stood out encircled in flames against the sky. The slates appeared to crumble up and melt as if made of lead, slipping down into the gutters, and revealing the flames speeding fiercely through the building.[20]

> Just before 1 p.m. an immense column of flame shot skywards, serving as a rocket to bring thousands of spectators to the scene, while great clouds of smoke and dust rose from the burning building. A continual mist of falling ashes and flakes of burned woodwork showered the surrounding area. The whole roof collapsed at this time just as the first fire engines arrived. More were continually summoned until twenty were finally gathered in battle against the gigantic conflagration. Before the last flame was extinguished thirty-five such were deployed to the task from all over London.[21]

Although the fire was controlled by firefighters to some extent, little could be done other than to preserve some surrounding buildings from destruction:

> Spectators arrived with still more rapidity, and continued coming till Newington Butts, and even the great space at the Elephant and Castle, were crammed with a vast sea of humanity, stopping all the traffic. The breeze was sufficiently strong to stimulate the power of the flames, but not to dispel the great volume of smoke which hung like a canopy at some distance above the doomed building. The gloom of the day only served to heighten the effect. In spite of the tons of water which were hurled by the steamers upon the great temple, the house being directed from all the neighbouring roofs and from every conceivable point of vantage, the fire burnt like a gigantic furnace. Columns of fire shot forth from every side, the great facade and Corinthian pillars, built of stone, were overlapped and encircled by the fire, and then, at a time when it seemed impossible that the din could be more terrific or the conflagration fiercer, the majestic roof crashed to the ground. . . .

> At first the firemen tried to enter the chapel, but they were at once driven back, one of them being burned, and another hurt by falling debris . . . their expulsion destroying all hope of saving any part of the structure. The iron pillars on which the galleries rested fell and twisted into fantastic shapes under the heavy streams of cold water.[22]

By a quarter after two, the Tabernacle had burned entirely. The huge portico now stood solidly set against gaping open spaces behind it. Bare and blackened walls on two sides loomed against the April sky amid the grotesque shapes of the heat twisted iron pillars. The space between the walls remained thick with choking smoke for many hours. For several days firemen and salvage crews patrolled the barricaded ruins, breaking down the more dangerous segments and securing areas considered likely to fall. While many of the steps had chipped and cracked, only the stone staircases leading to the galleries remained virtually untouched.

The Christian public reacted swiftly and with empathy. The *British Weekly,* the *Echo,* and other Christian papers opened restoration funds, as did Dr. Parker, Dr. Clifford, Dr. Meyer, and other notable leaders. The *Christian Pictorial* appealed for the replacement of the clothing stocks which had been destroyed in the Tabernacle basement, kept there for the Poor Ministers' Society securing 346 pounds of supplies for this cause.[23] The *Newcastle Daily Chronicle* of May 10 suggested that the impact of the loss sustained to London was comparable to the ruin of either Westminister Abbey or St. Paul's Cathedral.

By the time the hastily replanned college tea began at 5:30 PM (the same night of the fire, but moved to the buildings at the rear) Thomas had recovered some composure. He counseled faith and patience for the future. Referring to the sermon theme of the Sunday before as exalting God's providence, he said:

> The Lord works in a mysterious way His wonders to perform, But we can trust Him, brethren. (Cries of Amen) I am sure we should possess our souls in peace and patience in this trying time.[24]

His pain was evident, however, as he continued:

> I am bound to say that my heart is heavy with sorrow. I grieve to think that the house that echoed my dear father's voice has ceased to be, and that the very spot upon which he stood, and of which he and all of us were so fond, has indeed gone. (Sympathetic applause.) The Lord looks down upon us in this hour of trial, and will, I am sure, send relief. His ways may be past finding out, but if they are His ways, that is all we ask. Already the tide of sympathy has begun to pour in. I have been receiving telegrams ever since the news of the catastrophe got about.[25]

Offers of help poured in from many quarters. They decided to continue the conference meetings in the college buildings and scheduled the Sunday morning service also to be in nearby Exeter Hall. Tom announced that the building had been insured for twelve thousand pounds, but this was far less than it would cost to replace. The drama of his conference address can best be calculated by the press comment:

> Mr. Spurgeon was during the delivery of the greater part of his address in tears. As bravely as the Rev. gentleman tried to bear the trouble, it was obvious that his emotions were triumphant.[26]

On the last Sunday in April, Thomas, whose appearance still showed signs of the terrible ordeal, addressed a crowded congregation in Exeter Hall. He chose the text "Our holy and our beautiful house, where our fathers praised thee is burned up with fire, and all our pleasant things are laid waste" (Isa. 64:11).[27] Noting the loss of books and Bibles, and many other memorabilia of his father, Tom spoke of the comfort of heritages beyond the reach of the flames:

> If we have lost our hymn books we have not lost our songs; though our Bibles are burned the Word remains. Our pleasant things are those which nothing can destroy: the Church of God, the Holy Spirit, the fellowship of saints, the ordinances of the Sanctuary. I am glad to tell you that the old copy of the Declaration of Faith which hung in the pastor's vestry has been saved, but even if it had been lost our faith would have remained.[28]

By May 16 the insurance surveyors had examind the ruins more completely and determined on a very generous settlement of 20,000 pounds for the building and 2,000 pounds for its contents. Estimated building costs to reerect a similar structure on the same general lines as the old, incorporating the still-standing walls and portico, were calculated to be twice this amount. Although the insurance payment finally settled was far in excess of the original 12,000 pounds which it had been thought to be all the cover available, the gap seemed so huge that many were discouraged.

Services continued in Exeter Hall and in the Pastors' College for several months. But many thousands scattered to other churches. By the time the congregation was again finally gathered on Sunday, January 1, 1899, numbers were much smaller.

On Friday, May 27, 1898 a special meeting of the male members of the church (held at the orphanage) considered the steps to be taken to restore the Tabernacle. They agreed to clear the basement of the present building, erect a waterproof roof which would be the floor for the main auditorium above, and utilize the new basement areas immediately for the Lord's Day services.[29]

Although this structure cost almost 8,000 pounds, it proved a wise investment, resulting in a large assembly hall 142' by 80'. The design was pleasant. The new hall was lit by electricity, which had just been introduced to the district. A podium and baptistry were included. The parquet flooring, white ceiling and pillars, yellow and wood-paneled walls gave a warm and cheerful setting with near perfect acoustics. The area seated just over 2,000 persons. A series of receptions hosted by Tom and Mrs. C. H. Spurgeon graced the opening services.[30]

Some twenty-nine long months passed before the restored Tabernacle was complete. The work dragged on and James Spurgeon did not help it. Almost immediately after the fire, Thomas wrote, "J. A. S. has I fear, an opportunity to be nasty in the rebuilding of the Tabernacle; he is a trustee—worse luck. But the Lord is greater than he."[31] Tom had sung the doxology while the fire raged, he said, "but it wasn't easy."[32] By December of that year he referred to the opposition as a "diabolical war."[33]

Why did James Archer Spurgeon act so strangely at this time? The documents and reports give us little information. Like his elder brother, James was the son of an independent pastor. Three years younger than Charles, he had trained for the ministry at Regents' Park College. He had served the Portland Union Chapel in Southampton (an open-membership Baptist cause), resigning because of a difference with the congregation. After another short ministry at Bayswater, he took charge of a small group meeting in Croydon and remained their pastor for thirty years, building a large and commodious chapel which still functions strongly today. He served as London Baptist Association president in 1873, and had been slated to assume the presidency of the Baptist Union just a few months prior to his unexpected decease. In 1892 two American schools honored him; College University with D.D., and Olivet College an LL.D. Both honors recognized his attainments in the mastery of ecclesiastic law, a field in which he became an acknowledged expert. As the business manager and chief administrator of his brother's manifold Tabernacle ministries, he directed all the work of the orphanages, the Pastors' College, and the charity almshouses.

Unexpectedly, on March 22, 1899, James expired while returning from London. He died alone in a first-class carriage at the railway station in Preston Park. The funeral, held March 28, was attended by Thomas, his brother Charles, and their grandfather, John Spurgeon, then eighty-eight years of age. With genuine sincerity, the family paid respect and honor to a servant who, C. H. Spurgeon had often characterized as enlarging his own ministry beyond all description.[34]

James Spurgeon's attitudes, opposition, and attacks on Thomas and others at the Tabernacle, seem enigmatic today. His open advocacy of the Presbyterian A. T. Pierson as a candidate for the Tabernacle pulpit appears to have become an obsession at times, and this undoubtedly had an effect on all his future relationships. Thomas never castigated him publicly or privately, apart from one or two asides such as have been quoted in the personal letter above. It may be kindest to suggest that the loss sustained by James with the passing of his famous brother Charles seriously impaired his capacity for judgment.

W. Y. Fullerton and Archibald G. Brown held special evangelistic services in February 1900 for Thomas while the new Tabernacle neared completion. Costing 36,000 pounds, the auditorium seated 2,703 persons on the ground floor as compared to the original 3,600 of the old Tabernacle. When the galleries, designed largely along the lines of the former ones, were also completed, the whole building accommodated some 4,000 by official count. Of course, the crowd in both Tabernacles often exceeded the actual official limits.[35]

Rededication festivities began with an opening communion service led by Alexander Mclaren on September 19, 1900, and continued through October 18 of that same year. Despite the county council's proper insistence on improved safety features, which demanded more accessible exits, and the general desire for increased seating comfort, the new Tabernacle appeared remarkably similar to the old. Steel girders and brick walls replaced the wood and plaster ones. Broader aisles provoked the comment that the "general effect is rather of a renovation than a reconstruction."[36] One reporter poetically noted that "the sunlight streaming through the picturesque stained windows made the new Tabernacle infinitely more comfortable and fairer to look upon."[37]

The use of electricity for lighting and the steam radiators attracted attention. Acoustics were improved. The opening gatherings were not only characterized by large attendance and helpful addresses but also "by the old-time, wholehearted insistence on foundation truths, which has always been associated with the Metropolitan Tabernacle."[38]

Four thousand jammed the main auditorium an hour before the opening service, with 1,800 overflowing into the hall below. Thomas declared that " . . . as God enabled him he would go on preaching the Old Gospel, and working along the old lines."[39] Ira D. Sankey, musical associate of D. L. Moody, who had sung at C. H. Spurgeon's funeral in 1892, was featured musician for some of the services. His Saturday, September 22, service of song filled the house by 4:30 in the afternoon for a 7 PM meeting. The congregation packed into every available inch of space, even crowding onto the steps below the pulpit and onto the other platforms. A news picture of the occasion, taken by flashlight, shows Thomas and other notables crowded onto the rostrum, with Sankey seated at his harmonium. It endorses the newspaper comment, "there appeared not an inch of room in the pulpit!"[40]

Sankey told stories of how some of his hymns were written, and sang "The Ninety and Nine," recalled memories of the 1873 and 1874 Moody campaigns, and reminisced about those who had served in other years. He sang the verses of "When the Mists Have Rolled Away," asking that the galleries join in the refrain, each in turn.[41] In extending him a welcome, Thomas acknowledged how much Moody's preaching and Sankey's music had shaped his early years of faith. The press reported that Sankey was "received with prolonged cheers and interrupted with applause many times during his recital when he sang old gospel songs and told some of the stories that related to their beginnings."[42]

Tom had overseen all the building, raised most of the money by his own efforts, and had given himself unstintingly to the task. W. Y. Fullerton records the carrying through of such a vast undertaking successfully as "a notable achievement"[43] for the forty-four-year-old pastor. The Sunday services saw standing room only. Thomas's dedication sermon was a revision of the same ideas he had shared at the dedication of the Auckland Tabernacle fifteen years previously. He spoke from the text "Hear thou in heaven, thy dwelling place: and when thou hearest, forgive" (1 Kings, 8:30). His sermon followed the same divisions as he had used before. 1. This Is the House of God; 2. This Is the House of Prayer; 3. This Is the House of Mercy.[44]

Thomas stood firmly and uncompromisingly for the same truths which had come to the fore, heralded by his father during the Down Grade controversy of 1887. The emphases of this movement were altogether orthodox and supported the basic tenets of the faith common to all mainline denominational traditions. Ultimately, they caused C. H. Spurgeon to sever official connections with the Baptist Union, but he never broke personal fellowship with individuals, both Baptist and otherwise. Thomas also continued in a fellowship of openness and cooperation.

A striking example of this quality is his congregation's wholehearted participation in the Simultaneous Mission evangelistic meetings in London, scheduled near the end of January 1901, and sponsored by the Metropolitan Federation of Free Churches. The missioners who ministered at the Metropolitan Tabernacle were John McNeill, a fiery Scottish Presbyterian, Hugh Price Highes, the city's leading Methodist, and Rodney "Gipsy" (his spelling) Smith, the converted Gypsy boy who had first served with the Salvation Army and later was credentialed by the Methodists.[45] Thomas himself conducted a "Country Mission" for the program, allying himself with the Free Church Council in so doing, although neither he nor his church were official members of it.[46]

The combined churches sponsored meetings in selected centers within the boundaries of each of the sixty metropolitan councils of the London area, some simultaneously, and many overlapping. Local committees arranged for house-to-house visitation. They trained special choirs and inquiry room workers. Careful organization, sensible publicity and intensive prayer marked their preparation and fulfillment.

John McNeill, a graduate of Glasgow's Free Church College, originally served McCrie Roxborough Free Church in Edinburgh—situated in the lower parts of the city. He quickly filled it with the many new converts which his vigorous evangelism attracted. Gifted with a natural eloquence and wit not unlike C. H. Spurgeon's, his crowds soon outgrew not only his church, but also the Nicholson Street Public Circus ampitheater and the Free Church Assembly Hall. He then moved to London as the pastor of Regents' Square Church, and later entered an intinerant evangelistic ministry, working first as an associate with D. L. Moody, and later on his own. He ministered at the World's Fair meetings in Chicago in early 1893, and later settled as successor to the famed R. A. Torrey at the Church of the Open Door in central Los Angeles, California.[47]

Evangelist Gipsy Smith, then at the height of his ministry, missioned all over England as an appointee sponsored by the United Free Churches. He outlived all the other evangelists of his era, touring America thirty times in evangelistic meetings. Active in evangelism for seventy years, he died at the age of eighty-seven in 1947 aboard the liner *Queen Mary,* while again crossing the Atlantic for ministry. During his mission's first Sunday's services at the Tabernacle in 1901, 126 registered public decisions for Christ. On the following Monday and Tuesday almost the same number came to the inquiry rooms for counseling. His messages were strong calls to repentance and impressed Thomas so much that he wrote of them with great enthusiasm:

> Such mighty gatherings, such whole-hearted singing, such sweet "sermons in song" . . . such cheerful giving . . . such earnest Gospel messages, such startling and soul-searching home-thrust, . . . such loving and tender appeals, refuse to be told of adequately with pen and paper. . . . Gipsy Smith is an adept at drawing the net. He believes in eliciting a bold

confession, and very sweetly compels the people to respond to his call. The Father is "drawing" and the Spirit constraining. . . . And when the current began to set towards the inquiry rooms (we had eight of them fully-occupied), how persuasively that tender "Come along" rang out, as from a bell that was already ringing in the new order of things.[48]

Smith's appeals to conscience and heart pervaded the assemblies with an aura some characterized as approaching revival. Counselors described the work in the inquiry rooms as facilitating an unusual depth of reality and power among the seekers.[49] Thomas himself declared,

The names and addresses of no less than 1,200 were registered by the earnest band of workers. Many of these were very manifestly under deep conviction of sin. Old fashioned conversions came into vogue once more. God grant that this fashion may never die down again.[50]

F. B. Meyer declared that nearly every church in the locality had received some new converts, and that the quickened life of Christians brought untold benefits.[51] In the streets, trains, and trams of South London, someone seemed always to be whistling or singing "Count Your Blessings," the 1897 gospel song by Americans Oatman and Excell, which the Gipsy introduced to the huge crowds at the Tabernacle mission. Even the barrow boys and horse drivers of the markets were affected.[52]

So the successful years of ministry multiplied. Thomas never reached the 6,000 morning and evening that heard his father regularly each Sunday. Yet the 4,000 seats of the renovated Tabernacle were more often filled than empty, and great blessings continued. The church meeting of October 1901 recorded an extraordinary peace and harmony in the fellowship after the rebuilding.[53] The deacons' statement in September 1902 called for a celebration of the pastor's birthday with the invitation for members to visit him in the vestry between 4 and 7 PM on the twenty-second with gifts for the Tabernacle and its societies and institutions. It included this commendation:

Our pastor has now been with us for Nine Years, serving the Lord and the Church in all faithfulness. He has endeared himself to the hearts of us all; and there can be no better or more practical method of shewing our love to him, and our appreciation of his efforts, than by helping the great works so dear to him, and to his father before him.[54]

One "Jadi," writer for the *Morning Leader,* visited thirty-eight of the city's major churches and reported on their congregations and preachers in an extensive series of articles. He reserved the last of these for Thomas Spurgeon in 1903, and described his congregation as "gigantic," the singing as passionate and moving, and the pastor as having "the simplicity of his father's genius."[55] He found Thomas's voice to be "full, deep, and clear, eddying in easy circles of sound. A plain Cockney voice with racy Cockney vowelizations that chime musically with the dialect of the Elephantine zone, long drawn out in the true London cadence; a pleasant harmony of culture and democracy in its sweet, clear, treble tones.[56] "The Puritan spirit is strong in him. . . . John Bunyan would have nodded and amened approval to his homely points. . . . His style is Biblical. He thinks in texts. . . . His phrasing is very direct."[57]

The annual church report for 1904 revealed that 3,253 members served in active Tabernacle fellowship, seventy-six had come that year by baptism and forty-five by profession or transfer. Twenty missions to London's poor and twenty-two Sunday schools are officially connected with the church, the latter having 524 teachers and 8,362 scholars in attendance regularly.[58]

The official Baptist periodical marked Tom's completion of ten years of Tabernacle service with plaudits for his patient years of quiet preparation and service overseas, and for the refinements obviously evident in his present character and ministry:

> It is evident that no man could sustain such a ministry for ten years without being tested and revealed. Mr. Thomas Spurgeon has been tested, and has stood the ordeal. There has been the slow test of the years, the holding together of a vast congregation in a neighbourhood from which the wealthier inhabitants have long since removed, and there has been the sudden test of swift calamity in the burning of the older Tabernacle.[59]

The writer spoke of Thomas's composure when the news of the fire was first received in the midst of the pastors' conference meeting:

> It was such a moment as tries the strongest of men. Mr. Spurgeon knew what the fire must mean—what dislocation of plans, . . . what imposition of new burdens—but there was no moment of panic. He called upon us to pray, then to sing the Doxology of praise to Him Who doeth all things well, and then at last to pass out quietly from the room. His calm spread to the assembly. He was like a captain on the bridge, issuing his directions in perilous emergency and saving the ship. The first not only revealed the man, but it revealed the place he had now come to hold in the heart of Christendom. From all quarters, all classes, all churches, and from men of no church, came expressions of sympathy and gifts for restoration, until the second Tabernacle arose, . . . and Mr. Thomas Spurgeon was enabled, as his father had done before him, to open a Metropolitan Tabernacle free of debt.[60]

The accolade continued, lauding Thomas's presidencies of the orphanage and Pastors' College, mission societies, and other organization, and cites his authorship of six volumes and editorship of the monthly *Sword and Trowel* magazine. His contributions to the Temperance cause and many other social issues is also noted:

> If I were asked to name one quality which in my judgement distinguished him above all others I should name brotherliness. He is a man with a great heart, . . . which forgets its own in the cares of others. . . . Prominence has not spoiled him . . . in the Tabernacle, when he preaches, his tender interest in the people opens all hearts to him. The crowd sits hushed, softened, sometimes tearful, as the Pastor's voice trembles with loving emotion or earnest pleading. . . . With pleasant flowing speech and natural gestures he delivers sermons which bear the mark of careful preparation. Both of head and heart. Saturated with Scripture, and ever exalting Jesus, his messages have in them the power which only Truth can give. Now and then a flash of genial humour lights up a passage and relieves the tension of the audience, but the serious purpose of the speaker is never lost, and the theme sweeps on with gathering impressiveness to the final appeal.
>
> But the greatest thing with Mr. Spurgeon is not his humour, or his eloquence, or his earnestness, or even his brotherliness. It lies behind all these. It is found in the devoutness, the sense of spiritual realities, in the grip of things unseen of which we are conscious in his presence. . . . When C. H. Spurgeon passed away many said. "The last of the Puritans is dead." They were wrong. Thomas Spurgeon still lives.[61]

One illustration of Thomas's openness to Providential leading concerns a man who became one of Australia's best-known gospel ministers. The late Sidney M. Potter, who served Baptist pastorates into the 1950s, owed much to Thomas's intervention when all his previous hopes were crushed.

In 1902 Lila Spurgeon answered her front door to find a shy young man from the Aberdeen Street Baptist Church, Geelong, Victoria, asking to see her husband. Discovering him to be the son of one of her friends with whom she had grown up in far-off Australia, she welcomed him in to stay for lunch.[62]

Equally delighted to meet his unexpected guest, Tom, arriving from a funeral which he had conducted, proudly pulled his gold watch from his waistcoat pocket and informed the young man that the deacons of the Aberdeen Street Church had presented him with it in 1877 upon his twenty-first birthday. The pastor reminded his young guest how he had first started preaching there through the invitation of their minister, A. C. Bunning. "I know that," commented the young man. "My name is Sid Potter, and my grandfather was the senior deacon who presented the watch to you."

After luncheon, the two men retired to the pastor's study for more conversation. Sidney told how he had served with Baptist home missions in country pastorates in Victoria and Western Australia, and had now come to London. "I was about to enter the Baptist Theological College of Victoria this year for pastoral training," he said, "when I was advised that, owing to the resignation of the college principal, my entrance was deferred. They instructed me to come to London to enter your Pastors' College and said that Alan Webb, present pastor of Aberdeen Street, would write you in behalf of the denomination at home, and make all necessary arrangements."

"Have you been to our college yet?" Thomas inquired. "Yes, I have," Sid replied, grimly, "and they knew nothing there of my coming. Mr. Barlett, the secretary, showed me a huge pile of as-yet unprocessed applications for entrance, and informed me that 'Every applicant in that pile has a prior right of entrance."

"I have just heard that Alan Webb died at his bedside while at prayer in Geelong," Thomas interjected. Comparing notes, they discovered that the pastor's passing had occurred on the morning of the very day in which he had promised Sid that he would write to Mr. Spurgeon about the enrollment.

"That explains, then," commented Tom, "why we have had no information about your coming. And, as the college is now already in session, and we make it a rule never to receive students during sessions, you will probably have a chance to enter in twelve-month's time, if your credentials finally come through."

Sid grew quiet, greatly distressed at the news of Reverend Alan Webb's death, and further frustrated at the proposed delay. Then he reached into his pocket and thrust a calling card into Tom's hand, saying, "Oh, I was supposed to give this to you, when I saw you."

Tom's brow clouded. "How dare you go to Mr. Olney and secure his card to pressure me! You must know there is a proper way of college entrance, and that I will not respond to this kind of leverage."

Sid hastened to share the rest of the story.

"I left the college office annoyed and distressed. I wandered down the Borough, and along the busy thoroughfare which crosses London Bridge, towards the hotel where my lodgings were for that night. Suddenly the face of a man in the crowd arrested my attention.

"Impulsively I halted him and said, 'Pardon me, but is your name Olney?' 'My name is William Olney,' he replied, 'What can I do for you?' I looked at him in astonishment, and when I found my voice, I said, 'Sir, I have just come from Western Australia. I have never seen you before. But I have seen your photograph many times on the wall of the cottage of an old lady who was a member of my congregation in the Baptist church at Fremantle. She would talk of you often, and when she heard I was coming to London, she told me that if I ever came across you, I was to be sure to thank you for your kindnesses to her. I understand that you provided funds for her passage to Australia, and continue with some support, so that her health may improve there, after its failure here in England. She is most grateful. She gave me no address, and I never thought that I would meet you, and here we are face to face in the street!"

"'Why this is remarkable!' Mr. Olney replied. 'At the moment you accosted me I was thinking about Australia. I have been reading of the great evangelistic meetings being conducted there now by R. A. Torrey and Charles M. Alexander. Do you know anything about them?'"

"'I have just come directly from them in Perth, Western Australia!', I exclaimed. We spoke together for a few moments about the gospel meetings there and he invited me to come to the Haddon Hall Mission, which he serves as honorary superintendent, and to tell of the blessings in the Australian Torrey-Alexander meetings. I did. Then he and his brother took me to dinner and inquired as to my purposes in London. When he heard of the difficulties I had experienced with the Pastors' College entrance, he insisted that I seek you out and share the whole story with you. That is why I sought you out today, and that is why he gave me his card to hand on to you when I came."

Immediately Tom recognized the hand of God in these remarkable events, just as William Olney had. He quietly responded, "You did not know, then, that Mr. Olney is one of our senior deacons in the Metropolitan Tabernacle, and also one of my closest friends?" The surprised young man slowly shook his head. "I only recognized him as the benefactor of my Australian church member, from his photograph on her wall!"

"Potter," exclaimed Thomas, "When God opens a door we never close it! Meet me at the college at 10 AM tomorrow."

After the appropriate tests validating his admission levels were administered, the college immediately enrolled Sid.

The following Sunday, Thomas Spurgeon told the whole story to his Metropolitan Tabernacle congregation. He described Mr. Olney's picture in far-off Fremantle, and how Sid spoke with him just as he reflected on the Torrey-Alexander meetings from which Sid had so lately come. Thomas detailed the strange concurrence of other events in the story. He told of his wife's former membership in the same Aberdeen Street church in Geelong, and of Sid's grandfather presenting him with the watch he wore. He then spoke of the college opening its rolls to the young Australian lad, under the conviction that God's hand could be seen in such a bundle of details that all felt that His guidance could not be resisted.

Sid, present in the Tabernacle service, was quite overwhelmed. The events of the past week had left him shaken. Not the least among these was the discovery that deacon Olney was, at that specific period, the current chairman of the Pastors' College board of trustees![63]

Church historians, among others, commonly refer to a specific tide of spiritual blessing in the year 1905 as the "Welsh Revival." This movement attracted attention because of its phenomenal impact in Wales. Chapel services in that land would often continue all through the night, under no specific leadership, preacher, or organization, and with much fervor and many observable results in changed lives and communities. Few, however, realize that the Welsh segment was but an element in a larger movement of spiritual awakening which, after a peak in 1859, surged in continual waves on into the twentieth century, finally lessening in impact only with the outbreak of hostilities in World War I in 1914.

D. L. Moody, Henry Varley, Charles Haddon Spurgeon, Sam P. Jones, and John McNeill were among its early representatives. Ira D. Sankey, Charles M. Alexander, Amzi Clarence Dixon, Reuben Archer Torrey, Thomas Spurgeon, J. Wilbur Chapman, and Rodney "Gipsy" Smith were other prominent leaders who carried the movement's momentum into the 1900s. Billy Sunday campaigned into the 1920s with similar ardor, though his movement, through the ministry of Chapman, later became more prohibitionist that evangelistic. As in the ministry of Gipsy Smith (the only other one among these evangelists to continue past

Time-Line of Evangelical Leaders

C. H. SPURGEON   1834-1892

Henry Varley   1835-1912

D. L. Moody   1837-1899

Ira D. Sankey   1840-1908

Sam P. Jones   1847-1902

Charles M. Alexander   1848-1920

John McNeill   1854-1933

A. C. Dixon   1854-1925

THOMAS SPURGEON   1856-1917

R. A. Torrey   1856-1928

J. Wilbur Chapman   1859-1918

"Gipsy" Smith   1860-1947

Billy Sunday   1862-1935

World War I), however, such blessings as came appeared to be echoes from the past rather than fresh voices of the present.

A comparison of the life spans of these giants in evangelism sheds light on their interrelationship. We have no record of Thomas Spurgeon meeting Jones or Sunday directly, but we know of close friendships which he developed with Varley, Moody, Sankey, Alexander, McNeill, Dixon, Torrey, Smith, and Chapman. With some of these he worked at length, as they had with his father. All of them worked with one or more of the others in the grouping, and many extensively so.

To understand Thomas Spurgeon, and the time of his ministry, we must also understand these men, their perspectives, and the contexts of evangelism and spiritual awakening in which they moved.

C. H. Spurgeon died in 1892. D. L. Moody invited Thomas Spurgeon to participate in the multifaceted evangelistic outreach which he had organized in his home city of Chicago in 1893, in connection with the World's Fair Columbia Exposition. Chapman, Torrey, McNeill, Varley, and others, including Sankey and Alexander, were participants in the extended campaign. Meetings operated continuously in the northern, southern, and western areas of Chicago in eighty different locations, sometimes involving seventy meetings simultaneously. One hundred twenty-five separate meetings functioned on some Sundays, including some in a huge tent by the lake. Observers of the outreach calculated that some two million persons heard the gospel over this extended period.[64] Later Thomas preached for A. C. Dixon, who had also been a Chicago campaign participant, at his Hanson Place Baptist Church in Brooklyn, with great effect, an experience which began a deepening association between the two and which laid the groundwork for fellowship when Dixon ultimately succeeded Thomas as pastor of the Metropolitan Tabernacle in 1911.[65]

Recent research clearly documents the role of theology in Moody's ministry. Thoroughly grounded in the doctrines of grace, his theology stands in essence as Calvinistic rather than Armenian. He was by no means a rigid dispensationalist (although clearly premillennial in eschatology), but held his views with a liberal breadth of tolerance.[66] He came to England with the clear purpose in view of hearing C. H. Spurgeon as often as he could, and learning as much as possible from him.[67] Spurgeon was his hero and his model in doctrine, as well as in almost everything else, and the fellowship between the two became rich and productive.[68] Spurgeon often spoke in enthusiastic support of Moody's ministry.[69] The American evangelist wrote to Spurgeon twenty-two years after he first came to London, thanking him for a night of evangelistic preaching the Tabernacle pastor gave to the Moody-Sankey mission, and endorsing his effectiveness: "I wish you could give us every night you can for the next sixty days. There are so few men who can draw on a week night."[70]

Spurgeon thought so much of the U.S. evangelistic team that he called Sankey up into the pulpit in 1875 to sing "Ring the Bells of Heaven" for his congregation. He enlisted them to give special ministries for his college students, and conducted some noonday prayer meetings for their campaign, as well as preaching for their services himself.[71]

On Moody's second visit to Britain in 1872, after an all-night prayer meeting, Henry Varley said to him, "Moody, the world has yet to see what God will do with a man fully consecrated to him."[72] This challenged Moody to a deeper dedication of life and service. Moody saw elements of such dedication in Spurgeon, read everything Spurgeon had in print, and continued to do so all his life.

Varley, born in Lincolnshire in 1835, migrated to Australia in 1854, following his trade as a butcher in Melbourne and Geelong. By 1860 he had returned to London and expanded his previous lay preaching into a full-time ministry. He built the West London Free Tabernacle and engaged in evangelism with the working classes to great effect, serving there twenty years. He often used the Metropolitan Tabernacle for larger meetings, preaching for Spurgeon on occasions. Varley made many trips to overseas centers, creating a final base in Australia in 1890. He served with the other evangelistic giants at Moody's 1893 campaign in Chicago, and invited Spurgeon as pulpit guest for his own meetings from time to time. While Gipsy Smith was at the Tabernacle in 1901, he also missioned at Bloomsbury Chapel for the simultaneous mission meetings.[73]

Varley was neither quite Baptist nor Plymouth Brother, but drew his ministry ideas and organization from both. Thomas Spurgeon felt challenged by Varley's mature and successful evangelism, observed in Tasmania while he recovered from his second health breakdown there in 1878:

> When I see Mr. Varley preaching almost every day, I almost wish I could do the same, and thus devote my life. Perhaps the time may come when this shall be my proper course (evangelising), and if these quiet months' spell be the preparation for it, who shall call it wasted time?[74]

Among the more colorful evangelists of the era was Sam P. Jones. Jones held huge evangelistic campaigns all over the U.S.A., beginning in 1879 and concentrating in the South after 1898. He spoke powerfully to the social conscience of church and city, with an emphasis on behavior as the right outcome of genuine Christian faith—His best-known imperative was the phrase "Quit Your Meanness!"[75] On his fiftieth birthday, it was estimated that some seven hundred thousand had found Christ through his ministry, and he served nine years beyond that.[76] When his body lay in state in Atlanta, in the Georgia state capitol, some 30,000 people viewed the remains in tribute.[77] With an easy conversational style, Jones, who believed that fun was the next best thing to religion in life, quickly became known for his understanding of the right use of pathos and humor in the pulpit and for his wit and invincible repartee. Castigating church members who showed no zeal in their Christian service and criticized their pastors for a similar lethargy, he declared, "You pack your preachers in an ice-house all year and abuse them because they don't sweat!"[78]

After he criticized the excessive use of makeup, a woman accused him of dyeing his mustache (which was black while his hair was gray). He denied the accusation, saying, "Madam, my mustache is twenty-one years younger than my hair!"[79] He declared that he was afraid he might hurt somebody's feelings when he first began preaching, but afterwards was afraid he might not.[80] Some of his epigrams betray a keen insight into human nature. He once declared, "I have known women too poor to own a pair of shoes, but never too poor to own a looking-glass."[81]

When Moody heard him he said, "God has given you a sledge-hammer with which to shatter the formalism of the church, and to batter down the strongholds of Satan. The good Spirit is helping you mightily to use it."[82]

Major papers in St. Louis and Cincinnati leased Western Union wires in order to telegraph Jones's complete sermons from his Chicago crusade for their readers.[83] When he and Moody campaigned in different sections of Boston simultaneously, they heartily encouraged their hearers to support the other's meetings.[84] He was sponsored by A. C. Dixon,[85] J. Wilbur Chapman, and others. John McNeill praised him effusively.[86]

Jones began his ministry among the north Georgia mountains as a convert from wild living and alcoholism. His early training as a country lawyer helped him gather strong congregations in the little frame churches of the Methodists in an era when economic depression and post Civil War emotional stress was at its height.[87]

And the ministry begun with these eight years of apprenticeship had as its only preaching resources a copy of the Bible and one volume of C. H. Spurgeon's sermons![88] His son-in-law records that, "He would read until his soul was stirred. After reading a sermon he would say, 'If Spurgeon treated his text that way, how shall I treat my text?' "[89]

Jones's enthusiasm for the English preacher ultimately resulted in the twentieth-century rediscovery of Spurgeon's sermons, their entire republication, and sales of many hundreds of thousands of reprinted volumes in the past twenty years.[90]

A fresh wave of evangelistic leaders came to prominence at the turn of the century. Spurgeon, Moody, and the others, who launched the early years of spiritual awakening, later gave way to men such as Torrey, Chapman, and Dixon. Earlier momentum had given birth to a new focus on missions, with thousands of laymen trained in the Moody Bible Institute, and other similar institutions. The

Sunday School, until then mostly a children's organization, also blossomed into an outreach organization for adults and all ages. But a fresh impetus arose as an 1899 movement of prayer in Chicago, broke out in Australia in 1902, was kindled into a fire in England in 1903 and 1904, and "burst forth into a bright flame in Wales at the beginning of 1905."[91]

Reuben Archer Torrey, called to the superintendence of the Moody Bible Institute in 1889, came from a small Congregational church in Minneapolis, and also pastored the Chicago Moody church. Later, from 1912-1924, he served as the first dean of the Bible Institute of Los Angeles (now BIOLA University) and as pastor of the well-known downtown Church of the Open Door in that city.[92]

Spiritual awakenings of 1792, 1830, and those which ebbed and flowed from 1858 to the present age are now well defined and amply documented.[93] The 1899-1914 period appears, however, to be the least known, its description usually limited to the phrase "the Welsh Revival of 1905." But the movement originated around the ministry of R. A. Torrey in Chicago, amid a series of coincidences of unusual dimension.

In 1899 Torrey headed up the Moody Bible Institute. When D. L. Moody died in that year, it came into the hearts of several connected with the Institute to offer extended and sacrificial prayer for worldwide revival. The invitation to pray for such a blessing was extended by Torrey to his Saturday night Bible class at the Institute, and some 300 to 400 gathered regularly from 9 to 10 PM. After the larger prayer meeting concluded, Torrey and some of his closer friends and associates retired to his home or to some office in the school to continue in intercession, often until 2 AM Sunday mornings.

The meetings continued without slackening for about a year. Then Torrey suddenly and inexplicably found himself praying that God would lead *him* into worldwide evangelism. In his prayer, before the astonished group of close friends, he specifically asked that an international preaching opportunity might open before him and that thousands would be converted as a result. He named the lands of China, Japan, Australia, New Zealand, and Great Britain as places for such an opportunity, including very specific areas such as Tasmania, Ireland, Scotland, and also the U.S.A.[94]

After the prayer, Torrey found himself as surprised as his friends. He could not leave the church and the Institute for such a period. But like those who had faithfully prayed with him so often into the early morning hours, he firmly believed that the Lord had given special guidance in the utterance of the unanticipated prayer.[95]

They had not long to wait. Within two weeks, without prior notice of their coming, two men appeared as visitors in some of the Institute classes. Not much notice was taken of them as one was the father of a student. After a few days, the two men asked for a private interview with Torrey. Dr. Warren and Mr. G. P.

Barber were Australians, from Melbourne. They said they were commissioned by the United Churches of Victoria to visit Keswick in England, and other evangelical centers in the U.S.A., to select an evangelist to be invited to Australia for a series of meetings. They affirmed a clear leading to ask Torrey to be that man, indicating that they had traveled all over the world but until then had had no peace about approaching anyone for the task.[96]

Torrey made a full commitment to their call some months later. Well-known evangelical Baptist preacher A. C. Dixon, who was invited to substitute for him for twelve months, relieved him from the Moody church responsibilities. He was given leave from the Institute, and was soon engaged in evangelistic meetings in China and Japan, just as he had unexpectedly prayed so he would be.[97]

If the revival leadership arose in Chicago, its strength and fire burned brightest in Australia. John McNeil began prayer meetings for a spiritual awakening at about the same time as the Torrey Chicago prayer burden developed. Mrs. G. P. Barber, wife of one of the evangelical leaders who had enlisted Torrey, read the book on prayer which Torrey had written and became especially committed to his admonition to "Pray Through." She organized her friends into home prayer circles for the coming Melbourne meetings and within weeks the movement had spread over the entire city. In the two weeks before Torrey's Australian campaign began, over 40,000 persons attended these prayer circles in Melbourne.[98]

When Torrey arrived, he led in a four-week outreach which also involved some fifty other evangelists, modeled after the pattern of Moody's 1893 Chicago World's Fair meetings. Many of these meetings were simultaneous, and they culminated in Torrey's central campaign. Eight thousand six hundred converts were recorded, with a total of 20,000 decisions for Christ in all the meetings on the Australian mainland, in Tasmania, and also New Zealand.[99]

Mrs. Murray later visited the Keswick Convention in England and told the story of prayer at the center of God's blessing. The idea caught fire, and by the time Torrey arrived in the British Isles in 1904, groups of prayer circles in England, Ireland, Scotland, and Wales registered regular attendances of some 30,000 persons weekly.[100]

The blessings recorded in Australia moved the whole Christian world. Torrey seemed to be just the man for an evangelistic thrust into a world struggling through an era of destructive Bible criticism. He read the Bible constantly in English, Hebrew, Greek, German, and French. After his matriculation at Yale University (when only fifteen) Torrey showed remarkable intellectual prowess. A graduate in arts and divinity from Yale, he pursued post-graduate studies in the German universities, and passed through bitter struggles in his personal search for God. His doubts led him to a thorough skepticism, and to at least one serious attempt at suicide, before he found his way out of this barrenness and into a robust and joyful evangelical faith. He often told audiences that he owed his release to the faithful prayers of a devoted mother. In all he authored some forty books of theology, devotion, and exposition. His preaching was direct, forth-right, and unashamedly apologetic, defending the faith as reasonable and desirable.[101]

Torrey presented an impressive figure in the pulpit, tall, striking in appearance, with a full beard and dignity of demeanor. His powerful personality was embodied in his authoritative voice. He could be heard by crowds of up to 20,000 without amplification. He was forty-six when he ministered in Australia. A man of iron will and self-discipline, Torrey always spoke with crisp, logical precision in his denunciations of sin and pronouncements on the judgment of God and the way of salvation. Torrey was ruthless in his exposures of false teachings and religious sham; he constantly directed a fierce challenge to ungodly and unspiritual forces.

In Sydney, he stated that the Unitarians of Christ's day crucified him, thus linking current denials of the Deity of Christ to similar first-century attitudes. The local Unitarian pastor responded by challenging Torrey to debate the subject with advertisements in the daily press. This publicity greatly enlarged Torrey's crowds. He promised to deal with the matter at a certain noonday meeting, reserving special seats in the front row for the Unitarian pastor and his official board. At the appointed hour Torrey rose, outlined the controversy, and the request from the Unitarian pastor for a public debate. He also added that he held in his hand the record of a certain pastor, bearing the same name as his challenger, who had directed the affairs of a Unitarian church in Boston. This man had abandoned his wife, and later gone to New Zealand with another man's wife. He then moved to Tasmania, only to be driven from that island by an infuriated mob. "Until I am assured that this preacher is not that man I cannot allow him to speak from this platform,"[102] affirmed the evangelist. Of course there was no debate!

The subsequent history of this pastor included a conviction for fraud, and a seven-year jail sentence in Melbourne. J. Wilbur Chapman visited the jail, during a later evangelistic tour in Victoria, and found the man, who had now definitely accepted Christ as personal Lord and Savior and had renounced his former life and beliefs. He said that he had been led to this decision through Torrey's masterly addresses in Sydney on the deity of Christ. The compassionate Chapman arranged for him to return to the United States, where he later became the ordained pastor of an evangelical church.[103]

Moody and Sankey ministered in England and America but Torrey, with his song leader, Alexander, carried the thrust of spiritual awakening first around the world. In their initial tour, some 100,000 professions of faith were registered.[104] After a brief visit to India, ministry in Great Britain began at a scale which often surpassed the great Moody-Sankey meetings there of 1873.[105] The largest buildings proved inadequate to accommodate the crowds. Twelve hundred converts were listed in Liverpool, with 15,000 in attendance on the closing evening, and a further 20,000 persons outside.[106] Five months of London meetings in two iron tabernacles at different ends of the city culminated in a massive campaign in the Royal Albert Hall, yielding a total of 17,000 professions of faith.[107]

Thomas Spurgeon and his friends wholeheartedly supported the meetings. Thomas himself spoke words of farewell at the campaign's close, as he had from the platform where Torrey was welcomed at Exeter Hall in 1902.[108]

In 1904 Torrey held meetings in Cardiff, the first half of which seemed to have little blessing. (Wales was the only country he had *not* specifically named in his Chicago prayer!) After a day of special prayer and fasting, more blessings came, and the meetings continued after he left, every night for a year following, with many conversions.[109] Seven months after Torrey's campaign had ended, George Davis found the fires still burning in Cardiff and reached the conviction that the blessings merged into what later became known as the Welsh Revival of 1905.[110] It would be inaccurate to claim that Torrey initiated the revival, but Evan Roberts affirmed Torrey's contribution to it and also that Alexander's hymns, especially the far-famed "Glory Song," became favorites in all the Welsh 1905 revival meetings.[111]

When Torrey accepted the 1902 Australian invitation, he recruited one of his former students from Moody Bible Institute, Charles M. Alexander, a young gospel soloist from Tennessee, to help him. Alexander had worked with Moody, Torrey, Dixon, and others at Moody's Columbia Exposition 1893 Chicago meetings. His music ministry, especially in the leadership of congregational singing, had reached millions. Sankey was merely a soloist, Alexander mainly a song leader. He returned to Australia a second time, without an evangelist, found many converts of the Torrey meetings in the churches, and even in the ministry, and held meetings with almost as much proportionate blessing as those of 1902.[112]

Alexander became the link between Torrey and J. Wilbur Chapman. He enrolled thousands in well-drilled mass choirs, leading vast audiences in enthusiastic yet dignified worship through music. He had previously majored in music at Maryville College and had served on their faculty.[113] After further graduate studies, he had been introduced to the work of Moody and Sankey through their campaign in Knoxville, Tennessee. He had studied at Moody Bible Institute and had worked sucessfully with several lesser-known evangelists until called to join Torrey in the 1902 Australian campaign, working with him until 1908, when he joined in the team with Chapman.[114]

In 1909 Alexander and Chapman began four months of Australian ministries. Unlike the soldier-spirited Torrey, Chapman was a man of gentleness and quiet strength. His balanced gospel preaching, winsome charming in its delivery, graced by a personality evidently close in communion with God, wafted its way, on the wings of Alexander's music, into the hearts of thousands. Chapman had written 500 hymns by 1909, with the well-known "Jesus! What a Friend for Sinners" and "One day when heaven was filled with his praises" typical of those which expressed his gospel themes.[115] A friend of pastors, not an apologist as Torrey had been, Chapman easily won their hearts. He served his own local church ministries for eighteen years prior to his worldwide evangelism.[116] The power of his ministry equaled that of Torrey. Many thousands found Christ in Australia, the U.S.A., Britain, and elsewhere. According to documented evidence,[117] they stood firm and active in continuing church life.

Such blessing and interest developed in the Australian services that the *Australian Christian World* printed a month of daily newspaper editions just to share the day-by-day reports of awakening.[118] Meetings often overflowed into five or six city churches, in addition to the main assembly areas. Families pledged themselves to institute daily worship. The services in Adelaide brought a new Bible college to birth. Personal workers enlisted by the thousands in the Pocket Testament League, a special project of Mrs. Alexander. In four months in 1909, and again for fifteen months in 1912, the power of God shook the entire Australian nation, touching almost every city and major country center. Each time the meetings were characterized by enormous crowds, and undergirded with intensive prayer.[119]

D. L. Moody made the young Chapman his prótegé, advising and counseling him continually, always challenging him to a deeper surrender to God's will and a more committed evangelism.[120] Chapman had found his own assurance of salvation as a young man under Moody. He served not only as an effective pastor, but also as executive secretary for the American Presbyterian General assembly. He organized simultaneous crusades for them in 1,200 churches, and conducted many large citywide crusades himself. Under Moody's guidance, and using some of his resources, he lifted membership from 150 to 1,500 in one of his early pastorates.[121]

Chapman launched Billy Sunday into his ministry by lending him some of his old sermons to preach. Sunday had assisted him for some time, following his earlier conversion under Chapman's preaching. But Chapman found many of his own roots in Spurgeon, as much as in Moody. He quoted Spurgeon often, used his illustrations, read his sermons with high enthusiasm, and openly acknowledged his debt to him.[122]

The worldwide revival of 1905 crowded churches for several years. Torrey enlisted large numbers from the student body of Yale in prayer meetings and Bible study alone in that year. Southern Baptists showed a 25 percent increase in 1905. Two hundred forty stores closed in Portland Oregon from 11 AM to 2 PM each day to allow staff to attend prayer meetings for revival outreach in that city in that same year. The Grand Opera House in Los Angeles filled at midnight with drunks and prostitutes for a mission meeting. Eighteen hundred gathered in that same city for one service. The Korean outpourings in revival of that period continued also in waves of blessing for many years, as the researches of J. Edwin Orr have clearly documented.[123]

But the blessings in Wales seemed the most phenomenal. The wave of power which arose there in 1905 swept directly into the Metropolitan Tabernacle and lifted Thomas's evangelism to new heights as well.

Evan John Roberts, born in 1878, although widely-known as the leader of the Welsh Revival, always repudiated that honor. Often without stated leadership, designated preachers, and organized meetings, and always without advertising, the revival was basically a people's movement which kept the churches of Wales filled for many years after its peak of 1905. Churches, packed all day, often continued their informal services well into the small morning hours. Spontaneous prayer meetings burst into life in businesses and coal pits. Conversions occurred without the apparent involvement of any human agency. Saloons and police courts remained virtually empty for many months.[124]

But in its international expression, this awakening at the beginning twentieth century came after fifty years of evangelical growth, which was vitally linked with the previous 1858-1859 worldwide revival. Its emergence at this time, and especially its focus of power in Wales, has been described by the premier historian of the movement as "a blaze of evening glory at the end of the great Century."[125]

The effects of the Welsh upsurge included many blessings in Europe and the U.S.A.[126] Huge conferences of ministers gathered in New York, Chicago, and in other cities, to discuss what to do there when the awakening began in North America.[127] Spontaneous prayer and ardent evangelism burst forth in a great tidal wave of blessing, as the movement began to affect the American churches.[128] Results of the whole movement upon missions, and in society, are now amply documented.[129]

By the early months of 1905, the London papers began to note the rising tides of conversions across Wales as having some unexpected effects outside of that country:

> There are very few corners now in the principality that have not been touched by the Revival. Baptismal services, often held by the riverside in our rural districts, get conspicuous notices in the newspapers. It is questionable whether the ordinance of baptism was ever so much advertised in any country.[130]

The same report mentions Principal Edwards of Cardiff Baptist College receiving

200 members into a small pastorless church on the one Sunday, all of whom had found Christ during the revival meetings![131] Charlotte Chapel, in Edinburgh, Scotland, growing from fewer than 100 members to almost 400 in three years, reported experiencing a great ingathering in the first three months of 1905. Conversions every night and thirty or more on Sundays giving a total of 200 in one six-week period, with many striking cases of complete outsiders won into church fellowship.[132]

Glasgow reported continuous blessings from the beginning of 1905, with one suburb alone reporting 1,000 conversions in a mission conducted among railroad men. There were overcrowded churches, including one Baptist and Methodist in a suburban area, which combined services and had 500 professed conversions in three months.[133] Churches opened every night in Motherwell, with overflow crowds filling the town hall and other auditoriums in the city, and many were converted:[134]

> Customers in the various hostelries became so attracted to the testimonies of converted crowds that they were leaving the bars and rushing pell-mell to the revival meetings. The miners and steel workers have been going to and from the work in processional order singing revival hymns, and the power of the Spirit is witnessed at the furnace and at the coal fall.[135]

Thomas Spurgeon journeyed to Wales to experience something of the inspiration of the movement with Dr. McCaig as his companion. They found the prayers, the singing, the fellowship, and the testimonies as intense and delightful as anticipated.[136] Young converts told of their changed lives, old drunkards of new power in theirs, rough men gave clear evidence of softened hearts, and many who had before professed only a surface faith now testified to a new reality and power. The simple story of his own conversion told by Thomas encouraged half a dozen others to seek faith. Pastors shared long lists of new converts who had been brought to the kingdom through specific intercessory prayer offered in their behalf. The prayers and the singing proceeded with a spontaneous informality, providing a natural and unstructured context in which the blessings abounded:[137]

> A young woman prays very earnestly, then a young man in English and an old man in Welsh at the same time. A stirring Welsh hymn is then sung and a young deacon reads Joel ii. . . . A man under the gallery bursts out into passionate prayer "Here's another big drunkard saved during this Revival— here is the blest chapel where I was born, a sacred spot; Oh, what a happy home I have found." . . . and loud are the "Amens" when he cries, "Lord, may all the public houses be turned into chapels." That wonderful prayer, with its rough untutored eloquence, so touched the congregation that "Diolch Iddo" rang out with great gladness, the Welsh passing into the English "Songs of Praises" as the strains ceased. . . . At once a young man in the gallery pours out impassioned prayer for the salvation of sinners, and

another in the area starts simultaneously in the same strain. . . . During the
singing a woman prays in agony of earnestness, then several applicants plead
together and the tide of prayer sweeps through the house. . . . More than
twenty converts have professed in the course of the meeting.[138]

The local pastor of this chapel is listed as having no occasion to preach for
three months, so busy has he been occupied in the business of reaping![139] The
spontaneous prayer, witness, and worship of the crowded chapels, where those
attending responded to a sense of leadership in the Spirit, did its own sowing and
harvesting of the Word in what appeared to be a most natural, albeit inexplicable,
manner.[140] Miners meeting underground at 5:30 AM heard Thomas at the informal prayer service they themselves had arranged. McCaig commented:

> Perhaps this prayer meeting was the most wonderful thing we saw in Wales,
> and we heard that similar meetings are held in quite a number of the
> collieries, and where, formerly, oaths and blasphemies resounded all day
> long there are now heard songs of praise to the Saviour. Let critics of the
> Revival ponder such facts. But, Indeed, the Revival needs no defence, its
> good fruits are found on every hand, and the only explanations that "This is
> the Lord's doing, it is marvellous in our eyes."[141]

After Thomas returned from Wales, he began evening prayer meetings at the
Tabernacle for God's special blessings in what seemed to be a propitious climate
for spiritual outreach. These meetings continued for six weeks with high
attendances creating a context for the regular Sunday services in which it was
noted that the pastor's preaching seemed endowed with a new fullness of power.
Many Christians were quickened. Chains of services and conversions began what
was quickly recognized by the Christian press as a genuine awakening. Reports
in the denominational paper, and direct from the Tabernacle, describe the
blessing:[142]

> The breath of revival is beginning to be felt in the historic Church of the
> Metropolitan Tabernacle. For six weeks nightly, prayer meetings were held;
> many of God's people were stirred, and great power was realised. It was then
> felt that the time had come for prayer to be crystallised into special effort,
> and on Monday evening March 13 special services were commenced,
> conducted by six Welsh students of the Pastors' College.[143]

During their Christmas vacations all six of these men had been in close touch
with the revival movement and, stirred by its spirit, they resolved to accept the
pastor's invitation to mission at the church. They agreed to make a special effort
to try to reach some of the people living in the shadow of the Tabernacle
building, and in the immediate district surrounding it.

Their first meeting, in the Lecture Hall, was so overcrowded that the main
Tabernacle auditorium had to be used for Tuesday and Wednesday evening

services, with crowds gradually filling the main area, and creeping further up into the balconies each evening. Open-air meetings led by bands of the college students combined with special efforts of visitation. Processional marches to the Tabernacle, complete with banners and posters of invitation, managed to sweep large numbers of the interested and the curious into the gatherings each evening. By the time the first week of meetings had concluded 200 decisions for Christ were registered. By Tuesday of the second week the editor of the *Sword and Trowel* listed 540, as he excitedly put the story to press.[144] No less than 750 professions of conversion finally rounded out the twelve-night series.[145]

The brethren preached, sang, and opened some part of each meeting for free prayer. Sometimes they gleaned "twenty or thirty short, earnest prayers in the space of twelve minutes; the intensity of the pleading was very marked."[146] Troubled souls, upon whom conviction and need had settled, were invited into the inquiry room every night,[147] sometimes being challenged to stand in confession of their earnestness and concern before being led by workers for detailed counsel.[148]

One striking feature of the services concerned the midnight meeting held the first Friday. This lasted to 2:30 AM.:

> The students and others went out in procession and gathered hundreds in
> from the streets and public houses and a marvellous season was experienced.
> The power of God was present, many went into the inquiry room and thirty-
> nine definitely decided.[149]

Drunkards, harlots, and crowds originally bent for the theaters and music halls were among those intrigued by the enthusiasm of the four-deep marching men from the Tabernacle. Many of them crowded into the meeting and found Christ.[150]

This power and enthusiasm increased as the meetings progressed. Principal McCaig wrote a compilation of incidents of remarkable conversions during the Tabernacle meetings which fills seven closely typeset pages of the official Tabernacle report.[151] Some were stopped on the way to commit suicide, others were reached who had refused gospel invitations for fifty years. Atheists found faith, backsliders repented, and hundreds of the common people of London responded to the gospel invitations:[152]

> We might go on to tell of the work-girl who came night after night and would
> not surrender because she couldn't give up swearing! But on the closing
> Saturday found rest in Jesus. Of the young lady who came to buy a hat at a
> neighbouring shop, entered the Tabernacle out of curiousity, and left
> rejoicing in the Saviour; of a woman whose drinking habits had driven her
> aged father to attempt his own life, and who, shocked by the tragic event,
> determined to break away from her awful bondage, came to the Sunday

evening service, heard the preacher speak of the opening of the Books, went into the enquiry room in agony of soul, trembling in every limb, and was enabled to find hope in the Saviour's boundless grace.[153]

After one of the Welsh students had preached the gospel, the meeting was "tested" by asking for an open acknowledgement by those who felt God's conviction upon them. Those who stood up were then invited into a side room for such "inquirers," and each personally counseled by a trained worker who sought to interpret the experience of salvation in relation to each individual's need.[154] Fifty-two decided for Christ in the inquiry room on March 24. Many of the roughest sort were enlisted and, after the preaching, an effective gospel message in music " . . . deepened the impression made by the address, and when the meeting was tested, one after another rose and expressed his desire to accept Christ, some audibly saying, 'I will.' "[155]

The meeting continued until 3 AM with twenty-six definite decisions, in addition to the earlier ingathering![156] Twenty-five more came to Christ on Saturday, and fifty-eight under the pastor's preaching on Sunday evening. Another midnight rally on Wednesday, March 29 gathered in thirty-three more.[157]

The *Baptist Times and Freeman* reported the "Crowning Meeting" of March 30 by recording that " . . . responses to the appeals for decision came freely, some standing, others holding up their hands, and some shouting, "I will;" young men and maidens, boys and girls, old men and women went willingly into the inquiry room and over 60 definitely decided for Christ."[158]

This total, later revised to seventy-four, was the record for a single meeting.[159] Part of the blessing seemed directly attributable to the commitment of the workers who, led by Thomas and his wife, and often numbering up to 500 strong, marched in procession around the nearby Tabernacle streets garnering in those to midnight services who most needed to hear the gospel message. The outstanding feature of the meetings was defined as: " . . . the realization of the Divine presence, the consciousness that the Spirit of God was moving upon the hearts of the people. The speakers and singers have been marvellously under the influence of that Divine power, the Christians have realised it; the unsaved have yielded to it."[160]

On Monday evening, April 2, a praise and testimony meeting celebrated the blessings at the Tabernacle. A large and enthusiastic congregation responded with purpose to the many testimonies volunteered by mission converts. A meeting for converts and workers which followed the next evening filled the Lecture Hall. Such a spirit of concern arose for the reaching of others still lost that another midnight meeting was promptly scheduled for Friday, April 7, and yet another a week later.

Starting from the Tabernacle gates at 11 PM, the April 14 service gathered a similar crowd and recorded similar blessings. The lively scene impressed a visitor so deeply that he wrote a detailed description of the methods employed and the blessings resulting, and affirmed the validity of this invasion of enemy territory to rescue souls for Christ, concluding with a doxology: "Thank God for Spurgeon's men and others like them, who, copying their Master, go out and seek the lost sheep *until they find them.*"[161]

Just a month or so after the Tabernacle revival, and while much blessing still flowed, Baptists from many nations met in London to inaugurate the Baptist World Alliance, an international fraternity which chose Alexander Maclaren, long-time friend of both Spurgeons, as its first president (he was then seventy-nine years of age!). Thomas made a particular point of attending some gatherings and participating in the congress, leading one of the meetings in prayer from the platform when asked to do so. He loaned the commodious restored Tabernacle free of charge for the annual congress sermon on July 12, 1905, preached by A. H. Strong, of the U.S.A., on the theme, "The Greatness and Claims of Christ." As neither Thomas, nor the great church he pastored were in active affiliation with the British Baptist Union, these actions showed a brotherliness beyond the expectations of some.[162]

A. C. Dixon, for whom Tom had preached when visiting the U.S.A., and whose associations with the elder Spurgeon were very deep, was an American representative to the congress. He preached for Thomas at the Tabernacle on two midweek occasions, filling the pulpit also for both services on the two Sundays that he was in London for the Congress meetings.[163] He had preached there before, but this visit laid the foundation for a future association of significant dimensions about which neither of the men, nor any in Tabernacle congregations who listened to him, had any inkling.[164]

In early 1905, Thomas's twin brother, Charles Spurgeon, Jr., moved from his longterm pastorate at the Baptist church in Greenwich to a new task at the Nottingham Tabernacle.[165] During 1904 he and Tom had placed the bulk of their late father's library in the hands of an agent for sale to some college or theological school in Britain, but without success. A 1583 "Breeches" Bible, many works by old Puritan authors, and other aged leather-bound volumes of great value (some stretching back to 1525) constituted the bulk of the collection.

The group of just over 5,000 volumes was finally sold to the library of William Jewell Baptist College, of Liberty, Missouri, a school serving several Baptist conventions, located near Kansas City. J. T. M. Johnson, a college board member, negotiated the purchase, along with that of several thousand other venerable volumes, while he was in London for the Congress in 1905. The price averaged about fifty cents per volume.[165] The collection, which arrived in 1906, still displays its complexity and variety today to theological and historical researchers. It is housed in a $40,000 replica of the original study of C. H.

Spurgeon, built in 1965 as a family memorial to an alumnus of the school. Designers used plans and drawings from the original Spurgeon London residence and have even accurately reproduced decorative motifs, moldings, light fixtures, and furniture.[166]

By 1906, the strain of such a heavy pastoral ministry, including the extensive institutions under the direction of the Tabernacle pastor, had so wearied Thomas that, even though he was given some pastoral assistance, he found complete rest to be essential. He canceled plans for a series of preaching tasks at Tremont Temple, Boston, and in other U.S. centers with great reluctance, and ceased ministry altogether for several months, undertaking a quiet holiday instead.[167] Thomas reached his fiftieth year in September 1906, and his Tabernacle friends celebrated this jubilee with many festivities.

Of those fifty years almost twenty-seven had involved full-time ministries in New Zealand and London. Seven hundred invited guests rejoiced with him in the Tabernacle lecture hall on September 20 from 4 PM, bringing gifts for a testimonial fund. The packed Tabernacle meeting which followed testified to the respect and affection in which he was held. Thomas refused the money, handing it over for the work of the Pastors' College, the orphanage, and other Tabernacle institutions, just as his father had done years before with similar testimonials. He accepted with delight the grandfather clock, the silver tea tray given to Lila, and the promise that, if he would sit for it, they would have his portrait done in oils to hang beside that of his father in the Tabernacle vestry.

Letters and telegrams poured in from all over the world. F. B. Meyer brought greetings. G. Campbell Morgan, arriving unexpectedly from ministries in the U.S.A., did the same. Len G. Broughton, also from the U.S.A., offered a dedicatory prayer, and Dinsdale T. Young, warm-hearted evangelical Methodist pastor at Westminster, delivered an address of encouragement and congratulations.[168] In announcing the meetings the denomination paper affirmed:

> Probably no other living minister could have taken up such a work after such a predecessor and carried it forward successfully. It needed a preacher of ability and freshness, who was also a first-class organiser and a glutton for work; and at the same time it needed that he should secure and hold the affections of thousands of friends that C. H. Spurgeon had gathered round himself and his various institutions.[169]

The same journal later described the jubilee service on the Sunday following and Thomas's sermon in the most glowing of terms:

> . . . nothing has impaired that glorious voice which still without effort fills the Tabernacle with its melody. For the Scripture lesson Mr. Spurgeon read Psalm 90, and in his mouth, as in that of the ancient singer of Israel, it was a psalm of thanksgiving for the mercies of the Lord. The prayer carried on the

same note. There was a tell-tale inflection in the speaker's voice as he acknowledged the goodness of God in drawing His servant out of deep waters and putting a new song in his mouth. And though there were other and loftier strains in it, the deep undertone of the sermon was that of overflowing thankfulness to God for having brought him back once more to the place made sacred by so many memories.[170]

The *Christian World* reported that Thomas declared his one desire, next to the primary one of glorifying God, was to honor his father by maintaining the old-time traditions and methods, and "to declare the same grand and glorious, God-honoring, soul-saving truths which his father proclaimed from that pulpit."[171]

The *Baptist Times and Freeman* affirmed that the most striking feature of what was a most remarkable meeting, next to the open affection for "Son Tom," was the congregation's eager assent to these emphases as Tom declared them and the " . . . powerful sense of the Tabernacle as a stronghold of evangelical Christianity in the heart of London."[172]

By February 13, 1907 Thomas's health deteriorated to the point that he offered his permanent resignation to the Tabernacle leaders with much regret. He said in a letter which occasioned the calling of a special church members' meeting: " . . . I have long felt my powers overtaxed, and have many a time been on the point of resigning, but have struggled on again. . . . I am perfectly persuaded that the cause with its by no means diminishing difficulties, stands in urgent need of a leader who is not handicapped by physical weakness."[173]

The deacons prayerfully considered the matter for nine days, then sent him a letter filled with deep expressions of sympathy and affection, noting that his physical weakness had been largely brought on " . . . by your wholehearted and unstinted service of the church and its institutions."[174] They asked him to let the matter stand in abeyance for three months, inviting him to take a complete rest for that period. The members' meeting of March 18 concurred with the suggestion.

The church records of this period reveal an exchange of letters between pastor and people full of great affection and understanding. The physician's report indicated not only dispepsia and anemia, but a great deal of nervous depression, occasioned by the almost fourteen years of faithful service. Archibald G. Brown, one of C. H. Spurgeon's earliest protégés in the Pastors' College, and a preacher of considerable success at the East London Tabernacle was invited to serve with the title of assistant pastor to Thomas. He accepted, and the work continued in strength for most of the year. Thomas rejoiced especially over the baptism of his son and daughter on April 13.[175]

But by March 1908 Thomas's health had declined to such an extent that an official letter of resignation written from Austria, where he was visiting the warm sulphur springs, made the matter quite final. His retirement, accepted with regret, called forth a response resolution thanking God for his fourteen years of self-sacrificial service. Tabernacle members rejoiced that during his pastorate 2,200 new members had been added to the church rolls. They assured him of their esteem, affection, and conviction that his leadership had been in every sense providential. Archibald G. Brown, now the established copastor, continued in that role, and although sixty-four years of age his health and vigor was of such a measure that he was soon confirmed as the Tabernacle's future pastoral leader.[176]

Letters written by Tom at this period reveal that the "A. T. Pierson party" had remained critical throughout all of his ministry, and that some members of this group had been a continual stress to him. He said:

> A. G. Brown has been elected Pastor with virtual unanimity. He is a great preacher and teacher, and wonderfully vigorous for his years. I think the work will prosper under his leadership, despite the many difficulties. He has some advantages over his predecessor—he was not a rival to A.T.P. and he was not born and brought up from a child in their midst. Well—this business is a heart-break, but I'm not going to let it break any heart if I can help it. I stuck to the task as long as I conscientiously could, and wrought till my health was shattered. And yet some chide me for forsaking it. Ah well, God knows.[177]

In the light of such pressures the success of his fourteen years seems all the more worthy. Upon his resignation he was invited to return to New Zealand for extended evangelism but, of course, his health precluded any such plans.[178]

An illuminated manuscript presented to him upon his retirement speaks of overwhelming appreciation for his devotion and rejoicing in the blessings received under his ministry. (The full-color, hand-lettered address is still extant in a New Zealand collection.)[179]

After his official retirement from the Tabernacle in 1908, Thomas Spurgeon continued to occupy the presidencies of his father's most famous institutions, the Stockwell Orphanage and the Pastors' College. C. H. Spurgeon delivered twenty-seven annual addresses to the college conferences, and his brother, James Spurgeon, three. Thomas Spurgeon gave twenty-three presidential college addresses. Many feel that these are among his finest utterances. He was elected president in 1896, and every year thereafter reelected.[180]

The years between 1908 and 1917 were filled with such ministries as he was able to discharge. He supplied in Scotland and in Wales, occasionally served a brief interim in a pastorless charge, and was consistently busy as an honorary representative of the orphanage and the college. He raised funds, presented needs for prayer, and enlisted help in the undertaking of these two magnificent organizations. He remained as editor of the *Sword and Trowel*, the monthly magazine of the Tabernacle, which reached a large constituency in the whole Christian world, for four full years after his official retirement. He also continued to contribute articles for it after that. He also served as president of the Tabernacle Colportage Association, and occasionally lectured to the college students in areas of practical ministry on Friday afternoons, as his father had before him.[181]

It seemed to some that, with the 1908 retirement from full-time Tabernacle tasks, most of Thomas's work was complete. His deputation in behalf of the college and orphanage demanded almost full attention from 1911 to 1913.[182] A variety of organizational problems delayed its start from 1908 when first proposed, not the least of which was Thomas's slowly-recovering health. Archibald Brown's Tabernacle ministry, though effective, lasted only three years, by which time he was sixty-six and also in ill health.

Upon his retirement, the church called A. C. Dixon, from the U.S.A. to the pastorate, where he served eight years with distinction. He retired at age sixty-four, after carrying the huge church through times of great distress and tension during World War I, which savaged the program of London's best-known evangelical center. Though not an Englishman, Dixon gave himself wholeheartedly to the upholding of British morale and steadfastly refused to quit his effective leadership post in London. Only after the armistice in November 1918, did he return to America, offering his resignation in January 1919.[183]

Thus Dixon, Thomas's friend over many years, intimately associated with the elder Spurgeon and also with D. L. Moody, R. A. Torrey, and most of the others mentioned in this narrative, now became Tom's pastor. Thomas died in 1917, but before his death he fellowshiped closely with this one who became, with R. A. Torrey, the popularizer of the concept known as "Fundamentalism."

The story of Dixon's part in this movement, and in particular of the sources from which obtained his basic ideas, is also, surprisingly, the story of the Spurgeons and their ministries. This relationship may well serve as Thomas's most lasting contribution to theological immorality. While this story is diverse its complex documentation ties together several strands of evangelical history, which will be explored in the final chapter.

6 His Own Interpreter (1908-1917)

Blind unbelief is sure to err,
And scan His work in vain;
God is His own interpreter,
And He will make it plain.

orn in Shelby, North Carolina in 1854, Amzi Clarence Dixon graduated from old Wake Forest College.[1] After some studies at the original Southern Baptist Seminary in Greenville, he served churches at Warsaw, Chapel Hill, and Asheville in his home state. Later he pastored in Brooklyn, Boston, Chicago, London, and Baltimore. Ordained in 1876, he found personal salvation under the preaching of his father just after the close of the Civil War.[2] Literature was scarce in those days, and theological literature very scarce. But the name of C. H. Spurgeon stood as a household word among all Baptists in America.[3]

Next to the Bible itself, the young preacher-to-be eagerly devoured the sermons of Spurgeon, which were obtained from a colporteur who brought them to his father as soon as they were published. The hungry student not only listened with avid interest as his father read these aloud, but often shut himself off in a room to study them at leisure. His first impulse to preach came directly from these studies, and the theology which would characterize his life's ministry found its birth in these pages.[4]

Naturally he longed to be taught further by the one who had been his mentor. Although London was so far away, he applied (with his father's approval) for theological training at the Pastor's College. Spurgeon wisely advised training in the country where he expected to serve.[5] An impress of the beliefs and ministry of the London pastor continued as the major formative influence upon Dixon for the rest of his life.

From 1887 to 1889 Dixon followed Spurgeon's Down Grade Controversy reports with great interest, as his hero took a firm stand for orthodoxy. In 1889 the World's Sunday School Convention organized its second annual meeting in London. A. C. Dixon, who was president of his state chapter of the movement, responded with high excitement to the offer of his church (Immanuel) to pay his travel to the meetings. He was delighted over the opportunity to meet C. H. S. in person.[6] Called unexpectedly to make a public response to the Lord Mayor of London's welcome as a representative of the American visitors, he offered words of such caliber that they attracted the attention of Thomas Olney, one of the Tabernacle officers. Olney persuaded Spurgeon to invite the youthful pastor to offer the main prayer at the Tabernacle worship on the next Sunday. An invitation for him to preach to the crowded Monday evening prayer service quickly followed, where he declared with fervor, "For many years *your* pastor has been *my* pastor!" He told them of his own intimate acquaintance with Spurgeon's sermons even before he was quite able to read the daily newspaper, and now his first desire to preach the gospel had been kindled by that exposure.[7]

A week later Dixon addressed another prayer service. Spurgeon, whose eyes had dimmed with emotion at the thought of one called into ministry through his printed words, wrote of him with appreciation:

> He is a brother as great in heart as he is tall in body, and he is now considerably over six feet high. On two Sabbath mornings he offered the longer prayer, and so helped the minister. What prayers they were! His heart bubbled up with a good matter, and overflowed in fervent petitions of affection.[8]

Others who were also Convention delegates told Spurgeon of their conversion and entry into ministry from the reading of his sermons in their American editions.[9] But Spurgeon watched Dixon with special interest as he entered into the open-air outreach evangelism services which were a feature of lay-led Tabernacle activities. He then proposed that the American join him as a permanent associate in the Tabernacle pastoral team. This invitation Dixon felt unable to accept.[10]

Dixon served beside Moody in Chicago in the simultaneous evangelistic outreach campaign during the 1893 exposition which celebrated Columbus's discovery of America. There he fellowshiped with those mentioned previously, as well as D. W. Whittle, J. H. Brooks, A. J. Gordon, and others. Noting the effectiveness of the Chicago multiple services with preaching in Russian, German, French, and Polish, Dixon returned to his Brooklyn pastorate fired with a fresh desire to reach the masses. He started daily services which led to the organization of a campaign of effective united evangelism. Many blessings followed. He used some who had helped in the Chicago outreach.[11]

By 1905 Dixon had returned again to the London pulpit. Thomas had preached for him in Brooklyn in 1893, and their friendship had continued. After spending some time at Thomas's home, Dixon agreed to help him while in London for one weekday evening service, a pledge later stretched to embrace four separate addresses. Thomas spoke with warmth of the Baptist world meetings which occasioned Dixon's visit, and of the number of representatives who attended. He also wrote of Dixon with special affection:

> The Baptist World Congress has met, deliberated, and dissolved. Amongst the delegates were many good men and true, whom we honour for their work's sake. Of these none was more welcomed than our esteemed and

beloved friend Dr. A. C. Dixon, of Boston, whose helpful words at the
Prayer Meeting on Monday July 17, will not soon be forgotten. Again he
spoke to us on the following Thursday, and has kindly promised to occupy
the Tabernacle pulpit upon two of the Sabbaths of August, when we are on
holiday.[12]

In 1911, after Thomas had resigned, and as Archibald G. Brown's health
pointed to the certainty of his also resigning, the Tabernacle deacons invited
Dixon to conduct services for them in London for the month of January. A
growing conviction then arose that he should be approached to consider the
permanent charge there. Dixon secured temporary release from his Chicago
Avenue Church (which he had pastored since 1906), and visited for a third period
in the London pulpit where he had first ministered twenty-two years before.
William Olney, son of the deacon who had recommended Dixon to C. H.
Spurgeon in 1889, led in a move to consider him as pastor. He wrote to A. T.
Pierson, (by now elderly and ill) who replied that he felt the Tabernacle had some
Divine leading in the matter and that they should "trust God and call Dixon to the
pastorate!"[13] They did so. Dixon took some time to decide, but finally began
ministry on June 18, 1911, with Thomas beside him in the pulpit for the opening
meetings. Fresh from 312 additions to the Chicago church in the past year, and
some 800 in the past five years, Dixon's ardent evangelism stood out as his most
prominent characteristic.

"He preaches to win souls and expects to see results,"[14] said one significant
report. In Dixon's first service he affirmed again the place and power of C. H.
Spurgeon's ministry for his own, and the challenges wrought upon him by the
initial 1889 visit when he met and heard the great preacher for the first time.[15] His
style generated much enthusiasm during that visiting month."

> It was an impressive discourse, simple in character, yet wonderfully
> attractive in its appeal. Nothing, either in his manner or speech to suggest
> that he is an American. Dr. Dixon is a born preacher. . . . The preacher from
> America can scarcely be compared with anybody else, for his own
> individuality shines through everything that he says and does. He glorifies
> Jesus Christ, and uses all his gifts to bring men in willing subjection to His
> feet. All through, the sermon was a powerful and beautiful exposition of the
> text, and it closed with such a winsome appeal for surrender to Christ that
> one wondered how it could be resisted. With a preacher like Dr. Dixon in the
> heart of London there would be a new power for righteousness at work in the
> world's metropolis, and great things would be witnessed.[16]

Although the church constitution empowered the deacons and elders to elect a
pastor without congregational approval, they refused to exercise that right, and
even decided not to introduce Dixon's name for a call on their own volition.[17] A
regular church member introduced the matter, and, when it was opened for

discussion, particular note was taken that not one voice was raised in opposition.[18] At Dixon's welcome meeting, Olney declared that the current approach did not arrise from previous associations with both the Spurgeons, although the new pastor was known to be in an appropriate succession to the previous ones. He affirmed that a volume on the Holy Spirit, authored by Dixon, had been given to his father, Thomas Olney, ten years after the initial 1899 visit. It was the "coincidental" possession of this book, still in the family, through which the idea of approaching Dixon had first arisen.[19]

By the August after his June 1911 commencement, press headlines described blessings with precision:

DIXON IN SPURGEON'S TABERNACLE
Great American Champion of Orthodoxy and Evangelism
Grips the Hearts of Thousands in the Famous Metropolitan Pulpit[20]

The huge church, filled to welcome Dixon for opening services, saw Thomas by his side, found Charles M. Alexander leading the music, and heard the new pastor confess that:

> . . . he could not equal Spurgeon,—he was not so eloquent, he could not be Thomas Spurgeon, for he was not so poetic and artistic, he could not be Archibald Brown for he was never so robust and strong and expository. He just stood there with the text "work out your own salvation with fear and trembling, for it is God that worketh in you."[21]

Dixon declared that he would do his best to preach the gospel to the glory of God, in the power of God, and that he aimed for a church in which all were at work for the Lord.[22]

By November of that same year the secular papers discovered a movement of awakening which they compared with former days:

REVIVAL AT SPURGEON'S
Famous Tabernacle Again Crowded[23]

The report detailed Dixon's ministry as heralding a return to the church's former glory, suggesting that:

> . . . a revival (in, it must be confessed, a new form) of the dogmatic theology of its founder is in progress—quietly, unostentatiously, and, strange to say, successfully.[24]

This renaissance stood in stark contrast to some other contemporary efforts at local church relevance through outreach in social reforms. Rather the upsurge needed to be defined as:

> . . . A movement that points to a triumph of old-fashioned, straight-laced ideas of conversion, regeneration, and spiritual culture. Everyone knows that

the Tabernacle, since Spurgeon's death, has passed through the crucible of trial. At one time the voice of dissension was heard within its walls; now the "time of the singing of birds" has arrived. Empty pews saddened and depressed the fathers and elders of the church; now the stewards perspire in the aisles in their endeavors to pack newcomers into the space.[25]

The same report spoke of a Bible class scheduled during a midweek downpour where 1,200 sat spellbound at the quality of Dixon's biblical analyses and the contemporary application of the timeless truths he elucidated. After the service

> . . . costers and doctors, old maids and City clerks, South London tradesmen and servant girls—they faced the torrential darkness of South London with smiles.[26]

Often as many as 1,500 came to his midweek studies. There he stoutly defended teachings that modern thinkers had declared absurd. The Tabernacle rapidly filled for all Sunday services. His subject on one reported occasion was "Old-Fashioned Conversions":

> Then he took his South London audience to the United States, and described a camp-meeting with 20,000 men and women. All classes were present. Preachers, learned, and illiterate, took a part in the 14 day services, during which men and women were carried out prostrate and unconscious. Regaining consciousness they would shout "Hallelujah" and "Glory," and continue in a state of rapture for some time. "And all that" observed Dr. Dixon, quietly, "was organised under the good Presbyterians." Then came a surprise, for the camp was so sympathetically described, and the tone of the doctor's voice and allusions even to the prostrations so warm, that one expected from him a defence of these strange scenes. But no
> "I do not call these old-fashioned conversions," he said, "I call them modern conversions, and I consider their extravagances did the cause of evangelical religion much harm."[27]

The thrust of the sermon centered on the listing of New Testament examples of true conversion (Nicodemus and the woman of Samaria, Lydia and the jailer in Philippi, the Ethiopian eunuch, Saul of Tarsus, Andrew and Peter, and the conversions at Pentecost). The sermon and its delivery were characterized by simplicity, plainness, and clarity. Illustrations and logic seemed effective and interesting:

> The basis of all his argument is essentially Spurgeonic. He stands by the old Book. Facts clearly stated there are facts.[28]

These happy and prosperous days continued.[29] By 1915 the Tabernacle membership had gathered 540 additions over four years.[30] Dixon opened the London pulpit to J. Wilbur Chapman and Charles M. Alexander for evangelistic meetings,[31] and encouraged many others in like endeavors. The installation of a grand piano (to substitute for the ineffective reed harmonium which Thomas had introduced) fostered so much better singing that extra hymn leaflets were produced to supplement the variety offered, and to provide for the numbers attending.[32] (This also paved the way for the installation of a pipe organ in later years.)

Britain's darkest days began in 1914. Although greatly tempted to return to the U.S.A., Dixon bravely stuck to his London charge throughout World War I. He led the Tabernacle congregation into areas of compassionate ministry to servicemen and to the poor immediately around the church location.[33] Zepplin air raids provided an opportunity to open the lower hall of the Tabernacle as a shelter for bombed families night after night.[34] Dixon often preached evangelistic messages with the children gathered asleep at his feet while he proclaimed the gospel to their parents.[35] In one twelve months, during the peak of the war, he gathered 700 new converts despite these adverse conditions.[36]

Even when the United States came into the war in 1917, Dixon refused to abandon what he considered to be his post of duty in London. The armistice, signed on November 11, at 11:00 AM in 1918, brought him and his wife hurriedly to the Tabernacle where they found themselves thronged:

> . . . With a sobbing, laughing crowd, unable at first to suppress its emotions. Women, young and old, dropped their housework and hastened, unbonneted and adorned with their big kitchen aprons, to the place where they had so often fled for shelter. Workmen downed their tools, and by a common impulse all who could possibly do so rushed to join in the service of thanksgiving which they knew would take place in the dear old Tabernacle. All day long it continued, as the crowd ebbed and flowed, only to be resumed on the following afternoon and evening.[37]

His resignation in 1919 took the officers by surprise and led to a petition for reconsideration.[38] The church operated in a spiritual condition of unrivaled blessing and no record exists of the tension which some have imagined.[39] The Tabernacle treasurer's words offer a fine summation of Dixon's contributions:

> In the providence of God you have been called to a world-wide work on behalf of the spread of the Gospel and your Pastorate of this historic church which has covered a period of nearly eight years is now brought to a close. Your ministry amongst us has been in the power and demonstration of the Spirit and has brought a new inspiration to the lives of many who have come into the light and liberty of salvation, or who being already believers have entered the fuller Christian life. Your testimony to the integrity and supremacy of the Holy Scriptures, and the Divinity and Atonement of our Saviour Jesus Christ has been fearless, powerful and effective, and its influence has reached far beyond the limits of our own community. . . . your work and gracious influence will live in our hearts and lives long after we have been separated.[40]

Dixon received 1,000 new members into the Tabernacle in his eight years of service, according to an authoriatative witness.[41] In 1919 he returned to an extensive Bible conference and evangelistic ministry centered in America and continued therein until settling at the University Baptist Church, in Baltimore, in 1921. He died in that office in 1925. The previous year he had married Helen, widow of his old friend Charles M. Alexander, after the first Mrs. Dixon's unexpected death from a severe illness contracted in China during one of their missions tours.[42]

Loss of morale related to the Great War, 1914-1918, had left Britain greatly crushed and broken. One in every seven men of conscription age had died in the hostilities; three times that number received injuries. Some historians see this period as the ushering in of a new age of violence, from which our modern world never fully recovered. Certainly the bright days of the Great Century (1814-1914) will not easily be matched—a century in which humanity's strides forward in scientific advancement and social conscience accelerated. The Victorian Age (so named as the period of unparalleled peace and prosperity over which Queen Victoria reigned from 1837 to 1901) was one of peace coinciding with the greater portion of the 1814-1914 advances. Our current twentieth-century culture, society, politics, and philosophy were shaped in this age. The period thrust twentieth-century theology and religion into its current forms. A brief listing of the most significant social, political, scientific and industrial advances and events of this era highlights some of the elements.

HIGHLIGHTS OF THE "VICTORIAN AGE"

Social and Political	*Scientific and Industrial*
1790 French Revolution	
1805 Battle of Trafalgar	
	1807 Fulton's Steamship
1815 Napoleon Defeated (Waterloo)	
	1822 Gaslight Introduced
1824 Trade Unions	
1830 Oxford Movement	1830 First Railroad
	1831 Faraday's Electric
	Dynamo
1832 Voting Reform Bill	
1833 Slavery Abolished in British	
Empire	
1837 *Victoria Becomes Queen*	
	1838 First Ocean Steamship
	1844 Telegraph Invented
	1844 Sewing Machine
	Invented

1848 Marx—"Communist Manifesto"
1849 Penny Post Introduced

1850 Bessemer Steel
     Process

1854 Crimean War
1857 Indian Mutiny
1859 Darwin—"Origin of Species"

1857 Atlantic Cable Laid

1860 Internal Combustion
     Engine

1861 U.S. Civil War
1861 Albert Dies—Victoria "Retires"
1867 Voting Reform Act

1869 Suez Canal Opened
1871 Darwin "Descent of
     Man"
1876 Telephone Invented
1881 Germ Theory Proven
1885 Pasteur Cures Rabies

*1887 Victoria's Golden Jubilee
    and Reappearance*

1895 X-Rays Discovered
1895 Wireless Invented

1897 Victoria's Diamond Jubilee
1899 Boer War
1900 Boxer Rebellion in China
1901 Queen Victoria Dies

1903 First Airplane
     Flight
1905 Einstein's Theories
1909 Air Flight France to
     England
1909 Ford's "Model T"
1912 Vitamins Discovered

1914 Britain into World War I
1917 Russian Revolution/Communism

To understand the part which Thomas Spurgeon, A. C. Dixon, and others played, we must first understand the Victorian Age and its character.

This period embraced years of great discovery and controversy. It includes some immense and revolutionary changes. Many emerging factors reshaped society from the rural civilization of the previous centuries into a new culture of industrial might and affluence. New ideas, values, and systems resulted in great social upheaval. As one of Britain's contemporary historians commented, "The movement . . . is so continuous, the variety so great, that every historical comment seems fumbling and inaccurate, every generalization inconclusive and incomplete."[43]

1. *Industrial Revolution*—In this era Britain held the original monopolies on newly-developed manufacturing processes. Factories were filled with textile machines and locomotives and the steamships were operating while gas lighting replaced lamps and candles. Mechanization increased on every hand, as a variety and profusion of manufactured goods flooded the British Empire and the world, providing great wealth for the newly affluent middle classes. All nations responded to the new challenge of industrialization, but Britain led the way in the creation of an industrialized society from a previously agricultural one. Between 1850 and 1872, British exports doubled each ten years. New classes of industrialists and tradesmen emerged. Commerce became the most desirable of vocations as the materialistic society grew.

2. *Economic Revolution*—But the new affluence was based on the labor of the masses of the poor, who worked and lived in appalling squalor. Women labored in factories twelve to fifteen hours a day, six days a week for pittances. Children as young as seven or eight sweated as pit ponies, hauling heavy coal carts to feed the hungry factory furnaces. London, a city of narrow cobblestone streets, contained a vast mass of badly-housed, ill-fed, underpaid, and unskilled poor, who had been driven to the city as rural unemployment rose. Instead of fresh air and space, these Victorian families entered into a world of pea soup fogs with smokestacks belching black fumes from thousands of coal fires—a world of soot, grease, and grime.

London's classic buildings hid their majestic porticos and pillars under layers of filth. The dying foliage of black-streaked trees dripped with the grime and grit of the new society, thus adding to the general air of depression. This was a world of dysentery, typhus, gin palaces, harlots, jerry-built tenements, neglected children, and alcoholism. The slum dwellers bought their clothes from secondhand dealers in the open markets, and the lack of adequate drains and sewers brought three outbreaks of cholera between 1848 and 1868. London doubled its population to two million in the eighty years which followed the beginning of the century.

3. *Social Revolution*—The very rich fed at sumptuous feasts and relaxed in elegant drawing rooms. There were fashionable social evenings of dance and entertainment, while 30 percent of the populace remained hopelessly poor and 40 percent were clerks and tradesmen who eked out a miserable existence. The Great Exhibition of 1851 celebrated twenty-five years of unparalleled scientific advancement and prosperity but the 1870s poverty and economic depression had

become extremely oppressive. A growing middle class of the nation's shopkeepers, public-house proprietors, and their associates, gradually came to agree with visionaries within the ranks of the well-to-do, who asserted that society should act to protect those at the mercy of the emerging economic and social forces. Some aristocrats and landed gentry developed passionate interests in altruistic causes, perceiving that society should work for the benefit of every man and not merely for the good of the ruling classes. They reformed prisons, repealed cruel laws, fought child labor, and generally supported education and philanthropy. The struggle demanded great effort, and the victory did not arrive overnight. In 1800 the century began with 220 legal offenses for which the death penalty regularly was applied. Not until 1832 were such crimes as sheep stealing and house breaking removed from this list.

This emerging social climate brought the trade union movement to birth. The rights and privileges of the aristocracy stood challenged at all levels. Voices rose for the nationalization of property; reform became the order of the day. By the 1880s housing, paving, lighting, and transport had reached acceptable levels in London. Local councils administered controls for the public good and watched over the public's health. The period became a time of rival social theories and bitter domestic politics, with many reforms still remaining unsupported.

It was in this social climate that the Spurgeons and their associates ministered. One writer described the new East End of London, with its miles of squalid streets:

> Here lived the poor . . . countless outcasts of the industrial system. These were pallid and gin-sodden; their ragged reeking clothes . . . so vile that they left a stain wherever they rested; they stank. They herded together in bug-ridden lodging houses and rotting tenements; they slept under railway arches and on iron seats. They were the "submerged tenth," the skeleton at the rich Victorian feast, the squalid writing on the whitened wall.[44]

Conditions appear to have improved very little from similar description given of London thirty years before:

> The medical officer of health in London reported in 1849 that the Thames was a "rotten garbage dump," many of the busier streets were "ankle-deep in horse dung," Smithfield meatmarket slaughtered a million animals in the heart of the city each year and "a summer evening's walk often ended in fever and death in Paddington." Belgrave Park and Hyde Park Gardens rested on sewers abounding in the foulest deposits which blocked the house drains and emitted disgusting smells, spreading purlent throats, typhus, influenza and cholera.[45]

Poverty and moral degeneration often seemed to be locking the people into an impasse from which escape was possible only through death:

> "I recall," wrote Taine, "the alleys which run into Oxford Street, stifling lanes encrusted with human exhalations; troops of pale children nestling on muddy stairs; the seats on London bridge where families, huddled together with drooping heads, shiver through the night; particularly the Haymarket and the Strand in the evening. Every hundred steps one jostles twenty harlots; some of them ask for a glass of gin; others say, 'Sir, it is to pay for my lodging.' This is not debauchery which flaunts itself but destruction— and such destitution! The deplorable procession in the shade of the monumental streets is sickening; it seems to me a march of the dead. . . . The great social mill crushes and grinds here."[46]

Such conditions promoted new social ideas and movements. The American and French Revolutions, which set in motion a vast tide of new ideas concerning man and society had led to the development of Karl Marx's Communist Manifesto in 1848. Ultimately they generated the Russian revolution of 1917. With electoral power shifting slowly to the masses, and the shrinking of world markets, further upheavals followed.

4. *Political Revolution*—Marx wrote his flaming indictments of society and developed his radical theories in the London so movingly described above. But the rapid expansion of transportation and the desire of other nations to emulate British affluence, brought the same industrial, economic, and social pressures to bear across the world. Germany in particular, increased colonization and the manufacture of material goods. Britain, supreme as a world trade power partially because of her naval strength, suddenly found a large fleet of German naval and merchant vessels on the high seas in fierce competition.

Seeking the affluent society, Germany floated artificial credit systems which she could not sustain, expanded forcefully into Belgium, and sparked the Great War in 1914. France could not control her coasts on the Mediterranean, so the British forces moved into a police role here and also in the Middle East, remaining there for many years after hostilities ceased.

In 1900, although income tax was only six pence in the pound, 640 British strikes exploded in twelve months as labor and capital struggled to gain and retain power. Once again 25 percent of the population lived in poverty, as shrinking world markets and the demise of colonialism began to break up the once mighty British Empire. National confidence suffered well before the war, as evidenced in Kipling's classic poem, "Recessional," published in the London *Times* in 1897. The poet struck a sour but apposite note in the poem, written to celebrate Victoria's Diamond Jubilee. He wrote of the nation's forgotten glory and of the God of their fathers, beneath whose awful hand they *had* held dominion over palm and pine. He talked of tumults and shouting, of captains and kings departing, of a nation drunk with power, wild tongued, full of frantic boasts and foolish words. He included an unrestrained indictment of the nation's abuses with these words:

> Far-called, our navies melt away;
>   On dune and headland sinks the fire—
> Lo, all our pomp of yesterday
>   Is one with Nineveh and Tyre!
> Judge of the Nations, spare us yet,
>   Lest we forget—lest we forget![47]

Revolutions in industry, economics, society, and politics permeated the whole age, but reached a zenith in the last years of the nineteenth and early years of the twentieth centuries.

5. *Philosophical Revolution*—Poverty, materialism, social problems, international tensions, and the general mood of pessimism accelerated the stresses upon those who held to traditional values. Darwin's theories about evolution produced a philosophy which employed "Darwinism" to explain all of life and religion. German rationalists questioned the New Testament documents, suggesting that they were second-century forgeries, and alledging the Penteteuch to be post-Exilic and untrustworthy. New scientific methods applied to religion emphasized a naturalistic rather than a supernatural context.

Prior to 1880 most clergymen considered themselves orthodox in theology. But evolutionary philosophy taught that sin was a remnant of the animal instincts in man, which were on the way to eradication through evolutionary processes. It claimed that God and the Bible were also products of evolutionary changes in human consciousness, and rejected the fall as a indefensible doctrine in the light of contemporary scholarship. The death of Christ was viewed as an example but not as a substitution for the sins of men. Scholars attacked traditional values and concepts. The inspiration and authority of Scripture, previously accepted a *result,* now came under scrutiny in terms of its supposed developmental *process,* and was rejected.

P. T. Forsyth, James Orr, and other conservative Christian intellectuals stood firmly against these sweeping attacks. But the swirling maelstrom of a century in climax swept away the faith of many in the late 1800s and early 1900s. Popular religion became a weak blend of secular humanism, and ineffective Deism.

On both sides of the Atlantic, increasingly liberal perspectives brought to birth a revised system of beliefs, and the New Theology was born.[48] In this time of confusion and indecision, A. C. Dixon was determined to battle as well as he could under the terms demanded by the new century. He joined with Reuben A. Torrey in an ambitious and challenging program. His ideas were clearly founded on C. H. Spurgeon's concepts, the values articulated in the Down-Grade

Controversy of 1887, and the emphases evident at the Metropolitan Tabernacle, verbalized by Thomas so openly in the years which followed.

Perhaps no two words appear more regularly misapplied, both by scholars and by the press, than the terms commonly used to describe the conservative positions known as *Fundamentalism* and *Evangelicalism*. A *fundamentalist,* to many, suggests a belligerent iconoclast, a separatist, a sensational, disruptive, and divisive anti-intellectual, whose intransigent commitment to an unscholarly literal view of biblical inspiration brands him clearly as extremist. Names like Carl McIntyre, J. Frank Norris, and T. T. Shields are prominent, along with the Scopes Trial of 1925 with William Jennings Bryan versus Clarence Darrow and evolution, and positions like those espoused by Bob Jones University of Greenville, South Carolina. *Evangelicalism,* too, is far too often regarded as exemplifying the selfsame right-wing positions as those held by fundamentalists.[49]

Many historians, however, now acknowledge a distinct cleavage between turn-of-the-century Fundamentalism, and the movement it became in the 1920s and 1930s particularly in America. We use the title Evangelical for a segment of conservative thought, well represented by the journal *Christianity Today,* which parted company with the "fighting fundamentalists" in the early 1950s. Originally known as neo-Evangelicalism, this doctrine, espoused by an amalgam of scholars and church members, affirms a social conscience for the church, and denies that any special view of inerrancy and infallibility is essential for the acceptance of the inspiration and authority of Scripture. They refuse to apply this, or other points of finer doctrine (such as a particular view of millennialism) as a test of orthodoxy or of fellowship.[50] Quebedeaux confidently identifies today's evangelical moderates as the direct descendants of the early fundamentalists.[51] He classifies evangelicals as conservatives in theology and orthodox in practice, having a respect for scholarship and fellowship, and as being mainly devoted to the good news of the gospel and its publication.[52]

There is considerable literature which details how theological controversies drove the "fighting fundamentalists" of the 1920s into their separatist positions.[53] Ockenga believes that an erroneous exegesis of 2 Corinthians 6:14-18 was, in part, responsible for the deep divisions which developed through the third and fourth decades of the twentieth century, as extremists moved from conflict to separatism:[54]

> Contention was substituted for zeal in missions, evangelism, education, and worship. . . . Young Fundamentalists experienced an uneasy conscience in this situation. While remaining theologically committed to orthodoxy, they were reaching for a new position ecclesiastically and sociologically. By 1942 "evangelical" was equated with orthodox.[55]

"Modernism" (a popular name for the new theology of the late 1800s and early 1900s) can be clearly linked to the manifold changes within the great century which preceded it. Often militant in its demeanor, this movement generated a fierceness of conservative opposition equally as belligerent. Militant modernism together with fighting Fundamentalism helped to polarize American Christianity for almost forty years until Billy Graham began attracting attention as our most public evangelical practitioner. Similarly *Christianity Today* began in 1956 as a journal given to the scholarly defense of orthodox positions without the legalistic and judgmental attitudes so characteristic of extremists. Men like Carl F. H. Henry, E. J. Carnell, Bernard Ramm, Gordon Clark, H. J. Ockenga, and others led the way to a new day in transdenominational fellowship, and promoted a social ethic that allowed for the highest commitment to biblical inspiration and authority without eschatalogical encrustrations and bibliolatry. These men attempted to return to the *original* fundamentalist stance. Henry comments clearly on this perspective, affirming that the early scholars of neo-Evangelicalism, while strongly committed to scriptural authority, refused to rest their whole doctrinal understandings on such a pivot:

> While scholars disagreed whether inerrancy is explicitly or only implicitly taught in scripture, they did not make inerrancy a theological weapon with which to drive out those evangelicals not adhering to the doctrine into a non-evangelical camp.[56]

Many students of contemporary conservative theology seem quite blinded by the excessive focus of some within it on inerrancy. Few appear to know of the moderate perspective (which holds the possibility of a variety of understandings about inspiration, so long as the fact is itself asserted). There seems to be very little understanding that this moderation was the basic position of the early fundamentalists. This is true both in Britain and in the United States.

For ample illustration of this matter, we can turn directly to the series of twelve paper booklets issued by the group of defenders of orthodoxy, working out of Chicago, beginning in 1911. The three million copies of this publication that were finally distributed came from the Testimony Publishing Company, a group formed in A. C. Dixon's Chicago Moody Church. They worked with others at the Bible Institute of Los Angeles (BIOLA)[57] (which later republished the booklets in four hardback volumes,[58] under the same title *The Fundamentals*). But these documents, almost universally regarded as the earliest clear articulation of the movement's emphases, present a moderate (thoughtful, sensible, sensitive), positive defense of orthodoxy, without any extremism.

Benjamin B. Warfield's contribution to the series was not on inerrancy but on the Deity of Christ. One of the best modern evaluations of the movement firmly rejects the idea, advanced by Sandeen,[59] that the fundamentalist stance came on the simple bases of millennarianism and the Princeton theology alone.[60] He claims that these turn-of-the-century fundamentalists " . . . represent a movement at the moderate and transitional stage before it was reshaped and pushed to extremes by the intense heat of controversy."[61]

Such moderation shows forth, for example, in A. C. Dixon's article from the series entitled *The Scriptures,* in which he discusses the supernatural authority of the Bible without utilizing inerrancy and infallibility as rallying points essential for belief in inspiration.[62] In his article, James Orr calls the Bible "an infallible guide to the true knowledge of God and the way of salvation."[63] The Bible was simply viewed as "literature written by the command of God, under the guidance of God, and preserved by the providential care of God."[64] As the editor of the BIOLA newsmagazine affirmed at the same period, the views held by those he represented (who were also the sponsors of the huge publishing project of *The Fundamentals*) did not seek an analysis of inspiration as a *process* as is the fashion today, but these early fundamentalists accepted it by faith as a *result!* "By 'verbal inspiration' is meant the originals of the Old and New Testament scriptures were word for word the words of God. How 'holy men of old' were led to freely write his very words we need not enquire. We have to do with the result."[65]

With such an approach, concessions to problems and difficulties in inspiration could gladly be acknowledged. Writers were freed from arguing over the minutia of the inspiration process, and from the forging of shibboleths which divide.

In the area of eschatology, these early writers' restraint seems even more notable. A. C. Gaebelein wrote on the fulfillment of Old Testament prophecies in New Testament history, and not in the areas of millennialism for which he was best known. Even C. I. Scofield dealt with the subject of grace, not with the multitudinous interpretations of dispensationalism for which he was so well known. Philip Mauro, ardent eschatalogical enthusiast, discussed philosophy and life in Christ. No contributions were sought from the prima donnas of premillenialism, dispensationalism, or other areas in which conservative scholarship divided. Marsden affirms that mention of these topics, when they do appear, are so slight that for all practical purposes they may be regarded as absent.[66] Like A. H. Strong and Robert Stewart Macarthur of New York's best-known conservative fellowship, Calvary Baptist Church, many simply did not accept the fact that a commitment to absolute infallibility and inerrancy was essential for fellowship, or even right docrine.[67] Inspiration was the test, not any particular hard-line interpretation of the meaning of inspiration. A survey of these sources indicates that the current (neo) evangelical resurgence of today is a return to original perspectives. Today's "fighting fundamentalism" is an outgrowth of the Fundamentalism of the 1920s and 1930s, rather than a descendant of Fundamentalism's *original* precepts.[68]

The major challenges which *The Fundamentals* sought to raise existed in the areas of their contributors' concern over proper and responsible scholarship. They effected no dogmatic polemic against scientific inquiry; in fact, much of their work, as the articles clearly show, supported the need for such inquiry. They challenged the philosophy of scientism, with its naive naturalistic presuppositions, biased evaluation, and subjective conclusions. As Marsden affirms so clearly;

> The central unproven, unprovable, and wholly unscientific hypothesis or prejudice, everyone agreed, was the prejudice against the supernatural and the miraculous. While much specific evidence was marshalled to demonstrate the integrity of Scripture and the conjectural nature of the higher critical theories, the arguments always returned to this basic point. Without an *a priori* rejection of the miraculous, Scripture would always prove compatible with the highest standards of science and rationality.[69]

Original Fundamentalism, then, may be regarded as a responsible attempt to declare orthodoxy without belligerence and separatism. The sixty-four contributors to the original volumes included James Orr, B. B. Warfield, Sir Robert Anderson, G. F. Wright, H. G. C. Moulé, Charles R. Edman, H. Griffith Thomas, A. T. Pierson, G. Campbell Morgan, and others whose service as linguists, theologians, archaeologists, preachers, or lay leaders from industry and commerce gave them the highest reputation and honor. They labored in universities and pulpits stretching from Europe to America, seminaries and colleges of stature like Princeton, McCormick, Wycliffe, and Knox. Their perspectives in many theological areas were equally as diverse as their professional lives.

Southern Baptists also figured among the contributors. J. J. Reeve of Southwestern Baptist Seminary detailed his personal experience with the then predominant critical theories, offering a thorough discussion of their methods and presuppositions, and of the logical results of their adoption. Charles B. Williams, of the same seminary, presented a detailed rebuttal of the modernist denials of the reality of sin via a well-reasoned exegetical study. E. Y. Mullins, president of The Southern Baptist Theological Seminary, discussed the validity of Christian experience as an apologetic for the viability of faith. Other Baptists, such as T. W. Medhurst (C. H. Spurgeon's protégé) also made significant contributions.

In large measure *The Fundamentals* was a result of the vision and drive of its major editor, a Southern Baptist, and pastor of Moody Church, Chicago, and later of Spurgeon's Metropolitan Tabernacle—Dr. A. C. Dixon!

While serving in Chicago, Dixon sensed the pressures of the new theology and an increasing hostility towards orthodox gospel perspectives. Challenged to seek a means of awakening others to dangers inherent in this outlook, he began a prayer meeting for guidance in the matter. The whole concept of *The Fundamentals* grew out of a thirty-month prayer effort where Dixon met with ten others in extended intercession concerning these tensions. For two and one half years, the meetings continued in Chicago, as the group waited for some specific divine direction. They struggled with the question of how best to meet the flood tide of secularism and anti-Christian ideas which poured through the cracks of society now opening on every hand from the cataclysmic changes which had come before.[70]

An answer came decisively in 1909 when Dixon was unexpectedly called to minister in a series of special services in Los Angeles at the Baptist Temple. He chose to reply publicly to some previously-published statements from an ultraliberal professor at the University of Chicago, who had attacked traditional Christian beliefs.[71]

Lyman Stewart, who with his brother Milton, had founded the very successful Union Oil Company, heard him and sought an urgent interview. The Stewarts' Christian stewardship had already resulted in wide support of China missions, and in the founding of the Bible Institute of Los Angeles. Lyman Stewart attended the 1894 Bible Conference on Niagara-on-the-Lake and returned fired with enthusiasm at the idea of funding a series of booklets defending the orthodox faith, to be distributed across the world as far as his generosity would permit. Approaching Dixon with the offer, he told him of his own intensive prayer over many years, of his unsatisfactory search for someone who could edit such materials and supervise such an extensive project. He shared the conviction that God's leading at that point was clear. Dixon accepted at once, amazed at a proposal which he recognized to be the answer to the extended prayer of his Chicago group. Shortly thereafter he led them in forming a publications company, to which Lyman Stewart turned over $300,000 in stocks and securities to fund the enormous proposal.[72]

Within eighteen months, the first five volumes had circled the world. Dixon edited most of them. Louis Meyer succeeded him when Dixon moved to the London pastorate. In turn he was followed by R. A. Torrey, then academic dean of the Bible Institute of Los Angeles. By 1915, all twelve original booklets had been distributed. By 1917, they had become available as a four-volume hardcovered set published by the Institute, later to be reprinted several times.

By June 1920, a gathering at Buffalo for the consolidation of conservative positions with the Northern Baptist Convention led to a paragraph in the *Watchman-Examiner,* by Curtis Lee Laws. For the first time the term *Fundamentalist*[73] was suggested as a suitable term for those who stood by the essential doctrines of the Christian faith in the United States. Although the roots of the concept reached back into the past, this appears to be the initial occasion that the appellation was used in the American press.[74]

Dixon's address at this conference has been characterized as a balanced

intellectual refutation of opposing views.[75] The writer, somewhat critical of
Dixon in specific areas, states:

> Dixon did not fill the stereotype of a belligerent, irrational fundamentalist.
> His tone was calm, and he attempted to reject Darwinism on scientific
> terms.[76]

But the moderate voices of early fundamentalists had by now begun to fade
against the increasing pressures of a more radical element. Along with Fundamentalism's "going public," and the formation of the Northern Baptist fellowship of Fundamentalists, came the disruptive belligerence characteristic of the
coming years. By the time William Bell Riley had formed his World Christian
Fundamentals Association in 1921, he had added inerrancy and premillenialism
to their creed, elements studiously avoided by Dixon and his associates to this
point.[77]

By 1925 Dixon, aware that leaders in both the Northern Baptist and the
interdenominational organizations had shifted their emphasis from a sane defense
of orthodoxy to heresy hunting and extremism, determined that he would
withdraw his active support from them. Since so many of his Baptist brethren in
the South had never departed from an orthodox theological stance, Dixon felt
particularly uneasy. He was determined that loyalty to Christ and to the Bible did
not demand the antagonistic attitude towards the majority of his fellow ministers
that membership in these by-now-extreme organizations implied. He openly
rejected the new radicalism, and officially severed all association from both
movements, resigning his memberships. G. Campbell Morgan was among others
with comparable convictions who followed him in similar actions in the next
three years.[78]

The Fundamentals appeared first in 1911, but from 1907 to 1910, an extended
intercessory prayer program at the Chicago church, led by Dixon, had wrestled
with the proper way to meet the needs for which the booklets finally were
published. Only with Lyman Stewart's 1909 offer did they feel that the desires for
which they had prayed so long could be fulfilled with the blessing of God. We
have already noted the pressures of the age and the desire of Dixon to stand
squarely for orthodoxy, but from where did the momentum for such an effort
arise? The biographies and historical records of the period offer little insight into
this question. *But the general Spurgeon context, and its specific focus in 1865
and 1907, does exactly that.*

Called into the ministry through C. H. Spurgeon's published works, Dixon
continued a lifelong intimacy with the author and his emphases. As previously
noted, he expressed his enthusiastic support for C. H. Spurgeon's stand in the
Down Grade Controversy, as far back as 1878. In 1907 Thomas Spurgeon

focused on a stand for orthodoxy and used the term *fundamental* to express his perspectives. This actual term was the common one used in the Metropolitan Tabernacle to refer to the foundational doctrines of grace. In the absence of other evidence, given the continuity of Dixon's intimacy with Thomas, as well as with C. H. Spurgeon, his visit to London just two years before, and the affinities between all concerned, the conviction that Dixon found his source in the English expression seems inescapable.

In 1905 Thomas, asked to represent the free churches, spoke at a thanksgiving rally in the Royal Albert Hall, which concluded the five-month Torrey-Alexander mission in London. This followed the revival at the Tabernacle led by his Pastor's College Welsh students. It also came closely on the heels of the Baptist World Alliance, which Dixon had attended, and at which he had spent time in fellowship with Thomas, afterwards preaching for him at the Tabernacle several times. Thomas, at first overwhelmed at the ovation with which the giant assembly greeted him, spoke with delight of the thirteen thousand who had made professions of faith in the Torrey meetings. He lauded the spirit of brotherly love which had linked evangelicals of many differing communions together for the outreach campaign. The concerns closest to his heart at that time can be seen in the report that " . . . he greatly admired the bold and fearless manner in which Dr. Torrey had stated 'the *fundamental* doctrines' of Divine Grace, the inspiration of scripture, the efficacy of the blood of Christ, and the doctrine of substitution, having been constantly emphasised."[79]

1907 marked fifty years of service by the Pastor's College. Addresses delivered at the annual conference (April 15-19) were considered so crucial to the concerns which moved college president Thomas Spurgeon at that time that they were collected and published as a volume entitled *Fundamental Truths Re-Affirmed*.[80] Addresses on the authority of Scripture, the deity of Christ, the atonement, and associated doctrines, fill its pages. The articles are all standard, mainstream, orthodox expressions of these foundational concerns without any extremism, in all a perfect model for the later, much larger set of *The Fundamentals* edited by Dixon. Charles Spurgeon, Jr. recorded a brief testimony to the three "R's" of D. L. Moody ("Ruined by the Fall," "Redemption Through the Blood," and "Regeneration by the Holy Spirit") clearly linking his emphasis with the nineteenth-century revival movement. T. W. Mcdhurst attacked the new theology as "a sorry re-hash of old heresies refuted and exposed from the first moment they were taught by the father of lies."[81]

But the presidential address which begins the volume holds the most interest. Thomas based his remarks upon his father's words, penned beneath the motto he designed for the college. *Et teneo, et teneor (I both hold and am held)* had been C. H. Spurgeon's Latin crest for the work he loved. Beneath this, and the representation of a hand holding a cross high, C. H. S. had written the words:

> This is our COLLEGE MOTTO. We labour to hold the CROSS OF CHRIST
> with a bold hand among the sons of men, because that CROSS holds us fast
> by its attractive power. Our desire is that every man may both hold the
> TRUTH, and be held by it; especially the truth of CHRIST CRUCIFIED.[82]

Thomas's address gave weight to each phrase in his father's comments. Of the doctrine of substitution he declared:

> I need a "Substitute Saviour," who takes my place, bears my sins in His own
> body on the tree, suffers my penalty, and braves God's righteous wrath . . . I
> know this is counted blasphemy by the New Theology, but then the New
> Theology reduces sin to a matter mainly of selfishness, it lowers the Word of
> God to the level of Shakespeare, it degrades the blood of Christ to the spirit
> of self-sacrifice which may be in every man, and compares the love of Jesus
> to the love of John Smith. Wherefore we fling back the taunt of the New
> Theology, and venture to call *that* blasphemy which sneers at Christ's
> substitutionary work, and makes the death of Jesus only a barbarous murder,
> and the God-appointed Surety a martyr.[83]

Introducing the speakers who were to follow he endorsed their presentations by stating:

> We do well to reaffirm the fundamental truths of our most holy faith. We are
> not ashamed to preach them up, nor afraid to write them down. . . . We
> would rather be in a frail skiff in mid-Atlantic, rudderless, chartless,
> compassless, than on life's restless sea without this blessed Book. We shall
> go away established, and the Churches and the world will know that, God
> helping them, Spurgeon's men, come what may, will not lower the flag a
> hair's breadth . . .[84]

He saw the affirmations made at the 1907 conference as fundamental doctrines with an international relevance. Writing of the meetings the college principal, A. McCaig, declared that " . . . the Conference proved one of the best we have ever known, and evoked from the whole Brotherhood glad enthusiasm, and new devotion for the old truths."[85]

McCaig said that decisions relative to the themes of the 1907 conference were taken so that they could " . . . deal with distinctive points of the *Fundamental Verities*"[86] and that their reproduction in permanent published form was that they " . . . might be widely circulated among the people as likely to be eminently useful in the present crisis of theological opinion."[87]

The highest element of significance, however, arises with his reference to the first college conference of 1865, and to papers read at that conference by F. H. White and A. G. Brown, whose titles illuminate what he calls "these Fundamental Truths."[88] The titles of these two 1865 papers speak for themselves: "Unity in Fundamentals," and "Boldness in Distinctive Points."[89]

Thomas's 1907 emphasis then was but the echo of a forty-two-year-old emphasis which pervaded the Metropolitan Tabernacle and its auxiliaries thoroughly over that period! The use of the actual word "Fundamentals" is thus clearly documented to its origin in 1865. Hence the 1907 volume title "Fundamental Truths *Re-Affirmed*."

Without a clear and quotable statement from Dixon or Torrey indicating that their exposure to the Spurgeonic concepts specifically guided their own concept formation, absolute certainty of this source seems impossible to determine. However, in light of all the evidence (and particularly when the evidence is cataloged against a date line[90]), the burden of proof that these ideas and nomenclatures had their origins elsewhere would seem to rest on those who would contest this idea.

In 1912 president Thomas Spurgeon delivered what many regarded as the greatest of his annual conference addresses at the college. Entitled "Salvation by Grace," the address quotes authorities such as Dale, Maclaren, Jowett, and Alexander Whyte, and is altogether a characteristic utterance of the preacher, with his passion for evangelical truth and his poetic, imaginative prose. His pastor at the Tabernacle, A. C. Dixon, selected it as one of the articles to be published in *The Fundamentals* (where it appears in vol. IX pp. 48 ff.). Full of fire and gospel imagery, this clear affirmation that the way of salvation is a provision of free and unmerited divine favor ends with a peroration typical of Thomas's poetic illustration and love for ships and the sea:

> Toward the stout ships that have carried me across the seas I have ever cherished a grateful feeling. How much more do I love the good ship of Grace that has borne me thus far on my way to the Fair Havens. An unusual opportunity was once offered me of viewing the vessel on which I was a passenger, before the voyage was quite complete. After nearly three months in a sailing ship, we were greeted by a harbor tug, whose master doubtless hoped for the task of towing us into port. There was, however, a favorable breeze which, though light, promised to hold steady. So the tug's services were declined. Anxious to earn an honest penny, her master ranged alongside the clipper, and transshipped such passengers as cared to get a view from another deck of the good ship that had brought them some fifteen thousand miles. You may be sure that I was one of these. A delightful experience it was to draw away from our floating home, to mark her graceful lines, her towering masts, her tapering yards, her swelling sails—the white wave curling at her fore-foot, and the green wake winding astern.

> From our new view-point items that had grown familiar were invested with

fresh interest. There was the wheel to which we had seen six seamen lashed in time of storm, and there the binnacle, whose sheltered compass had been so constantly studied since the start, and there the chart-house with its treasures of wisdom, and yonder the huge-fluked anchors, and over all the network of ropes—a tangle to the uninitiated. Even the smoke from the galley fire inspired respect, as we remembered the many meals that appetites, sharpened by the keen air of the Southern Seas, had demolished. And yonder is the port of one's own cabin!

What marvelous things had been viewed through that narrow peephole, and what sweet sleep had been enjoyed beneath it, "rocked in the cradle of the deep." Oh! it was a brave sight, that full-rigged ship, so long our ocean home, which, despite contrary winds and cross-currents, and terrifying gales and tantalizing calms, had half compassed the globe, and had brought her numerous passengers and valuable freight across the trackless leagues in safety. Do you wonder that we cheered the staunch vessel, and her skillful commander, and the ship's company again and again? I can hear the echoes of those hurrahs today. Do you wonder that we gave thanks for a prosperous voyage by the will of God, and presently stepped back from the tug-boat to the ship without questioning that what remained of the journey would be soon and successfully accomplished?

Let me apply this incident. The good ship is FREE GRACE, and I have taken my readers aboard my tug-boat to give them opportunity to view the means by which they have already come so near—(how near we know not)—to the Haven under the hill. We have sailed around about her, and told the towering masts thereof, and marked well her bulwarks. We have seen the breath of God filling her sails brightened by the smile of His love. We have noted the scarlet thread in all her rigging, and the crimson flag flying at the fore. We have seen at the stern of the wheel of God's sovereignty by which the great ship is turned whithersoever the Governor listeth, and on the prow the sinner's sheet-anchor: "Him that cometh unto Me, I will in no wise cast out." The chart-house is the Word, and the compass is the Spirit, and there are well-plenished store-rooms, and spacious saloons, and never-to-be-forgotten chambers wherein He has given His beloved precious things in sleep, and outlooks whence they have seen His wonders in the deep. Through stress of storm and through dreary doldrums; through leagues of entangling weed, and past many a chilling and perilous iceberg, with varying speed and zigzag course, and changing clime, FREE GRACE has brought us hitherto.

We have, perchance, a few more leagues to cover. We may even stand off and on a while, near the harbor mouth, but, please God, we shall have abundant entrance at the last. We have circled the ship, and I call on every passenger to bless her in the name of the Lord, and to shout the praise of Him who owns and navigates her. All honor and blessing be unto the God of

Grace and unto the Grace of God! Ten thousand, thousand thanks to Jesus!
And to the blessed Spirit equal praise![91]

*   *   *

In September, 1916 the Tabernacle was again crowded to celebrate Thomas's
diamond jubilee of the orphanage. Three of the eight years which had passed since
his official retirement were filled with active service when, as president of both
college and orphanage, he had stumped the country raising funds and pleading
their cause before the Christian public. But for most of the period a lifelong
respiratory weakness and increasing nephritis had found him in such constant
indisposition that work was impossible. His rest was continually disturbed by
insomnia and depression.

Although confessing himself to be in "something of a backwater at this time,"
the valiant warrior showed something of his calibre by releasing a jubilee
message to the press, which reaffirmed his faith at sixty years of age. He praised
God for the mysterious ways of his providential leading, and for the grace, which
he declared had always been sufficient for the task, and was so still, in these days
of weakness.[92]

Before 1917 ended, a final stroke crippled him for a period and then ushered
him quietly into his reward in late October. Tenderly nursed by Lila during the
last weeks of illness, he died at age sixty-one, a life span exceeding that of his
father's by only four years. Tributes in the secular and religious papers spoke of
his authentic godliness, devotion, integrity, and brotherly spirit as dynamic
elements which made his ministry great and his life successful. The denominational paper concluded, "   he is worthy of honor for his own personal character
and achievements under conditions of difficulty which are only possible to a very
few."[93]

With the funeral service of Friday, October 26, 1917 completed, and the body
of her beloved husband laid to rest in Norwood Cemetery, near that of his father,
Lila returned to the family home, at 20 Prentis Road, Streatham, with a small
group of close friends. Though grateful for the help they had provided for the
evening meal, she was relieved when most departed early in the evening. She felt
the need of a closer and more personal support; inviting three of the oldest in the
group to remain with her for more intimate conversation. F. A. Jackson, Tom's
companion in vacation times for many years,[94] W. Y. Fullerton, the elder
Spurgeon's protégé, whose colorful Irish ways were now in great demand as he
ministered in successful evangelism,[95] and J. C. Carlile, one of the Pastors's
College most distinguished graduates,[96] made up the little company.

Beside the bright sitting room fire Lila sat quietly embroidering, enjoying their
welcome chatter. Occasionally she replenished their cups with fresh tea brewed
from the iron kettle which breezed beside her on the hearth. She smiled to note

how much more freely the conversation flowed with fresh vigor at each pouring. As one or the other spoke of Thomas, or of his father, with a perceptive comment, or a pleasant reminiscence, she would nod approvingly, or offer a shy smile.

At first they talked of Thomas's most recent successes, expressing delight at the ease with which he had reached back to early skills in art learned forty years before at South Kensington College.

"I viewed both of his large exhibitions of 1909 and 1911, as well as the watercolors offered every year for sale at the orphanage," Jackson enthused. "Those shipping scenes and seascapes were lifted right from the coasts where he and I rambled on many a happy holiday together. I would read while he sat by the hour, brush in hand, on some high bluff overlooking the sea. The light and action he conveyed on canvas always matched his moods of delight at picturing God's glories in nature, now that he was unable to preach with his mouth."[97]

"And let me tell you that he had his father's wit!" exclaimed Fullerton. "You remember C. H. Spurgeon's story about how his mother had expressed her Congregationalism, when she learned that he had walked eight miles as a sixteen-year-old to be immersed in confession of his newfound faith? I see you do! She remarked, 'Charlie, I always prayed that you might become a Christian, but never that you might be a Baptist,' and he replied, 'God has answered your prayer, Mother, with his usual bounty, and given you more than you asked!' "[98] All present chuckled at the recollection. "Well, C. H. Spurgeon spoke of using humor as a teaching tool, comparing it to tickling an oyster with a feather, and saying, 'I should never get the knife into some people if they were not first opened by the feather.' "[99]

"And Tom's humor was just as sharp," Fullerton continued. "I do not think he used it much because so many looked for every excuse to criticize him. But I recall that when he left college for his second health trip to Australia he quipped a line still quoted by students there today: 'I have read in Scripture that Enoch was translated by faith, but I have discovered in college that Homer can only be translated by hard work!' That matches his unusual response when as a young lad, out walking with his father, he was pressed to confess which tree he liked most. Smiling up into his father's face, the quick lad said, 'Yew, Father!' An answer which delighted C. H. S. for the rest of his life."[100]

Lila quietly interrupted their reminiscences. "My husband left many good memories for us all, but for Vera and for Harold and for me, his love of life in all its dimensions focused here in the home. Many is the Saturday or holiday when he would take the children to a museum, or Harold to a cricket match, or in some other way enlarge their education or appreciation of the world around them. He used to sit for hours reading Dickens and Milton to them, and especially the great literary histories of England. I am sure Harold's love for literature was born from his father's."[101]

"Of course, you are right there," Fullerton affirmed. "Thomas really knew the literary classics. Why, this bookshelf in front of us has all the names you have just mentioned, and here is Samuel Taylor Coleridge's *Rhyme of the Ancient Mariner*, which I know was a favorite of his, and beside it Bunyan's *The Pilgrim's Progress* which he was always quoting, as he father did before him. Did you know that the last address he gave was filled with quotations from Francis Thompson's poem the *Hound of Heaven*? And that was at a missions meeting where he worked them into his own personal testimony! Like his father, Thomas had a mind which spanned oceans of thought. Think of his literary productions! For ten years he was full editor of the monthly *Sword and Trowel*, and made many other contributions to its pages in other years. The *Gospel of the Grace of God*, his first book of sermons, was published as well in 1884. *Light and Love* followed in 1897, and a book of poems in between!"[102]

"And the sermons of 1897 were selections from weekly publications in *Word and Way* and other periodicals," Lila reminded him, "as was his other sermon volume, *My Gospel*, of 1902."

"Personally, I prefer his 1906 devotional volume *Down to the Sea*. It reveals him at his best, working with analogies and figures of speech which picture spiritual truths," Fullerton commented.

"You have a point there," Carlile opinioned. "Tom was always his best working with metaphors and analogies."

"Indeed he was!" Fullerton interjected. "Only this year he wrote me about his beginning the jubilee history of the orphanage and said just that, 'I must have an analogy, you know!' He chose the title *A Goodly Cedar*, and was working on the institution's story as the record of something good planted by God, nurtured, and fruitful. Unfortunately, now, others will need to complete this history."[103]

"What you fellows are saying helps me to understand Tom's preaching much better," asserted Jackson. "Some always criticized his methods, complaining that his sermons were not as doctrinally strong as his father's, but he *wasn't* his father! He was one who gave free rein to his poetic and imaginative nature, and often preached heartwarming messages which were really only extended metaphors. However, I must say there were many times when his sermons were every bit as theological and standard as you could ever wish that they should be."[104]

"Thomas is to be commended for being his own man," Carlile agreed. "He never spoke of his father without a tear in his eye, and with the deepest affection, but he refused to ape him just because others wanted that. It is impossible to disentangle his life from his father's. Tom was one who humbly claimed his heritage and followed steadfastly in his father's steps, but who nevertheless dared

to be himself. It remains a matter of wonder that he was able to sustain the
Tabernacle work for fourteen long years.

"And I believe his sermons were all so evangelical," continued Carlile,
"because of the depth of his own conversion experience. I loved to hear him
quote his father's favorite hymn:

> There is a fountain filled with blood
> Drawn from Immanuel's veins,
> And sinners, plunged beneath that flood,
> Lose all their guilty stains.

"And I was especially delighted to hear him testify how he had found faith
through those words learned at his mother's knee. He loved to share how the next
time he sang the refrain to that hymn, his heart almost burst with joy at the
newfound faith he held in Christ as Savior:

> I do believe, I will believe,
> That Jesus died for me;
> That on the Cross He shed his blood,
> From sin to set me free.[105]

"That also explains his commitment to the great truths of the atonement. His
theology was Calvinistic to the fingertips. He reveled in the doctrines of grace.
The sermons and the conference addresses have all been characterized by a
strong Calvinistic flavor."[106]

"Anyone who reads his article in *The Fundamentals* can see that," Fullerton
confirmed. "I don't know how some people insist on saying that his theology
differed from C. H. Spurgeon's. The Tabernacle officers introduced him to the
congregation in 1893 as one following the beliefs of his father and this was after a
thorough investigation. And W. J. Mayers asserted that 'he kept the old flag
flying and was faithful to the Spurgeon tradition.'"[107]

"Well some folks expected too much from him, that is true," Jackson asserted.
"Why, they even claim that Thomas introduced evangelistic methods which his
father refused to approve, despite clear evidence to the contrary!"[108]

"When C. H. Spurgeon died, it was difficult to find any preacher with a ghost
of a chance of succeeding at the Metropolitan Tabernacle. The building was so
vast, the congregation so varied. When God created C. H. S., he broke the mold.
The emperor of the Christian pulpit had no competitor, he stood alone, and when
he went a great gap was made that no man could fill,"[109] Carlile mused.

"Hold it, Charlie!" said Fullerton, "that paragraph sounds suspiciously like
good press copy!"

"That's exactly what it is," the author replied, "and I have brought the printer's
proof with me to share with you tonight! The words already are set for *Baptist
Times and Freeman* for their issue of this week, under the headline, 'The Death

of Pastor Thomas Spurgeon'—An Appreciation and a Tribute." He began reading from papers drawn from his coat pocket:

> Thomas Spurgeon was a man of considerable parts, a gentle personality, retiring in spirit, and modest in manner. He inherited a great name and a brilliant tradition but he could never be his father, for the simple reason that no man ever could. As a preacher he had gifts and graces far beyond the average, and some of his sermons showed not only spiritual insight and poetic imagination, but originality of thought and freshness of treatment. Had his name been other than Spurgeon he would have stood up as a preacher of considerable power. But the truth is he was overshadowed by the surpassing splendour of his father's reputation.
>
> No man could follow "C. H. S." and hope to do more than fairly well. The Tabernacle Church had been built up by the great Spurgeon. His personality was evident in everything connected with it. Its organizations were so complete and far-reaching that there was not room for additions. The most a successor could hope to do was to sustain, if only in part, the great work created by the genius of the English pulpit. Thomas Spurgeon did well, but the task was hopeless. Had it been possible for Dr. Pierson and Thomas Spurgeon to have united in a joint pastorate the result might have been otherwise, but no one can tell. Thomas held the fort with a diminishing following for years, until his health made the task impossible.
>
> Thomas Spurgeon had the artistic temperament. He was subject to moods and suffered great depression, as well as enjoyed periods on the mountaintops with the clear air and exhilaration of spirit. He was not morose, neither did he spend time in useless regrets. He had enough humour to save him from the tragedy of the situation into which the pastorate of the Tabernacle necessarily brought him. He inherited the legacy of controversy with which he had nothing to do. It was a calamity that he did not come into touch with the larger life of the Baptist denomination. There were many brethren who might have helped in some little way to share the burden that he shouldered so bravely, but which was so great for any one man's strength. He had a genius for friendship and was a loving soul, but the tradition of the "Down-Grade" controversy, with its dark shadow, fell heavily upon him and shut him off from some comradeships which must have been a matter of regret.[110]

"That says it well, doesn't it?" Fullerton exclaimed. "Tom was a man who dared to be himself; he built a great congregation on the other side of the world; he maintained his father's work in incredible strength. While others fought for truth, he was willing most to live it. I see him as a model for so many others in his behavior, so full of integrity, godliness, and patience with the providence of God. Retirement found him unsoiled in temper and unsoured in disposition."[111]

"For me," Carlile responded, "his magnificent leadership in rebuilding the

Tabernacle after the fire was his greatest achievement. Yet I cannot escape from the memory of his refusal to manipulate for the call to the Tabernacle, leaving his family in New Zealand, and giving no indication that he had carried the letter from his father for so long. That letter would have secured him the pulpit immediately had he chosen to reveal it, you know!"

"You are right again," Fullerton cried. "I do not know another who could have handled two or three major breakdowns in health, and continued as he did, shaking both sides of the world for Jesus Christ. And his warm pastor's heart beat with a stability of faith unshaken by life's toughest times. I recall the sincerity of his relations with James Spurgeon, and the grace he always showed to critics and antagonists. The vigor of his stand for the fundamentals of the faith in the latter years may well be the bridge that will carry C. H. Spurgeon's ministry forward into this new century."

"I walked down to Westminster yesterday," Jackson suddenly interjected. "A friend asked me the time, but before I could pull out my expensive gold watch, Big Ben suddenly began to chime the full hour behind us. We looked at each other and laughed. With that enormous timepiece besieging our ears, and claiming our vision, neither of us bothered to consult my watch! I have not thought of it until now—but perhaps that is what we should say about Tom? Had he not been overshadowed by the enormity of his father's ministry, we may well have regarded him with better attention. No matter how valuable, useful, correct, or wonderful my watch is (and it cost the better part of a month's salary, mind you!) in the light of Big Ben, it seemed less significant than I know it truly is."

Silence filled the room for several minutes, as each was busied with his own thoughts. Finally, Fullerton quietly asserted, "That settles it! My mind is decided! I will write a biography of Tom. It will take a year or two to gather the materials, but the record should be made, and made now, while so many of the facts are fresh. I do not think it will be a great biography, but it will at least be a true one, and written from the heart of a friend.

"Greatness needs distance. Little things sometimes appear great when they are close at hand. And great things are often dwarfed by nearness. Heroes are generally exaggerated or appreciated by the estimates of their own generation. The calm judgment of history, though not infallible, is fairer.[112] Nevertheless I shall do what I can."

His words remained with Lila long after they had left. As she tidied the books and papers still scattered over Tom's desk, she glanced at the light pencil underlinings in the worn copy of *Familiar Quotations* Tom kept so often at his side. Besides Shakespeare's line from *Hamlet*—"There's a divinity that shapes our ends, Rough-hew them as we will," she deciphered Tom's scrawled comment. "The Lord has a way of edging our rough beginnings to dovetail perfectly into His eternal plans."

Lifting the huge teapot, hugged it to her as she stepped outside to add the spent tea leaves to the garden compost heap. Soft moonbeams struggling against the swirling fog highlighted the black smoke belching from a dozen nearby chimney pots around her. Across the valley and up the hill she watched the ever-changing contours of light and darkness swallow up village streets and lanes and then slowly reveal the bright rows of terraced houses, lights twinkling in their windows.

A chill breeze startled her. Drawing her blouse collar up against the damp air, she stumbled back towards the warm kitchen. Unexpectedly, her knees buckled just as she reached the kitchen table, as a fountain of sadness welled up afresh within her at the thought of a future without Tom.

Memory rushed her back to the garden gate of Quambatook in the long ago when she as a twelve-year-old had watched twenty-one-year-old Tom walk out of her life. With unchecked tears, she recalled the rediscovery of his friendship, and its ripening into love, eleven years later in New Zealand. She lived again the Auckland years, the death of Daisy, the Tabernacle ministry, the fire, and all between. She sat thus, for twenty minutes, sobbing quietly into her apron. Glad for the emotional release after the long hard day, she lay limply with her head pillowed in her arms, cheek down, against the hard table.

Was it memory then, or imagination, that hurled those words of William Cowper's suddenly into focus? Tom's fervent tenor seemed to ring afresh in her ears, just as it had so often in the Tabernacle pulpit, as he gave out the words:

> Blind unbelief is sure to err,
>   And scan His work in vain.
> God is His own interpreter,
>   And He will make it plain.

"Dear Father," she agonized, fighting back a fresh upsurge of tears. "Make it plain, Oh, *do* make it plain! I know that Will's biography will be a tribute of love, that he will seek to glorify thee, but we are so close to Tom's time. So much ought to be said, and I fear it cannot. And so much cannot be made plain from love alone!

"Please, please, dear Lord, do bless Will's efforts! But if others can build on them in later days, make it then so plain that none can fail to see thy providence and thy purpose in it all. Magnify thy grace, oh God, through Tom's witness in the years ahead, as thou hast in his life now gone."

*   *   *

Presumably, so Lila prayed.

Indubitably, so Will Fullerton began.

My part in all the rest is but ungarnished obedience.

God is His own interpreter,
And He will make it plain.

finis

Author's Afterword

Too many biographies bore by beginning with weary family histories and ending with somber funeral orations. I have tried not to over romanticize, but have integrated other historical facts and human emotions only into the opening and closing portions of this narrative, and into an occasional reference concerning Tom's relationships with Lila. These are simply those that the evidence suggests and the heart declares suitable. In so doing, I have done what any biographer is expected to do:

> . . . a biographer is a story teller who may not invent his facts but who is allowed to imagine their form. . . . a biographer fashions a man or woman out of the seemingly intractable materials of archives, diaries, documents, dreams, a glimpse, a series of memories.[1]

And I have needed to do less than most to make this story live.

Patient research yields rich treasures, as, for example, the detail of Tom's acceptance meeting (at the London Tabernacle). In these, and in other areas where the reader may be tempted to protest the veracity of the actual words and events recorded, I suggest a careful study of the endnotes and references.

In all this work I affirm unhesitatingly that a divine sovereignty and a benevolent providence have been my constant companions.

The subsequent history of C. H. Spurgeon's congregation has been well detailed elsewhere.[2] The building, destroyed again in World War II, was rebuilt in 1959, and its large auditorium considerably shortened in 1980. The present congregation remains an independent fellowship under the pastoral leadership of Peter Masters. Visitors to services are welcome, and an evangelical spirit prevails. Theologically the group has more affinity with the remnant "Strict and Particular" Baptists than any other and, indeed, operates a part-time theological study course in which young men from the congregation are graduated into pastoral service with churches of that order, as well as into other independent Baptist causes.

One has the feeling, however, that both C. H. and Thomas Spurgeon, if they visited that fellowship today, might experience some discomfort at the astringency of the congregation's separatism, and concern over the rigidity in evangelistic programming. Nevertheless the Metropolitan Tabernacle ministry continues largely in the theoretical tradition of the Spurgeons, albeit numbers and visibility are small.

The great stone portico remains, frowning crablike amidst the busy traffic and renewed affluence of South London. But do not look for Spurgeon's greatest heritage here. It is to be found, literally, everywhere else.

Although an independent chapel, Westminster Chapel near Buckingham Palace, captures in its physical interior much of the "feel" of the original Metropolitan Tabernacle. (Of course it is much smaller.) Nor is the present ministry there unlike that of the Spurgeon tradition. The Auckland Tabernacle continues as the central Baptist Union fellowship in the North Island of New Zealand. Like all city churches it suffers the limitations imposed by changing times but is nevertheless vital and robust. Charles Spurgeon, Jr. (Thomas's twin) died in 1926. His descendants, and James Spurgeon's, are scattered throughout the British Commonwealth of Nations, as well as Britain. Principal Harold Spurgeon led the Irish Baptist College in strength for many years. He possessed his father Thomas Spurgeon's gift for poetry and imagination, and was known to all as an outstanding classicist and Greek exegete.

C. H. Spurgeon's sermons continued in publication until 1918, when the metal shortages of World War I caused the breaking up of many messages already set from the hundreds not as then printed. (Had all been published, their number may well have reached towards 10,000, as he preached three times per week for most of his life, yet only published one of these addresses in the Metropolitan Tabernacle series.) The demand for their republication in recent times has brought astronomical sales once again, and many publishers continue to find them to be an essential part of their productive lists.

The influence of the graduates of what is now known as Spurgeon's College is probably incalculable. Today this seminary stands as the leading Baptist seminary, in numbers and in its growing influence in the British Isles. Its emphases, under Principal Raymond Brown, remain evangelical, as well as suitable to the high academic accreditation which the school now enjoys with the secular authorities.

Thirty-three years ago G. W. Harte researched statistics which indicated that, despite a closure of the college during World War II, a total of 465 graduates had served in overseas ministries. Two-thirds served in the British Isles, and the overseas appointments included eight to miscellaneous countries, twenty-six to China, thirty-two to Europe, fifty-five to India, eighty-seven to Africa, 106 to the South Pacific, and 151 to North America.[3] Spurgeon's men undoubtedly shaped the evangelical ethos of Baptists and many others in Australia, and their influence upon the nations named above remains. In the years since this analysis was obtained, many more graduates have also served.

C. H. Spurgeon expressed his views on church architecture clearly. He affirmed:

> It is a matter of congratulation to me that in this city we should build a Grecian place of worship. There are two sacred languages in the world, the Hebrew of old, and the Greek that is very dear to every Christian's heart. The standard of our faith is Greek, and this place is to be Grecian. Greek is the sacred tongue, and Greek is the Baptist's tongue. We may be beaten in our version sometimes; but in the Greek never. Every Baptist place should be Grecian, never Gothic.[4]

With the completion of the Metropolitan Tabernacle in 1861, Greek porticos, Corinthian pillars, and amphitheatrical seatings appeared to increase among evangelical churches of many denominations. Across Britain, in the United States of America, Asia, Africa, and the South Pacific, miniature "tabernacles" sprang up, and other houses of worship, not so named, clearly reflected the impress of Spurgeonic ideals.

In 1955-56 I pastored the Wallsend Baptist Tabernacle, a timber building in the Newcastle area 100 miles north of Sydney, Australia, which was a copy in miniature of the London building, reflecting its features in pulpit and external design. The main church of that area is still the Newcastle Baptist Tabernacle (1861), a much more faithful miniature replica of the original. Other major cities and country centers reflect a similar influence. The tourist driving today through parts of England and Wales or traveling through the great centers of United States commerce and the county seats in the South, often begins to feel that almost no other design than this appeared acceptable for churches erected between 1860 and 1900.

To such lasting effects must be added the weight of Spurgeonic theology and style. The detailing of these areas of influence would require another volume larger than this one. The lives of many evangelical leaders of the late nineteenth and early twentieth centuries not mentioned in detail in this work interweave intimately with the Spurgeons. Among such are W. Robertson Nicoll, James Denney, P. T. Forsyth, F. B. Meyer, G. Campbell Morgan, J. H. Jowett, F. W. Boreham, and Alexander Whyte. The twentieth century's best-known English expository preacher, the late D. Martyn Lloyd-Jones, often acknowledged his Spurgeonic indebtedness. The story of how one of Germany's most respected contemporary theologians rediscovered Spurgeonic literature in recent times, and his delighted response, also highlights the current relevance of these resources.[5]

Numerous individuals, scholars, historians, university faculty members, and theological school personnel have cooperated with me in the collation of materials for the research which undergirds this volume.

Lynn Litherland (Auckland, New Zealand) and Grace Muir (Forster, New South Wales) both gave rare, otherwise inaccessible, Thomas Spurgeon volumes.

Mrs. Dorothy Spurgeon (Dublin, Ireland), second wife of Harold T. Spurgeon, Thomas's son, gave much encouragement. Ian T. Adams (Kerang, Victoria), F. J. Church (Sydney, Australia), E. W. Batts (Dunedin, New Zealand), Don Christensen (Hobart, Tasmania), Evangelist Michael Gott (Texas), David Morley (Launceston, Tasmania), J. T. Soundy (Hobart, Tasmania), and Hawley Stonecombe (Launceston, Tasmania) all gave much valuable help.

Raymond Brown (Spurgeon's College) and R. J. Thompson (Baptist Theological College of New Zealand) gladly granted access to archival and other resources of inestimable value for this work.

Some of these have read portions of the manuscript, and J. Edwin Orr (Fuller Theological Seminary) and W. Morgan Patterson (dean and professor of history of my own faculty) have also given me the benefit of their careful perusals. My good friend and internationally-known Spurgeonic authority, Eric Hayden, former pastor of the Metropolitan Tabernacle, has also helped in a multitude of ways. Of course, all responsibility for materials remains mine.

Barrington R. White of Oxford has not only encouraged me in the project over several years, but has also consented to introduce it with his gracious foreword.

J. Richard Chase, now president of Wheaton College, encouraged the awarding of a 1981 Summer Research Grant from BIOLA University when he was its president. This helped greatly with needed travel costs to London at a critical period in the task.

The photographs and illustrations in this volume are culled from a group of 300 which I assembled for this purpose. They come from historical collections, out-of-print and out-of-copyright periodicals, and century or more old volumes. The search for these and for the basic research materials of the work, both exhausting and exciting, was a task demanding my presence on three continents, several times. Many originals come from my own private collection. A number are my own contemporary exposures and/or copies given directly to me, or personally reproduced.

The custodians and librarians of the following archival and historical collections deserve special thanks for their ready permission to research and reproduce materials from their resources.

    Aberdeen Baptist Church, Geelong, Victoria, Australia
    Auckland Baptist Tabernacle, New Zealand
    Auckland Institute and Museum, New Zealand
    Australian National Library, Canberra
    Auckland Public Library, New Zealand
    Baptist Union and Baptist Historial Society Archives, London
    Baptist Union of Victoria, Melbourne, Australia
    Baptist Union of Tasmania, Launceston, Australia
    Ballarat City Library, Victoria, Australia

BIOLA University, La Mirada, California
British Library, British Museum, Bloomsbury, England
British Newspaper Library, Colindale, England
Evangelical Library, London
Geelong City Library, Victoria, Australia
Hocken Library, University of Otago, Dunedin, New Zealand
Metropolitan Tabernacle, London
National Portrait Gallery, London
New Zealand Baptist Historical Society, Auckland
New Zealand Baptist Theological College, Auckland
Regent's Park College Library, Oxford, England
Southern Baptist Convention Historical Commission, Nashville, Tennessee
Spurgeon's College, Archives and Heritage Room Holdings, Norwood, England
Tasmanian State Library, Launceston
Tasmanian State Library Archives Office, Hobart
Whitley Baptist College, University of Melbourne, Victoria, Australia
William Jewell College Library, Liberty, Missouri

The discerning reader will note considerable reference throughout to W. Y. Fullerton's small biography entitled *Thomas Spurgeon*, published in 1919. Obviously I have needed to depend upon his work where other primary source materials were not extant. However, Fullerton's work is by no means duplicated herein.

His volume, now so long out of print that only about fifty copies appear extant across the world, was published just three years after Tom died. It says nothing about the impress of his ministry in the area of Fundamentalism, naturally, and little about many other areas. The whole "Tabernacle Tempest" is dismissed in a page or so, due to the obvious desire not to disturb protagonists still living when it was written. Many of the assertions in the story are undocumented, and facts often very incomplete. Almost fifty pages are given over to detailed listings of Thomas's conference addresses, letters, and vacation travels, etc., and the whole leaves a great deal to be desired as a definitive work.

But Fullerton makes it plain that his little volume is offered as a tribute to Thomas, his friend. Without it I should have had little direction as to how to "port my helm," and almost no compass to enable the constant checking of my "longitude and latitude," to use metaphors that would be close to Thomas's own heart.

I suppose that if there is one thought with which I should conclude, it would be the fact that William Cowper's hymn captures Thomas's life and ministry so succinctly. The message for today is simply that if God can use one who served so well, with such humility, despite four major health breakdowns, under the shadow of expectations above his capacities, and amid the loneliness of repeated partings, then the Lord may also use some of us.

Thomas served his part with faithfulness, and left the Lord to take care of the results. The only greater epitaph would be to couple it with the Cowper poem, a stanza of which I have used to launch each chapter. If you wish to anchor Thomas's beliefs, and mine, you may read our joint confession by reviewing the poem.

APPENDIX A.

A Summary of Spurgeon-Dixon Reciprocity

1854   C. H. Spurgeon Begins London Ministry. A. C. Dixon born.

1856   Thomas and Charles Spurgeon, Jr., born.

1864/74 Dixon reads C. H. Spurgeon's sermons, is converted, and called to preach, thereby, continues to study them for life.

1865   First Pastor's College Conference; papers on *the fundamentals.*

1875   Dixon applies for entrance to Pastor's College, but goes to Wake Forest College and Southern Baptist Seminary.

1878/92 Dixon follows Down Grade Controversy and approves.

1888   Dixon visits London, associates with C. H. Spurgeon while there, refuses invitation to join in his permanent London ministry.

1893   Thomas Spurgeon visits with D. L. Moody, R. A. Torrey, A. C. Dixon, and others in Chicago campaign. Preaches for Dixon in New York.

1894   Thomas begins London ministry.

1899   Moody dies. Prayer for revival begins under Torrey through 1901.

1902   Torrey begins worldwide evangelism. A. C. Dixon goes to Moody church as interim.

1905   Torrey in Britain. Welcomed and farewelled by Thomas, with public reference to *fundamentals.* Dixon visits London, ministers extensively at Tabernacle, and fellowships with Thomas.

1906   Thomas's London Golden Jubilee. A. C. Dixon begins permanent Moody Church pastorate in Chicago.

1907   Full Pastor's College conference on the *fundamentals.* Extensive Chicago prayer, under Dixon, begins concerning issues of Fundamentalism, etc.

1908   Thomas retires. Chicago prayer continues.

1909   Publication plans for *The Fundamentals* instituted, helped by Stewarts.

1911   *The Fundamentals* volumes into high circulation. Dixon begins London Metropolitan Tabernacle pastorate.

1912   Thomas's address at Pastor's College Conference is "Salvation by Grace." Published also in *The Fundamentals* (Vol. IX).

1915   *The Fundamentals* publications completed.

1916   Thomas's Diamond Jubilee.

1917   Thomas dies. *The Fundamentals* reprinted into four hardback volumes.

1919   Dixon returns to U.S. ministries.

1925   Dixon dies.

APPENDIX B.

AN EXCURSUS ON FAITH-ASSURANCE INSPIRATION

Those who hold a high view of biblical authority and inspiration appear to act from one of two foundational positions.

1. **The Evidence-Judgment Position—**
in which the authenticity of the Scriptures is a verdict, assessed as an outcome from the responsible examination of factual material;

and 2. **The Faith-Assurance Position—**
where the authenticity of the Scripture exists as a given element of revelation, which is verified by its effective functioning to fulfill the purposes of its intention.

The first position is a view of *inspiration-as-process.*

The second position is a view of *inspiration-as-result.*

Until the dawning of the Victorian Age most preachers accepted what I have named the faith-assurance position with little question. The original autographs of the Scriptures were deemed as developing under divine initiative, through divine supervision, and for divine purposes. While humans were God's instruments (and their humanity was not compromised by being merely a channel for a divine dictation), the Word was nevertheless God's Word, possessing its own intrinsic authenticity and supernatural authority.

For somewhat more than a century now the focus has shifted to the *process* of inspiration and away from its simple application as an axiomatic certitude. Evaluations of veracity now involve the modern worlds of history, philosophy, literature, philology, and the empirical sciences. Such a movement yields many values for our contemporary understanding and cannot be attacked as wrong in essence. But the effect of a fresh focus on the method and process of inspiration places a restraint upon the functional power of inspiration.

But to presuppose inspiration to be a debatable possibility rather than a revealed result jeopardizes clear Scriptural teaching. Inspiration should be validated by its effective function, not its method.

Where real or imagined tensions appear, between what we understand the Scriptures to affirm and what we understand other areas of contemporary knowledge to affirm, some tend to deny the biblical revelation. Or we may, at least, defer judgment upon its dependability in the light of such unresolved problems.

The most that the Bible says about inspiration-as-process is that *"men, moved by the Holy Spirit, spoke from God" (2 Pet. 1:21, NASB)*. It says a great deal, however, about inspiration-as-result, reminding us that the Scriptures are capable of making us wise unto salvation, (2 Tim. 3:15), that they produce an outcome of profit in teaching, reproof, correction, and training (2 Tim. 3:16), that they cut sharper than a double-edged sword, having a life and power that divides soul and spirit and judges the thoughts and intents of the human heart (Heb. 4:12), and that they exist for the planting of faith and the increase of assurance (John 20:30-31, Rom. 10:17, 1 John 5:13).

Confusion of Terms

Infallibility is a word possessing a long and honored history of valid use by the Reformers and such early Puritans as Bunyan and Keach. *Inerrancy* is a more modern term which, while it has been used in the past, appears most used by some today who desire to affirm a precise description of factual accuracy about biblical information as it relates to history and secular human knowledge. Infallibility means simply possessing a quality of truth that negates the possibility of failure concerning the designed purpose. (That word is still present in some current confessions of faith, and extant in ancient ones.) For many inerrancy means true in every part, or wholly without error of any kind. *Because many contemporary protagonists now use these words to refer to their own interpretations of the Scriptures as beyond any challenge both terms have become very wooly, and are best avoided in discussions about inspiration.*

They can, however, be used in a much less polemic manner as James A. Packer has asserted.

> This is to say that the infallibility and inerrancy of Scripture are relative to the intended scope of the Word of God. Scripture provides instruction that is true and trustworthy, not on every conceivable subject, but simply on those subjects with which it claims to deal. We must allow Scripture itself to tell us what these are. The concepts of inerrancy and infallibility express one aspect

of the conviction that the teaching of Scripture is the authoritative teaching of God, and call attention to the fact that it is always a wrong approach to treat anything that Scripture actually says as untrue or unreliable.[1]

We may, then, view the Bible as a factual record *from the perspective of those who wrote it*. Although we commonly use imaginative and poetic expressions (such as those about the sun setting and rising) to describe erroneously the facts about the earth orbiting the sun, it took the church many years to discern such elements in the biblical record. Destructive critics rejected any idea of the possibility of a Mosaic authorship of the Pentateuch some years back on grounds that writing was unknown in Moses' time. The discovery of written records in the tomb of the boy-king Tutankhamen (which antedate Moses) make such an assertion no longer tenable.

Such experiences have been repeated in manifold variety over the years. They should teach us that *where apparent tensions exist between our understanding of biblical assertions, and the problems they pose against our understandings of contemporary knowledge, we should regard them first as measures of our human limits, rather than as problems related to an erroneous text.*

Spurgeon and Inspiration

As usual Spurgeon goes directly to the heart of the matter.

> If I did not believe in the infallibility of the Book, I would rather be without it. If I am to judge the Book, it is no judge of me. If I am to sift it, like the heap on the threshing fllor and lay *this* aside and only accept *that*, according to my own judgement, then I have no guidance whatever, unless I have conceit enough to trust to my own heart. The new theory denies infallibility to the words of God, but practically imputes it to the words of men; . . . [2]

C. H. Spurgeon consistently appears to treat inspiration as a *result*. His major sermon on infallibility is given over entirely to how Jesus treated the subject in just such a manner, and how he thus set a model for us to follow with a like attitude.[3] The story of how one of our most erudite contemporary German theologians discovered the value and power of Spurgeon makes absorbing reading.[4] After analyzing and applauding the strength of C. H. Spurgeon's intellectual, spiritual, and practical disciplines, Helmut Thielicke defines the real secret of Spurgeon's power as centering exactly on this understanding.

> He worked only through the power of the Word which treated its own hearers and changed souls. Now this was not *his* word, the product of his

own rhetorical skills. It was rather a word which he, himself, had merely heard. He put himself at its disposal, as a mere echo, and it brought to him the Spirit over whom he did not himself dispose. His message never ran dry because he was never anything but a recipient.[5]

Baptists and Inspiration

In Spurgeon's sermon, "The Bible Tried and Proven," he affirms that mistakes of translation are possible as "translators are not inspired." In asserting the historicity of the biblical facts Spurgeon uses a most interesting phrase.

> It is also a pure book in the sense of truth, being without admixture of error.[6]

This exact phrasing appears in the New Hampshire Confession of an earlier date and in the 1925 Southern Baptist confession document. It is expressed also in the current SBC 1963 statement:

> It (the Bible) has God for its author, salvation for its end, and truth, without any mixture of error, for its matter.[7]

The main architect of this current confession of faith, Herschel H. Hobbs, comments on this statement with clarity.

> What is the infallibility of the Bible? It is infallible as a book of a religion. While Southern Baptists hold to the inerrancy of the Scriptures, their infallibility rests upon the fact that they do what they are designed to do.[8]

Validation by Function, Not by Argument

In asserting the inspiration-as-result position as a faith-assurance perspective on inspiration I am protesting that without this the authority of the Word is too often made subject to the solution of problems which arise in the minds of some of its readers. In my own view, biblical authenticity and utility are never compromised by such tensions. Inspiration exists as a free entity completely apart from such concerns.

An enemy may jeer at my fighting sword, repudiate its quality, and affirm its dullness and entire unsuitability for effective warfare. He may consider it rusty, weak, and useless. *But one hearty swing of the blade against his throat, with the hasp held by a firm grasp, will determine its viability once and for all!*

And the Bible *does* cut to the thoughts and intents of the heart! It *is* alive and powerful. The Word of God continues to be profitable for the purposes for which it declares itself to exist. Isaiah's testimony (55:10-11) insists that the return is as dependable as is the harvest from the rain. "So shall My word be which goes forth from My mouth, it shall not return to Me empty without accomplishing what I desire, and without succeeding in the matter for which I sent it" (NASB).

Such success-power, inherent in the Scriptures, verifies its truth. This assurance of a validity about the faith position arises from the Bible's effective functioning as the powerful Word of God, rather than from any analytical discussion. The values and truths of Scripture reach into supernatural rather than natural levels of human life. Their authenticities are not irrational. They are beyond rationality.

The Evidence-Judgment Position

But where inspiration is a reasoned conclusion, drawn from the examination of evidence, there appears little escape from a continually defensive and often fluctuant posture. In this position, apparently logical tension between our interpretations of biblical teaching and those we hold about contemporary thought *must* be reconciled. Without this harmony this theory of inspiration remains jeopardized.

It would seem then that, ultimately, there is little escape from a faith-assurance perspective. (Most of us revert to this when we cannot harmonize a specific discrepancy.) This does not mean, however, that we are excused from the effort to research, discuss, and attempt every possibility that may lead to such harmonization. We should welcome all serious study of the Scriptures and their relationships to contemporary knowledge. We may rejoice in corroborative materials.

Yet we need not be embarrassed by seemingly irreconcilable difficulties. Our authority for a high view of Scriptural inspiration and authenticity remains independent. It rests on faith verified by function, not on an analysis of evidence and the rational judgment of a human nature whose interpretations and discernments are highly liable to serious error.

If the faith-assurance perspective appears paradoxical this is no more than other standard positions held by those justified by faith. Any individual in our society who claimed to possess both a divine and a human nature in the one person would be regarded as insane. The rationality of human intellect operates under a system of logic that will not allow the same person to be both God and Man. These two ideas cannot be held simultaneously in the human mind without conflict. *But we accept this as true about Christ because of its revelation in the Scriptures.*

In a similar manner we alternately observe salvation from the perspective of God's elective and eternal choice of his own, and then from the aspect of man's free-will responsibility through faith. No one can "reconcile" these twin revelations of the nature of salvation reported in the Scriptures in a manner entirely satisfactory to the human intellect. But we accept the paradox, and the positions, and leave it to God to work out the details.

So the faith-assurance perspective on inspiration allows us to function with an authoritative Word. In such an allowance it does not require us to harmonize all tensions, but accepts these as part of some normal limitations to the human condition.

Ability to function depends upon a faith-assurance position. Without accepting inspiration as a result, unaffected by the (proper) discussion of inspiration as a process, few will be able to function in effective ministry.

Both the total-innerancy position (correct in all scientific and historical details) and the limited-innerancy position (correct where we can show it compatable with contemporary knowledge) are, at heart, evidence-judgment perspectives.

The faith-assurance position might be best described as a *functional-infalli-bility* perspective.

This functional-infallibility view has characterized a variety of effective service for Christ across the centuries. R. A. Torrey was known to express it.[9] D. L. Moody clearly affirmed it.[10] Billy Graham has constantly stated that his position in this matter lies at the foundation of all his theological thinking and evangelistic practice.[11] Karl Barth has also made a rather large point of its centrality within his perspectives.[12]

No one said it better, however, than Charles Haddon Spurgeon. Asked if he would defend the Bible his response was:

"Defend the Bible? Would you defend a lion? Loose him; and let him go!"[13]

Notes

Chapter 1

1. Two verbatim reports by Reverend James Voller are extant. They have been blended for this written story. (*Baptist Magazine* 1854: 32-36, 293-300; and *Sydney Morning Herald*, January 13, 1854.) Voller began his Sydney ministry at Bathurst Street Baptist Church on January 12, 1854, when a number of citizens from the young colony gathered to hear the account as reported here. They subscribed a purse of four hundred guineas (420 Australian pounds) to assist in his resettlement. The meeting was chaired by John Fairfax, editor of the *Herald*.

While Thomas Spurgeon's personal knowledge of Voller remains undocumented, the story of this shipwreck and Voller's faithful service was so well known in England we may confidently assert Tom's awareness of it. This is especially so as the Spurgeons were readers of the *Baptist Magazine*, and supporters of the Baptist Missionary Society. In light of Thomas's lifelong fascination with the sea and ships, and his Australian interests, it seems unlikely that he was unaware of Voller. When he later visited Queensland, Voller was there as one of its best-known pastors. He preached at Sandgate where Voller was then serving, as this chapter later records.

2. Fullerton, 1919: 41-42.

3. C. H. Spurgeon, *Autobiography*,1899: Vol. 1. 324-325.

4. Ibid.

5. Ibid.

6. Fullerton, 1919, pp. 49-50.

7. The words are Bunning's own but they were published in the *Victorian Baptist*, March, 1892, as part of an obituary article for C. H. Spurgeon.

8. Fullerton, 1919: 62.

9. Ibid., pp. 62-63.

10. *Geelong Advertiser*, September 4, 1877.

11. Fullerton, 1919, p. 41.

12. From 1 Corinthians 6:19-20; Cf. Fullerton, 1919, pp. 45-46.

13. Full details exist in the *Geelong Advertiser*, September 21, 1877, and in the *Victorian Freeman*, October 1877.

14. Fullerton, 1919, pp. 58-59.

15. Ibid., p. 63.

16. Ibid., p. 64.

17. Ibid.

18. Ibid.

19. Ibid., p. 66.

20. Eric. J. Daley, (ed.) *Great Is Thy Faithfulness*, 1977, pp. 1-23, passim.

21. See bibliography under *Australian Life and Times*, for volumes which picture these, and similar, conditions.

22. Fullerton, 1919, p. 67.

23. Ibid.

Chapter 2

1. *Geelong Advertiser*, November 12, 1877: *Victorian Freeman*, November 1877.

2. Fullerton, 1919: 70.

3. Pryor, 1962, 105*ff.*

4. Ibid., pp. 108-109.

5. Fullerton, 1919, p. 65.

6. Ibid., p. 68.

7. Hughes, 1937.

8. Fullerton, 1919, p. 71.

9. Ibid.

10. Ibid., p. 72.

11. Materials relating to Baptist beginnings in Tasmania will be found listed in the bibliography. The archival records of the Tasmanian Baptist Union and the Tasmanian State Library have all been helpful in researching this information which has hitherto been unpublished.

12. The volume by Dowling (1871) and other unpublished manuscripts in the Tasmanian Baptist Union archives suggest that the full story of this amazing pioneer remains one of the untold gems of South Pacific evangelical history. It deserves more attention than can be given to it here.

13. See Reed (n.d.) in bibliography and note 11 above. Also the *Day Star*, September 1886, and the *Launceston Advocate*, December 10, 1966, "Weekend Magazine."

14. Fullerton, 1919: 74.

15. See note 13. This church is not to be confused with the Memorial Baptist Tabernacle which was erected in 1884 in Launceston by the Gibsons, under the mistaken belief that Thomas would accept that pastorate. This story is given in more detail in chapter 3.

16. Fullerton, 1919: 75-76.

17. *Sword and Trowel*, 1878: 550.

18. Fullerton, 1919: 78.

19. Fullerton, 1919: 79.

20. *Sword and Trowel*, 1878: 550.

21. J. J. Voller served the Sandgate church from 1875 to 1878. He retired from the active ministry in 1889 but later started another Baptist church at Taringa, in Brisbane. A man of incredible energy and farsighted vision, he had served as the first president of the Queensland Baptist Association (now the Baptist Union), formed the Colonial Missionary Society, started the Baptist churches at Parramatta and Hinton in New South Wales, while pastoring the Sydney Bathurst Street church, and helped other fellowships in Brisbane and Rockhampton also while stationed in Sydney. He was also instrumental in fostering work in Melbourne. Little has been researched about him other than the famous shipwreck story. His life is another example of the immense effect one dedicated life can have upon an entire nation and denomination. (Cf., Cramb, 1975 and Bollen, 1975.)

22. Fullerton, 1914: 79.

23. Ibid., pp. 79-80.

24. Fullerton, 1919: 83-85.

25. Ibid., p. 85.

26. Blackwood, 1941: 9.

27. *New Zealand Baptist*, March 4, 1934.

28. *Christian Bookseller*, Feb. 1980.

29. C. H. Spurgeon, 1954: 138.

30. *C. H. Spurgeon—The Early Years* (Vol. 1), *C. H. Spurgeon—The Full Harvest*, (Vol. 2), Autobiography, revised, 1962. This is the definitive biography, and the most interesting.

31. Orr, 1974: 81; Orr, 1949: 270-271.

32. *Sword and Trowel*, 1865: 68.

33. Ibid., p. 70.

34. Ibid., 1866: 522.

35. *Metropolitan Tabernacle Pulpit*, 1886: 237.

36. Ibid., 1903: 43.

37. Brown, n.d.: pp. 149-150.

38. *Metropolitan Tabernacle Pulpit*, 1875: 441.

39. Williams, n.d., p. 134.

40. Ibid., p. 201.

41. Ibid., p. 166.

42. Ibid., p. 148.

43. Ibid., p. 201.

44. Ibid., p. 138.

45. Ibid.

46. Ibid., p. 172.

47. Fullerton, 1966: 196.

48. Allen, n.d.: p. 61.

49. *Victorian Freeman*, December, 1879.

50. Ibid.

51. R. McCullough's words, quoted in Fullerton 1919: 95.

52. C. H. Spurgeon, *The Early Years*, 1962: 426-451.

53. Fullerton, 1919: 87-88.

54. Ibid., p. 93.

55. Ibid., p. 95.

56. Cf *Sword and Trowel*, October, 1880.

57. Cf. Chapter 3 for a summary of Tom's Tasmanian influence.

58. *Victorian Freeman*, February 1880.

59. *Sword and Trowel*, December 1880.

60. *Ballarat Courier*, July 12, 1880.

61. Fullerton, 1919: 12.

62. *Banner of Truth*, August 4, 1880.

63. *Der Wahreitszeuge*, January 1881 (The Queensland German Baptist magazine) reports their delight at joining with other Baptists to hear Thomas on August 24, 1880. Pastor Straughen was also a graduate of the London Pastors' College. He was then working among these German Baptists whose antecedents originally had come to settle as part of Zinzendorf's Moravian missionary outreach at Nundah in early days of the colony. More and more came in later years and ultimately began their own German Baptist Convention. This was amalgamated with the Queensland Baptist Union in later days. (Cf. White, 1977.)

64. *Sword and Trowel*, 1881: 9-12.

65. Ibid., p. 170-173.

66. Ibid., p. 44.

67. Ibid.

68. *Victorian Freeman*, November 1880.

69. Clemens, 1973: 287.

70. *New Zealand Baptist*, April 1881.

71. Ibid.

72. Kendon, 1955.
73. *New Zealand Baptist*, August 1881.
74. Ibid. November 1881.
75. Fullerton, 1919: 100.
76. Ibid., pp. 101-102.

Chapter 3

1. Powell, 1970: 103.
2. Fullerton, 1919: 103.
3. Ibid.
4. *Baptist Builder*, December 1882.
5. Ibid.
6. Ibid.
7. Ibid.
8. Kendon, 1905: 15-16.
9. Fullerton, 1919: 103-104.
10. Ibid., p. 107.
11. Circular in New Zealand Baptist Historical Society archives, Auckland.
12. *Baptist Builder*, December 1882.
13. Ibid.
14. Undated and undesignated newsclip, New Zealand Baptist Historical Society Archives, Auckland.
15. Cf. Williams, Muriel, 1979: 169.
16. Ibid. passim.
17. Ibid. passim.
18. Cf. "What Is Art—The Power of the Picture," Auckland *Star*, Sept. 27, 1925. The last article in a Blomfield series, and very typical.
19. *New Zealand Baptist*, April 1883, (article by Thomas describing the trek.)
20. Ibid.
21. E. E. Morris, 1889: 98.
22. Ibid.
23. *New Zealand Baptist*, April, 1883.
24. Lysnar, 1915: 229.
25. *New Zealand Baptist*, April, 1883.
26. Williams, Muriel, 1979: 74.
27. Ibid. 67.
28. Ibid, 68 ff.
29. *Thames Observer*, Sept. 24, 1910.
30. Williams, Muriel, 1979: 83-85.
31. The poem appears on page 32 of *Scarlet Threads and Bits of Blue*. An original small exercise book is in the archives of the New Zealand Baptist Historical Society, Auckland, which appears to be copies made of most of Tom's poems, in his own beautiful copperplate hand, given to the Blomfield family.
32. Ibid.
33. Page 40, *Scarlet Threads*.
34. The poem is so inscribed to Mary Blomfield in the New Zealand Baptist Historical Society manuscript referred to in note 29.
35. Oral information from Muriel Williams, author of *Charles Blomfield*, Op cit.

36. Thomas Spurgeon, 1919: (preface, viii-ix).

37. Ibid.

38. Ibid., pp. 23-24.

39. Ibid., p. 25.

40. Ibid., pp. 31-32.

41. Thomas Spurgeon, 1895.

42. Details of his speech and of the stone laying are given in full in the *New Zealand Baptist* of June 1884, and in the *Auckland Weekly News* issue of the third week in April 1884.

43. Ibid.

44. Ibid.

45. Ibid.

46. Ibid.

47. Auckland *Evening Star*, May 6, 1884.

48. *New Zealand Baptist*, July 1884.

49. Auckland *Evening Star*, May 6, 1884.

50. *New Zealand Baptist*, August 1884.

51. *Victorian Freeman*, June 1884.

52. *Daily Telegraph*, Launceston, May 26, 1884.

53. Ibid.

54. Ibid.

55. *New Zealand Baptist*, October 1884.

56. Ford, 1884: 46.

57. *New Zealand Baptist*, October, 1884.

58. *Christian World*, July 31, 1884.

59. Transcript of speech by Mrs. W. Lambourne at Auckland Tabernacle Centenary Banquet, August 17, 1955, in archives of New Zealand Baptist Historical Society.

60. *New Zealand Baptist*, October, 1884.

61. Lambourne, see note 56.

62. Hood, 1876: 186.

63. A. W. Blackwood in *C. H. Spurgeon-Great Pulpit Masters*—1959: 14

64. Quoted in Fullerton, 1966: 247.

65. *Christian Endeavour World*, December 13, 1900.

66. Ibid.

67. Hood, 1876: 187-188.

68. Wilbur H. Smith in *Treasury of Charles H. Spurgeon*, 1954: 12.

69. *Sword and Trowel*, August 1934.

70. Cf. Payne, 1959, passim.

71. *C. H. Spurgeon—the Early Years*, 1962: 27-31.

72. The sermons appear in the New Park Street Pulpit.

73. Quoted in Carlile, 1933: 102.

74. Quoted in Fullerton, 1966: 105.

75. *C. H. Spurgeon—The Early Years*, 1962: 164.

76. *C. H. Spurgeon, the Full Harvest*, 1962: 12 (italics mine).

77. Ibid. 393 (italics mine).

78. *New Park Street Pulpit*, 1859: 424 (italics mine).

79. Toon, 1967: 15.

80. *C. H. Spurgeon—The Early Years*, 1962: 171 (italics mine).

81. Ibid., 173 (italics mine).

82. *New Park Street Pulpit,* 1860: 113*ff.*

83. The clock still serves in the church today, marked with the name of the town of its origin (Greenwich).

84. Thomas Spurgeon, 1884: 65-66.

85. Ibid., p. 26.

86. Unclassified press clipping, Baptist Historical Society of New Zealand archives.

87. Reports of the opening and building details appear in Fullerton, 1919: 121-122, in the *New Zealand Baptist*, October, 1883, and in the *New Zealand Herald*, March 2, 1885, as well as all the Auckland papers of the week of May 12 and following.

88. Ibid.

89. *Sword and Trowel*, 1886: 332-336, 347-352.

90. Fullerton, 1919: 126.

91. *Chicago Standard*, August 25, 1887.

92. Ibid.

93. Quoted in Fullerton, 1966: 245-246.

94. Ibid.

95. Cf. chapter VI.

96. *Sword and Trowel*, August, 1877.

97. Ibid, March 1887. So also many letters in the Spurgeon's College archives attest.

98. Ibid, April 1888.

99. Letter in Spurgeon's College archives, March 2, 1888.

100. Cf. The references in *C. H. Spurgeon, the Full Harvest*, 1962.

101. Ibid.

102. Cf. R. J. Helmstadter "Spurgeon in Outcast London" in Phillips, 1978: 60 ff.

103. Carlile, 1933: 64-69.

104. Thielicke, 1963: 44; Cf. 42-44.

105. See chapter 6.

106. Fullerton, 1919: 103.

107. *New Zealand Baptist*, May 1887.

108. Ibid.

109. Fullerton, 1919: 133-134.

110. Copy of letter from church in New Zealand Baptist Historical Society archives, dated June 13, 1819.

111. Auckland *Leader*, November 8, 1899.

112. *Sword and Trowel*, 1890: 249.

113. Cf. Fullerton, 1919: 137-143, *Sword and Trowel* reports 1890-1892, and the *New Zealand Baptist* issues of the same period.

Chapter 4

1. *Daily Chronicle*, February 12, 1892. All the other London papers of that date carry further information, as do most of that same week. See also *New Zealand Baptist*, May 1892 and *Victorian Baptist*, May 1892.

2. *The Standard*, February 12, 1892.

3. Ibid.

4. *New Zealand Baptist*, May 1892.

5. *The Standard*, February 12, 1892.

6. Pierson, 1912: 228.

7. Ibid., p. 241.

8. *Daily Chronicle*, February 12, 1892.

9. Ibid. passim.

10. Ibid., pp. 128-129.

11. Ibid., p. 142.

12. Ibid., p. 134.

13. Ibid., pp. 138-139.

14. Ibid., pp. 101-102.

15. Ibid., pp. 228-229.

16. Ibid.

17. Ibid., p. 230.

18. Ibid., p. 231.

19. Fullerton, 1919: 150.

20. Pierson, 1912: 244.

21. Ibid., p. 245.

22. Ibid., p. 244.

23. Ibid., p. 245.

24. Ibid.

25. So stated "a member for 34 years" in a letter to the editor published in the *Daily Chronicle* September 27, 1892.

26. Ibid.

27. Quoted in the obituary article on James in the *Baptist Times and Freeman*, of March 31, 1899, written by G. Holden Pike. The statement was made on January 22, 1860 on the occasion of the reopening of the Union Chapel where he was pastor (after renovations).

28. Letter to the editor from "A Provincial Watchman." Published in *The Baptist*, October 21, 1892.

29. *The Standard*, February 12, 1892.

30. Pierson, 1892: preface.

31. *The Freeman*, June 24, 1892.

32. Ibid.

33. Letter to the editor of *The Baptist* from Lambeth, dated August 20, 1892.

34. *The Standard*, Chicago, September 8, 1892.

35. *The Echo*, October 21, 1892.

36. *The Baptist*, October 21, 1892.

37. Ibid.

38. Fullerton, 1919: 150-151.

39. Letter to the editor of *The Baptist*, from "a member," in the issue of August 12, 1892.

40. Unclassified news clipping in archives at Spurgeon's College, London, titled "A Sunday in London."

41. Ibid.

42. Letter by S. Chandler, written August 30, published in *The Baptist* the next week.

43. *Christian Commonwealth*, August 25, 1892, editorial notes.

44. *Morning Leader*, September 28, 1892.

45. Ibid.

46. Ibid.

47. Letter to the editor of *The Baptist,* August 9, 1892, from "an old member."

48. Ibid.

49. Letter of A. Brookman to *The Baptist*, September 26, a similar letter was also published in the *Daily Telegraph*, September 27, and the *Daily Chronicle* of the same date. Mr. Brookman appears determined to publicize James's apparently unethical conduct!

50. Ibid.

51. *Daily Chronicle*, October 25, 1892.

52. *The Times*, November 5, 1892.

53. Pierson, 1912: 294, 296.

54. Ibid., p. 295.

55. *The Baptist*, editorial, October 21, 1892.

56. Letter from Pierson, August 30, 1892, included in call petitioning officers for the special church meeting. Copy of the leaflet containing these materials from New Zealand Baptist Historical archives, Auckland.

57. Report in *The Baptist*, October 14, 1892.

58. *South London Press*, October 15, 1892.

59. *Sword and Trowel*, 1892: 668-669.

60. Ibid.

61. Ibid.

62. Details of this remarkable farewell can be seen in the reports of the *Daily News, Daily Chronicle,* and *Morning Leader*, of October 15, the *South London Press* also reported on that same date. The *Christian Commonwealth* of October 20 and *The Baptist* of October 21, also presented reports, and the whole is summarized in the *Sword and Trowel* of 1892:669. The scenes described appear remarkable in their excitement and interest.

63. Ibid.

64. Ibid.

65. *The Baptist*, October 21, 1892, "Personal" column by the editor.

66. Ibid.

67. *Victorian Baptist*, August 1892.

68. *New Zealand Baptist*, January, 1893.

69. *Sword and Trowel*, 1893: 295.

70. Fullerton, 1919: passim.

71. Letter in the Ellis collection in the archives at Spurgeon's College, London.

72. Fullerton, 1919: 156.

73. *Sword and Trowel*, 1893: 244. The church minute book records details on pages 333-336 in the 1887-1894 volume in the archives at the Metropolitan Tabernacle, London.

74. *New Zealand Baptist*, July, 1893.

75. *Sword and Trowel*, 1893: 372.

76. Ibid., p. 427.

77. Ibid.

78. *New Zealand Baptist*, August 1893.

79. Day, 1977: 301*ff.*

80. Ibid. passim.

81. Ibid.

82. The Thomas Spurgeon memorial sermon by A. C. Dixon, in *Sword and Trowel*, 1917: 367.

83. Fullerton, 1919: 170.

84. *New Zealand Baptist*, October 1893.

85. Fullerton, 1919: 165.

86. *Sword and Trowel*, October 1893.

87. Ibid., Nov. 1893.

88. Ibid.

89. Fullerton, 1919: 172.

90. Annual Report in *Sword and Trowel*, 1893: 195.

91. Fullerton, 1919: 173, cf. pp. 327-399 of the 1887-1894 members' minute book, Metropolitan Tabernacle archives.

92. Fullerton, 1919: 172.

93. Ibid.

94. From the printed letter distributed to Tabernacle members, copy in the archives of the New Zealand Baptist Historical Society, Auckland.

95. Ibid.

96. (to 109). These references are sometimes paraphrased for contemporary clarity, but obvious in the text of the following materials: Fullerton, 1919: 172-175; *Sword and Trowel*, 1894: 231-236; *Christian World*, April 5, 1894; *Daily Telegraph*, April 13, 1894; and *Christian Pictorial*, April 19, 1894.

97. Ibid.

98. *Christian World*, April 5, 1894.

99. Cf. reference 96.

100. Ibid.

101. *Christian World*, April 5, 1894. This statement by Thomas fulfills the three conditions for an acceptable pastor as required by the Tabernacle trust deed.

102. *Sword and Trowel*, 1894: 235-236.

103. Ibid.

104. Ibid.

105. Ibid.

106. *Christian World*, April 5, 1894.

107. Cf. reference 96.

108. *Christian Pictorial*, April 19, 1894.

109. Ibid.

110. Fullerton, 1919: 176.

111. Ibid., (paraphrased from words in *The Echo*).

112. Ibid., p. 158.

113. Ibid., p. 157.

114. William Cowper (1731-1800). These words appear in virtually every church hymnal over the years; often some words are altered.

Chapter 5

1. *The Freeman*, February 28, 1896.

2. Letter dated February 12, 1894, in the Ellis collection, archives of Spurgeon's College, London.

3. *The Freeman*, February 28, 1896.

4. Ibid.

5. *Sword and Trowel*, 1894, pp. 419-424.

6. Letter dated January 18, 1895, in Ellis collection, archives of Spurgeon's College, London.

7. Ibid. This appears the only time, in all the history I have researched, when Thomas gave expression to some of the very human feelings he must have harbored for his uncle. Even this was only in a private letter. He made no public allusions to tension whatever, but consistently strove to be cooperative and positive.

8. W. Y. Fullerton, 1919: 179.

9. Ibid.

10. Quoted by Fullerton, 1919: 179.

11. Ibid.

12. A full report exists in *The Baptist* for February 7, 1896, and discussions raged in *The Christian Pictorial* and similar papers for several weeks around the early weeks of February.

13. Ibid.

14. Ibid.

15. Ibid.

16. Letter dated November 15, 1897 in the Ellis collection, archives of Spurgeon's College, London.

17. Letter dated February 20, 1896, in Ellis collection, ibid., also quoted in Fullerton, 1919: 177-179.

18. *Baptist Times and The Freeman*, 1917: 647. Reminiscence by J. C. Carlile in an obituary written about Thomas Spurgeon.

19. Ibid.

20. *South London Press*, April 23, 1898.

21. Cf. *South London Press*, April 23, 1898, and *Christian Pictorial*, April 28, 1898.

22. The *South London Press*, April 23, 1898.

23. *The Baptist*, September 1898.

24. *The Christian Pictorial*, April 28, 1898.

25. *South London Press*, April 23, 1898.

26. Ibid.

27. Fullerton, *Thomas Spurgeon*, 1919: 185-186.

28. Ibid.

29. 1898 members' minute book of the Tabernacle, p. 236.

30. *The Freeman*, December 23, 1898.

31. Letter dated April 25, 1898, Ellis Collection, Spurgeon's College archives.

32. Ibid.

33. Ibid., letter dated December 27, 1898.

34. G. Holden Pike, "James Archer Spurgeon," obituary article in *Baptist Times and Freeman*, March 31, 1899.

35. Fullerton, 1919: 196-197.

36. *The Christian Pictorial*, September 27, 1900.

37. *The Daily Telegraph*, September 20, 1900.

38. *The Christian*, September 27, 1900.

39. Ibid.

40. *The Christian Pictorial*, September 27, 1900.

41. *Christian Pictorial*, September 27, 1900.

42. *Baptist Times and Freeman*, September 28, 1900.

43. Fullerton, 1919: 199.

44. *Christian World Pulpit*, September 26, 1900.

45. Reports about the mission occur in the *Sword and Trowel* for 1901: 11-12; 1902: 125-128; and the other religious papers of the period.

46. *Sword and Trowel*, 1901: 11.

47. *Word and Work*, October 21, 1892.

48. *Sword and Trowel*, 1902: 127.

49. Ibid.

50. Ibid. By such statements, and other quotations which appear in Gipsy Smith's autobiography, the lie that the Spurgeons did not countenance open public invitations for "inquirers" to come forward is exposed. C. H. Spurgeon supported Moody's work and invitations, although he himself used them seldom, and Thomas gave hearty and unqualified endorsement to the practice by his participation and use of the method, often called in thoses days "testing the meeting."

51. Smith, 1923: 281.

52. Ibid., p. 276.

53. *Metropolitan Tabernacle Member's Minute Book* for 1901, entry dated October 22. Tabernacle archives.

54. Copy of printed letter dated September 1902, Spurgeon's College Archives.

55. *Morning Leader*, August 10, 1903.

56. Ibid.

57. Ibid.

58. *The Baptist*, January 21, 1904.

59. *Baptist Times and Freeman*, January 1, 1904.

60. Ibid.

61. Ibid.

62. This remarkable story is detailed in a handwritten manuscript by Sid Potter (undated) entitled *When God Opened a Door*, supplied to me by his son, Ross Potter, of St. Ives, Sydney, Australia. The facts have been documented from other sources, specifically an article in which Sidney M. Potter was interviewed when he was ninety-eight years of age, in Victoria, Australia. The article is entitled "Sid Potter—God's Working in One Man's Life" by the editor of *On Being* magazine, Hawthorn, Victoria, Australia, June 1978.

63. Ibid. The conversational elements in the above are given substantially as Potter has recorded them.

64. Day, 1977: 301ff.

65. The "Thomas Spurgeon Memorial Sermon," preached by A. C. Dixon, in the Metropolitan Tabernacle, and published in *Sword and Trowel* for 1917: 367.

66. Gundry, 1976: passim.

67. Ibid., pp. 117-118, 141-142.

68. Ibid., pp. 44, 46, 68.

69. C. H. Spurgeon, *Metropolitan Tabernacle Pulpit*, 1875: 335; 1897: 516; 1905: 342; these are all passages in which Spurgeon supports not only the Moody-Sankey efforts but specifically defends their inquiry-room methods and motives!

70. Fullerton, 1919: 4, quotes the letter concerned.

71. Needham, 1883: 107.

72. Gundry, 1976: 141.

73. Varley, n.d., and Varley, 1916: passim.

74. Fullerton, 1919: 58-59.

75. Holcomb, 1947: passim.

76. Ibid., p. 12.

77. Ibid., p. 20.

78. Ibid., p. 126.

79. Ibid., p. 20.

80. Ibid., p. 59.

81. Ibid., p. 136.

82. Ibid., p. 70.

83. Ibid., p. 75.

84. Ibid., p. 143.

85. Ibid., pp. 84, 150.

86. Ibid., pp. 147-148.

87. Ibid., p. 35*ff.*

88. Ibid., p. 176.

89. Ibid.

90. *The Christian Bookseller* for February, 1980, includes a testimony by Bob L. Ross, of *Pilgrim Publications*, Pasadena, Texas, telling how he found an old volume of Jones's sermons and

how his references to Spurgeon sent Ross off to find original Spurgeon volumes, from which many hundreds of thousands of volumes have been reprinted and sold since the 1970s by *Pilgrim Publications*.

91. Davis, 1905: 9.
92. Ibid., Alexander and McLean, 1920: Harkness, 1929; Martin, 1976; Davis, n.d., all passim.
93. Orr, 1973, 1974, 1975.
94. Davis, 1905: 10-12; Harkness, 1929: 19; Martin, 1976: 131ff.
95. Ibid.
96. Harkness, 1929: 20; Davis, 1905: 13; Martin, 1976: 133-135.
97. Ibid.
98. Davis, 1905: 15-16; Martin, 1976: 140.
99. Martin, 1976.
100. Davis, 1905: 16..
101. Cf. note #92, passim.
102. Harkness, 1929: 37-40.
103. Ibid.
104. Davis, 1905: 18.
105. Ibid., p. 17.
106. Ibid., p. 18.
107. Ibid., p. 19.
108. Ibid., p. 93.
109. Martin, 1976: 173.
110. Davis, n.d., pp. 106-107.
111. Ibid.
112. Ibid., pp. 19-23, 349, 358.
113. Ramsey, 1962: 115-116.
114. Ibid.
115. Ibid., p. 120.
116. Ibid. passim.
117. Ibid., pp. 137-238, 172-173, etc.
118. *The Australian Christian World*, Sydney: A.C.W., Souvenir Volume for 1909.
119. Ramsay, 1962: 87.
120. Ibid., pp. 9, 36*ff*, 78.
121. Ibid., p. 89.
122. Ibid., pp. 41, 74-75, Ford; 1920, passim.
123. Orr, see note #93, especially *The Flaming Tongue*, 1973.
124. Orr, 1973: 1-18.
125. Ibid., p. 191.
126. Ibid., pp. 58-69.
127. Ibid., p. 195.
128. Ibid., pp. 95*ff*.
129. Ibid. passim.
130. *Baptist Times and Freeman*, April 14, 1905.
131. Ibid. April 7, 1905.
132. Ibid.
133. Ibid.
134. Ibid.
135. Ibid.
136. *Sword and Trowel*, 1905: 122-129.

137. Ibid., p. 123, passim.

138. Ibid.

139. Ibid., p. 126-127.

140. Ibid.

141. Ibid., p. 129.

142. *Baptist Times and Freeman*, 1905, March 24; *Sword and Trowel*, 1905: 179*ff.*

143. *Baptist Times and Freeman*, March 24, 1905.

144. *Sword and Trowel*, 1905: 180.

145. Ibid., p. 1905.

146. Ibid., p. 179.

147. Such notations nail the falsehood often proposed by some today who affirm that public professions of faith should never be called for in evangelistic services. The method can be abused, and should not be. Here it was handled responsibly, and was greatly blessed.

148. Thomas's pattern in all his ministry followed this same procedure. His letters collated in the archives of Spurgeon's College contain many such references relative to his regular Sunday services at the Tabernacle.

149. *Sword and Trowel*, 1905: 180.

150. Ibid.

151. Ibid., pp. 232-238.

152. Ibid. passim.

153. Ibid., p. 238.

154. Ibid., pp. 222-226.

155. Ibid., p. 223.

156. Ibid.

157. Ibid.

158. *Baptist Times and Freeman*, April 7, 1905.

159. *Sword and Trowel*, 1905: 224.

160. Ibid., p. 226.

161. Ibid., p. 240.

162. *Sword and Trowel*, 1905: 414-415.

163. Ibid.

164. See the next chapter for details.

165. Ibid., p. 241.

166. *The Christian*, London, 1905, November 9; Descriptive leaflet, William Jewell College Library, n.d.

The context and setting of the library deserves a better display than its current basement location provides. Among its treasures one will find an amazing breadth and variety of volumes on natural science, geography, and general literature, testimony to the wide interests of C. H. Spurgeon, and the source for many of his apt illustrations. One unusual element is a collection of handwritten poems, of C. H. Spurgeon's own composition, in an exercise book, in his own handwriting. The entire holding would be much more useful in a seminary setting, or at the least in a more visible and prominent one.

The residue of the Spurgeon library at William Jewell College still contains the following volumes: Literature 528, sermons 519, New Testament studies 488, theology 422, biography 319, mission 266, science 265, hymnology 200, history 203, commentaries on the Psalms 159, general Bible commentaries 156, homiletics 45 volumes and seventeen books on jokes and humor. (L. Klose, 1956, appendix.)

167. *Daily News*, July 2, 1906; Fullerton, 1919: 247.

168. *British Weekly*, September 28, 1906; Fullerton, 1919: 200-201.

169. *Baptist Times and Freeman*, September 14, 1906.

170. Ibid. September 21, 1906.

171. *Christian World,* September 27, 1906.

172. *Baptist Times and Freeman,* September 21, 1906.

173. *Sword and Trowel,* 1907: 191.

174. Ibid.

175. Cf. Fullerton, 1919: 206. I examined the deacons, elders, and members' minute books in the Metropolitan Tabernacle archives to confirm the lack of any official criticism or disappointment with his leadership. They are redolent with affectionate expressions and loving concern for the pastor in every way.

176. Fullerton, 1919: 210-211. Of course Thomas often spoke as a pulpit guest in the Tabernacle during his years of retirement.

177. Letter dated March 21, 1908, to an unknown confidant, in the historical archives, Spurgeon's College, London.

178. *Sword and Trowel,* 1908: 392. He traveled extensively in Europe during the years 1908 through 1917, vacationing and occasionally preaching for missions friends. Fullerton, 1919: 241-250.

179. This calligraphic masterpiece, now part of the archival collection at the Baptist Theological College of New Zealand, in Auckland, is undated, but obviously refers to the 1908 resignation. How such a priceless original ever came to be housed in that institution is a mystery. Since it was there, it was spared the destruction common to other memorabilia of both C. H. and Thomas Spurgeon which were lost in the World War II bombing of London, when the Tabernacle was burned for the second time. Some have said that this address originally reposed in that collection, but this cannot be proven.

180. Fullerton, 1919: 215.

181. Ibid., p. 214 ff. passim.

182. Ibid., pp. 282-283.

183. Cf. Chapter 6 and Dixon, 1931.

Chapter 6

1. Later he refused to assume the Wake Forest presidency when invited and apparently did not see himself as potentially attaining such a position of eminence. As an active pastor involved with denominational matters at state and national levels, he was known first and best as a strong Southern Baptist. He helped develop the strengths of the infant Woman's Missionary Union of the denomination. He never seemed truly comfortable with Moody's interdenominational church (where he pastored in Chicago), and moved back fully into Baptist life, after his five years of service there, with enthusiasm.

Memorabilia and historic documents pertaining to Dixon's life and ministry are now stored in Southern Baptist archives at the Dargan-Carver Library of The Baptist Sunday School Board in Nashville, Tenn.

2. Dixon, 1931. Mrs. Dixon, author of the biography, was the former wife of singer Charles M. Alexander, marrying A. C. Dixon in 1924 after the decease of his wife and of her husband. English-born heiress to the Cadbury-Fry-Pascall confectionery fortune, she became an American citizen after marrying Alexander. Her full name, which she continued to use until her death was, Helen Cadbury Alexander Dixon.

3. Ibid., p. 195.

4. Ibid. passim, especially pp. 39, 106, 107.

5. Ibid., p. 39.

6. Ibid., p. 104.

7. Ibid., p. 108.

8. *Sword and Trowel,* 1899: 487.

9. Ibid.

10. Dixon, 1931: 109-110.

11. Ibid., pp. 133-134.

12. *Sword and Trowel*, 1905: 144-145.

13. Ibid., pp. 192-193.

14. *Life of Faith*, January 11, 1911. Most of this article is direct quotation from the *South London Press*.

15. Ibid.

16. Ibid.

17. Ibid. In 1973 an exponent of a restricted form of reformed theology published a revised edition of his previously very useful work with some additions critical of the whole Tabernacle history after the death of C. H. Spurgeon (Murray, 1973). This revision included an extra chapter and also the reproduction of an interesting pamphlet, dated 1918, by Charles Nobel, a Tabernacle member.

In this document Nobel complains that the Tabernacle deacons and elders have abused their leadership rights, and that A. C. Dixon has departed from the Spurgeonic tradition in his ministry.

He claims the pastor was forced upon the people (despite the public records of congregational acceptance and no opposition). He objects to the pastor's use of a blackboard for Bible study classes, and to his leadership in abolishing pew rents to allow the poor to attend worship. He also complains about humor in the pulpit (despite C. H. Spurgeon's fame for this). He demands that the elders be elected by the congregation and not by a committee (although this was already a change toward participative election from Spurgeon's custom of choosing elders himself), and objects to the pastor's stewardship preaching, which he can only see as legalism.

The material is most self-revelatory. Not only does Nobel spit and sputter a most English aversion to anything American, as such, but it appears to picture him as a disgrunted individual, unwilling to change, and petulant when things did not go exactly to his liking.

This confirms an estimate of Nobel, given by a former pastor of the Tabernacle, Eric Hayden, who quotes both his father and grandfather, long-time members there, as affirming Nobel was "a confirmed trouble-maker." (Interview with Hayden at Longhope, Glos., England, by me, July 18, 1981.)

The strangest aspect of Nobel's letter is the fact that neither his voice, nor that of any other, was raised against Dixon in objection to the initial call, and that no other hard evidence for the charges he raises are extant. The opposition which Nobel articulates appears, at this distance, to be the result of frustration that traditional methods of a previous century could not be applied in exactly the same manner in the new one. It reveals a seeming inability to adjust to changing times. The blessings documented by the facts about Dixon's ministry (as detailed above) *including the Metropolitan Tabernacle minute book records,* cannot be gainsaid by such an expression of dissatisfaction.

One could compose such a letter, equally as vituperative, complaining that better modern translations of Scripture, the use of public-address systems instead of pulpit shouting, and the radio and television broadcasting of the gospel instead of street meetings were all quite "wrong" today because we did not do them yesterday! A principle or method is not wrong of itself just because it may be subject to abuse. All changes need disciplined application, but such changes there must be as persons and their contexts continually change.

18. Ibid.

19. Ibid.

20. *Golden Age,* August 24, 1911.

21. Ibid.

22. Ibid.

23. *Daily Telegraph,* November 14, 1911.

24. Ibid.

25. Ibid.

26. Ibid.

27. Life of Faith, January 11, 1911 (This report concerns a service during the initial months of preaching while his call was under consideration.)

28. Ibid.

29. Dixon, 1931: 204-205.

30. Ibid., p. 219.

31. Ibid., p. 212.

32. Ibid.

33. Ibid., p. 200*ff.*

34. Ibid., p. 232.

35. Ibid., p. 233.

36. Ibid.

37. Ibid., p. 236.

38. Ibid., p. 240. The minutes of the Tabernacle deacons still in the Tabernacle archives indicate this quite clearly as well.

39. Murray's claim that Dixon was the object of great dissension cannot be supported from the Tabernacle minutes. The copies of the correspondence therein seem most explicit—" . . . we cannot face the prospect of a separation without deep sorrow and regret filled with expressions of thankfulness for the ministry and its blessings" (1919 Deacon's minute book). In replying to their request for reconsideration, Dixon's letter expresses his inability to do so, stating that he is not resigning because of any discouragement and that prospects as he views them are brighter now than ever before. (Ibid.) In my discussion with some in present Tabernacle membership, I found it a common misunderstanding that Dixon was forced to resign from the Tabernacle because of American excesses. This appears to be a position created almost solely by Murray's perspective, which the evidence above does not sustain. Charles Nobel, and perhaps some others, were undoubtedly unhappy. I believe the reasons to be largely due to the difficulties created by the impossibility of anyone successfully following C. H. Spurgeon, and that such opposition was minor, and of a significance common to most successful pastors. (Cf. note #17.)

40. This letter, dated April 3, 1911, appears to be that which accompanied the official check from the Tabernacle members who subscribed to a farewell gift. The original is preserved in the A. C. Dixon memorabilia in the archives of the Dargan-Carver Library, Baptist Sunday School Board, Nashville, Tennessee (SBC), as are many other clippings and materials Helen Dixon used for her biography of her husband.

41. Dixon, 1931: 238, *ff.*

42. Letter from Dr. C. T. Cook, quoted in Hayden, 1971: 43.

43. Clark, 1969: 275.

44. Bryant, 1940: 165.

45. Ibid., p. 47.

46. Ibid., p. 166.

47. Kipling's masterpiece still appears in some hymnals today with the first line beginning "God of our Fathers, Known of Old . . . "

48. The whole movement is often referred to by conservatives as "Modernism." Any treatment of

this age and its importance seems inadequate (see quote given for note 43). Clark and Bryant give the best introduction to the period for the general reader. Further reading would be best in the following order—

Latourette, 1953: 1063-1079; Benson, n.d.; Phillips, 1978; Longford, 1969; Payne, 1951; Thompson, 1950; then Reardon, 1966.

49. Cf. Barr, 1978, and E. Glenn Hinson "Baptists and Evangelicals" in *Baptist History and Heritage,* April, 1981: 20ff, for examples of such confusion.

50. The emergence of Billy Graham and the founding of *Christianity Today* can both be affirmed as evidences of a healthier mainstream position rather than as reactions of defense for Fundamentalism. The 1976 issuance of Henry's, *God, Revelation and Authority* shows how far the scholarship of this movement has progressed, and its approach has earned the grudging admiration of the bitterest opponents to neo-Evangelicalism. Quebedeaux, 1978: 34-35, sees Henry's work as a view of propositional revelation which is sound philosophically and theologically, and that is rationally defensible at the highest of levels. Other evaluators share such a perspective. (Bernard Ramm, "Carl Henry's Magnum Opus," in *Eternity,* March, 1977. Cf. The whole of Quebedeaux' work.)

Earlier Henry had articulated the evangelical conscience in areas of social ministries and clarified some of the concerns which mark them off from Fundamentalist extremists. His work has stimulated further expressions. (Henry, 1965, 1973, 1976, and Wirt, 1968.)

51. Quebedeaux, 1978: 8-9.

52. Ibid. 6. He affirms that evangelicals today are those who hold a full authority for Scripture, but do not necessarily want to battle over inerrancy questions (1978: 7). He characterizes today's fundamentalists as still exhibiting the marks of their 1920 excesses, and as advocating a "belief in inerrancy or everything else is wrong" attitude (7-8). [For him *evangelical* is a word which expresses the theological stance which lays stress upon personal salvation by faith through the atoning death of Christ, rather than on doctrinal shibboleths] (7). This seems to be a fair and reasonable analysis.

Further reading in this area could begin with Nash, 1963; and Jorstad, 1970: 19-37. See other materials under note 53.

53. Cf. Dollar, 1973; Cole, 1931; Gasper, 1963; Kantzer, 1978 (especially p. 36); Sandeen, 1970. The latest and best evaluation of the whole movement is undoubtedly Marsden, 1980. Russell, 1976, is also a most interesting recourse. The Moral Majority movement (an extension of fighting Fundamentalism into political areas) has just produced a volume which explains their concerns and philosophies. Edited by the group's major spokesman, its perspectives have great significance and show how neo-Fundamentalism continues to keep to its rightist extremisms, quite apart from most mainstream Evangelicalism. (Falwell, *et. al.,* 1981.)

54. Kantzer, 1978: 37-38.

55. Ibid., p. 38.

56. Henry, 1976: 54.

57. This institution, now known as BIOLA University, the largest interdenominational evangelical university in U.S.A., enrolls 3,000 students in a large liberal arts college along with two well-known graduate schools *(Talbot Theological Seminary* and *Rosemead Graduate School of Psychology).* It relocated from downtown Los Angeles to La Mirada, an Eastern suburb of the city, some years ago. The emphasis of some on its faculty lies within premillenial and dispensational views of eschatology but this is neither overt nor total (as it is, for example, in Dallas Theological Seminary). Many who teach there moderate significantly from extremes in these areas.

58. This was in 1917. The original booklets were published by Testimony Publishing Company (the name of the Chicago group headed up by A. C. Dixon and funded by the Stewarts). They were sent to every pastor, missionary, evangelist, theological teacher, religious lay worker, and Sunday School superintendent for whom an address could be obtained in the English-speaking world! Of the three million copies published one third went outside the United States.

59. Sandeen, 1970.

60. C.f. Marsden, 1980, passim, especially pp. 118-123.

61. Ibid., p. 119.

62. Volume V, of the original publications (pp. 72 ff.), published (as the heading indicates) while he was then pastor of Spurgeon's Tabernacle, London, following Thomas Spurgeon and Archibald Brown.

63. Ibid., Vol. IX: 32.

64. This is the threefold phrase used by Dixon as headings for first portion of his article.

65. *The King's Business,* Feb. 1912: 25.

66. Marsden, 1980: 119.

67. Ibid., p. 107-108.

68. One can read a large majority of the works on the history of Fundamentalism, such as some listed in note #53 above, and never arrive at an awareness of the original fundamentalist stance for what it was, *a moderate and orthodox perspective.* Perhaps the extremes of later days were so great that these have overshadowed all else. This does raise the very serious question, however, as to whether some who have so written ever actually read and evaluated the original articles in *The Fundamentals.* Many appear simply to have repeated the assumptions of others as to their radicalism. For the simplest modern evaluation which does perceive this original openness Cf. Marsden, 1980, pp. 118-123.

69. Marsden, 1980: 121.

70. Brenda M. Meehan, *"A. C. Dixon—An Early Fundamentalist,"* Jan-March, 1967, passim; Dixon 1931: 181-185; James O. Henry, "Black Gold and Souls to Win" in *The King's Business*—50th Anniversary Edition, Feb. 1958: 17 ff.

71. Ibid.

72. Ibid.

73. Dixon 1931: 246.

74. Meehan, 1958: 57.

75. Ibid., p. 65.

76. Ibid., pp. 58-60.

77. Dixon, 1931: 302-311; Cole, 1931: 282, 316.

78. Morgan protested further against a Fundamentalist narrowness that he could not espouse by resigning from the faculty of BIOLA in 1928 out of sympathy with a colleague (J. M. MacInnis), unjustly accused of liberal views by the institute board. This appears to be the only incident of extreme Fundamentalism in the BIOLA history and is not characteristic of their general perspectives then, or now. (Cf. Morgan, 1951: 173-275.)

79. Report in the *Sword and Trowel* for 1905: 414. Cf. Fullerton, 1919: 282.

80. *Fundamental Truths Re-Affirmed, being Addresses Delivered at the Conference Held in the Jubilee Year of the Pastors' College, April 15 19th, 1907.* London; Passmore and Alabaster, 1907. Copy inspected in the archives of Spurgeon's College, London.

81. Ibid., p. 82.

82. Ibid., p. 2.

83. Ibid., p. 6.

84. Ibid., p. 14.

85. Ibid. preface, p. 3.

86. Ibid., pp. 3-4.

87. Ibid.

88. Ibid.

89. Ibid. 3. Cf. *Sword and Trowel 1865* for the actual papers. The *Sword and Trowel* for 1890 talks of public meetings then and some months earlier " . . . at which clear testimony upon the

fundamental doctrines of the gospel has been given by various members" (an undoubted reference to the *Evangelical Alliance* meetings of this character in which C. H. Spurgeon was most prominent) (pp. 85-86). The *Sword and Trowel* for 1889, page 75 presents John Tuckwell's suggested London Baptist Association amendment as being that "the Scriptures of the Old and New Testament . . . be an infallible and sufficient guide in all matters of religous faith and practice." C. H. Spurgeon's acceptance of this suggestion as a worthy one underlines the conviction of infallibility as meaning that there was an unfailing confidence in the Scripture's ability to fulfill the purposes for which it was created, chiefly, the "making wise unto salvation" purpose. There is no discussion of the historical/scientific accuracy/inerrancy question in all of Spurgeon's convictions regarding inspiration.

90. See Appendix.

91. Thomas Spurgeon, "Salvation by Grace" in *The Fundamentals,* Vol. 3, 126-128.

92. Cf. *The Christian,* Sept. 21, 1916; *Baptist Times and Freeman,* October 26, 1917.

93. Ibid.

94. Jackson is so described in Fullerton's 1919 work, passim.

95. Fullerton wrote the original Thomas Spurgeon biography, 1919.

96. J. C. Carlile wrote the C. H. Spurgeon centenary biography in 1933. He was a Spurgeon's College graduate, and one of the "inner circle" for many years.

97. Of course the conversation here, and following is literary conjecture for the sake of focusing facts. However, an attempt has been made to reproduce the actual words of each respondent in so far as they have been recorded elsewhere. The comments are all in line with those made by these men at other times, and mostly report the actual words, as the notes which follow indicate. Sometimes the words of others also are used.

98. This story appears in most of the biographies.

99. William Higglett, "Reminiscences of C. H. Spurgeon," in the *Australian Baptist,* May 22, 1934.

100. Cf. Fullerton, 1919: 278-279, 32.

101. Ibid., pp. 291-293.

102. Ibid. Also p. 301.

103. Ibid., pp. 285-286.

104. See volumes by Thomas Spurgeon in bibliography.

105. Fullerton, 1919: 35-36.

106. J. C. Carlile, "The Death of Pastor Thomas Spurgeon—An Appreciation and a Tribute," in the *Baptist Times and Freeman,* October 26, 1917.

107. Ibid. Mayer's words were actually spoken at Thomas's memorial service and reported in the *Baptist Times and Freeman* of November 23, 1917.

108. Murray, 1973, rejects the whole validity of any nineteenth-century revival. He charges Thomas, and others, with introducing inquiry rooms and other suspect invitational methods which C. H. Spurgeon abhorred. He quotes a report from Poole-Connor suggesting nonapproval of Moody's meetings, without indicating that his quotation is partial, and that Poole-Connor (a strong Calvinist) is actually speaking in favor of Moody's ministries. Murray also ignores evidence collated by Hayden, 1973, showing how C. H. S. clearly supported Moody's work. He ignores supportive references to inquiry room methods in Spurgeon's lectures, and the fact that Spurgeon and many others have always worked out some method to get inquirers into face-to-face personal counseling about spiritual issues. Spurgeon spoke against the abuse of many methods (including inquiry rooms) but did not attack them. He preached for Moody at his meetings and gave widespread public support to their programs. (Cf. Poole-Connor, 1933, passim, 1941; 98.ff.; also Murray, 108 ff., and Hayden, 1973: 130-131. The references in Spurgeon's sermons that Hayden quotes include "Beware of Unbelief" (1875), "Declaring the Works of the Lord" 1897, and some comments on p. 342 of the 1905 volume.)

Murray also criticizes Thomas for not repeating C. H. Spurgeon's extended emphasis on

Calvinism's "5 points" at the dedicaton of the restored Tabernacle as his father had done some forty years before. By such remarks Murray appears to misunderstand the whole historical theological context of the times. Combat against the New Theology was found best in the powerful and genuine revival spirit through which lives were being changed. C. H. S. had championed the doctrines of grace and they now needed declaration in terms of their power to apply to human need rather than mere defense of their validity in theological terms. Each Spurgeon spoke to his own age and its specific needs. Murray's castigations of Moody's supposed Arminianism simply cannot be sustained, as recent research has clearly validated (Cf. Gundry, 1976).

109. J. C. Carlile, "The Death of Pastor Thomas Spurgeon" in *Baptist Times and Freeman*, October 26, 1917.

110. Ibid.

111. Fullerton, 1919, passim.

112. These are words written by Fullerton about Spurgeon senior, not junior, in his biography completed twenty-nine years after the elder Spurgeon's death, 1966: 278 (reprint of 1920 edition).

113. Fullerton, 1919.

Author's Afterword

1. Packer, 1979: 20.

2. Thielicke, 1963.

3. Harte, 1951.

4. Fullerton, 1966: 118.

Appendix B.

1. Packer, 1958: 98, Cf. 95-110.

2. From his sermon, "The Bible Tried and Proved" (M.T.P. #2084) published with four others on inspiration as *The Scriptures—Five Sermons by C. H. Spurgeon*, n.d.

3. In the collection above, from the sermon on *Infallibility* . . . (M.T.P. #1208).

4. Thielicke, 1963.

5. *Ibid.*, p. 1.

6. See note #2 above.

7. *The Baptist Faith and Message*, 1963: 7.

8. Hobbs, 1971: 29.

9. "It doesn't matter whether a person believes the Bible. It is the Sword of the Spirit so just stick them with it!"—R. A. Torrey, quoted by Martin, 1976: 158.

10. Grundy, 1976: 212-213.

11. Pollock, 1966: 80-81.

12. " . . . were I driven to choose between (the historical/critical method) and the venerable doctrine of Inspiration, I should without hesitation adopt the latter, which has a broader, deeper, and more important justification." Karl Barth, 1975: 1.

13. Spurgeon, 1878: 17.

Bibliography

a) *General Publications*

Adams, Jay E., *Sense Appeal in the Sermons of Charles Haddon Spurgeon*, Grand Rapids, Michigan: Baker, 1975.

Alexander, Helen C., and Mclean, J. Kennedy, *Charles M. Alexander—A Romance of Soul-Winning*, London: Marshall Bros., 1920.

Allen, James T., *Mighty Messengers of Christ*, London: Pickering and Inglis, n.d.

Allyn, Russell C., *Voices of American Fundamentalism*, Phil., Pa.: Westminster, 1976.

Bacon, Ernest W., *Spurgeon, Heir of the Puritans*, Grand Rapids, Michigan, Eerdmans, 1968.

......*The Baptist Faith and Message*, (Statement adopted by the Southern Baptist Convention), Nashville, Tenn.: Baptist Sunday School Board, 1963.

Barr, James, *Fundamentalism*, Phil., Pa.: Westminster, 1978.

Barth, Karl, *The Epistle to the Romans* (translated by E. K. Hoskins) Oxford, England: University Press, 1975.

Bateman, Charles T., *John Clifford*, London: S. W. Partridge, 1902.

Benson, E. F., *As We Were—A Victorian Peep Show*, New York: Blue Ribbon Books, n.d.

Blackwood, A. W., *Preaching from the Bible*, New York: Abingdon, 1941.

Boyce, James Montgomery, *Does Inerrancy Matter?* Oakland, Ca.: International Council on Inerrancy, 1979.

Brastow, Lewis O., *Representative Modern Preachers*, New York: Macmillan, 1904.

Brown, Archibald G., *God's Full-Orbed Gospel and Other Sermons Preached at the Metropolitan Tabernacle*, London: H. R. Allenson, n.d. (but assumed 1009.)

Bryant, Arthur, *English Saga, 1840-1940*, London: Collins, 1940.

Carlile, John C., *The Story of the English Baptists*, London: James Clarke, 1905.

Carlile, James C., *C.H. Spurgeon—An Interpretive Biography*, London: Religious Tract Society, 1933.

Clabaugh, Gary C., *Thunder on the Right—The Protestant Fundamentalists*, Chicago: Nelson-Hall Co., 1974.

Clark, G. Kitson, *The Making of Victorian England*, New York: Artheneum, 1969.

Cole, Stephen G.U., *The History of Fundamentalism*, New York: Richard R. Smith, 1931.

Conwell, Russell Herman, *Life of Charles Haddon Spurgeon*, Boston: Hastings, 1892.

Cook, Henry T., *What Baptists Stand For*, London: Kingsgate Press, 1947.

Cook, Richard Briscoe, *The Wit and Wisdom of Rev. Charles H. Spurgeon*, Baltimore, Maryland: Woodward, 1892.

Cunningham-Burley, A., *Spurgeon and His Friendships*, London: Epworth 1933.

Davis, George T.B., *Torrey and Alexander—The Story of World-Wide Revival*, New York: Revell, 1905.

Davis, George T.B., *Twice Around the World with Alexander*, New York: Christian Herald, n.d.

Day, Richard Ellsworth, *Bush Aglow—The Story of Dwight Lyman Moody,* Grand Rapids, Michigan: Baker, 1977.

Day, Richard Ellsworth, *The Shadow of the Broad Brim,* Philadelphia, Pa.: Judson, 1934.

Dixon, Helen C.A., *A.C. Dixon—A Romance of Preaching,* New York: G. Putnam's Sons, 1931.

Dixon, A.C. and Torrey, R.A., *et al.* (eds.) *The Fundamentals*—(12 volumes), Chicago: Testimony Publishing Co., 1911, ff.

Dixon, A.C. and Torrey, R.A., *et.al.* (eds) *The Fundamentals*—(4 volumes), Los Angeles: Bible Institute of L.A., 1917.

. . . . . . *The Down-Grade Controversy,* Pasadena, Texas: Pilgrim Press, n.d. (reproduction of original articles by C. H. Spurgeon and others in booklet form).

Ellis, James J., *Charles Haddon Spurgeon,* London: James Nisbet, 1891.

Evans, R.J., *The Victorian Age—1815-1914,* London: Edward Arnold, 1950.

Falwell, Jerry, *et.al. The Fundamentalist Phenomenon,* Garden City, N.Y.: Doubleday, 1981.

Ford, C. Ottman, *J. Wilbur Chapman, a Biography,* New York: Doubleday, 1920.

Ford, Samuel Howard, *The Life and Labors of Charles H. Spurgeon,* St. Louis, Mo.: Christian Repository, 1884.

Fountain, D.J., *E.J. Poole-Connor, 1872-1962,* London: Henry E. Walter, 1966.

Fullerton, W.Y., *Charles Haddon Spurgeon—a Biography,* Chicago: Moody Press, 1966, (reprint of 1920 edition).

Fullerton, W.Y., *Thomas Spurgeon,* London: Hodder and Stoughton, 1919.

Gasper, Louis, *The Fundamentalist Movement,* Paris: Mouton and Co., 1963.

Gundry, Stanley M., *Love Them In—the Proclamation Theology of D.L. Moody,* Chicago: Moody Press, 1976.

Harkness, Robert, *Reuben Archer Torrey,* Chicago: Bible Colportage Association, 1929.

Harte, G.W., *Historical Tablets of the College Founded by C.H. Spurgeon in 1856 and First Called the Pastors' College,* Southport, England: Thomas Seddon, 1951.

Hayden, Eric W., *A History of Spurgeon's Tabernacle,* Pasadena, Texas: Pilgrim Publications, 1971.

Hayden, Eric W., *Searchlight on Spurgeon,* Pasadena, Texas: Pilgrim Press, 1973.

Hayden, Eric W., *Spurgeon on Revival,* Grand Rapids, Michigan: Zondervan, 1962.

Henry, Carl F., (ed.), *Baker's Dictionary of Christian Ethics,* Grand Rapids, Michigan: Baker, 1973.

Henry, Carl F., *Christian Social Ethics,* Grand Rapids, Michigan: Baker, 1965.

Henry, Carl F., *Evangelicals in Search of Identity,* Waco, Texas: Word, 1976.

Henry, Carl F., *God Revelation, and Authority,* 4 vols. Waco, Texas: Word, 1976 ff.

Hobbs, Herschel H., *The Baptist Faith and Message—A Doctrinal Study Course Book,* Nashville, Tenn.: Convention Press, 1971.

Holcomb, Walt, *Sam Jones—An Ambassador of the Almighty,* Nashville, Tenn.: Methodist Publishing House, 1947.

Hood, E. Paxton, *Lamps, Pictures, and Trumpets—Lectures on the Vocation of the Preacher,* New York: Dodd and Mead, 1876.

Horne, C. Silvester, *A Popular History of the Free Churches,* London: Kames Clarke, 1903.

Jorstad, Erling, *The Politics of Doomsday—Fundamentalists of the Far Right,* New York: Abingdon, 1970.

Kantzer, Kenneth, (ed.), *Evangelical Roots,* Nashville, Tenn.: Thomas Nelson, 1978.

Latourette, Kenneth Scott, *A History of Christianity,* New York: Harper and Row, 1953.

Lazell, David, *Gypsy Smith: From the Forest I Came,* Chicago: Moody Press, 1973.

Lorimer, George Claud, *Charles Haddon Spurgeon—The Puritan Preacher of the Nineteenth Century,* Boston: Earle, 1892.

Longford, Thomas A., *In Search of Foundations—British Theology 1900-1920,* New York: Abingdon, 1969.

Marsden, George W., *Fundamentalism and the American Culture*, New York: Oxford University Press, 1980 (The Shaping of Twentieth-Century Evangelicalism).

Martin, Roger, *R.A. Torrey—Apostle of Certainty*, Murfreesboro, TN: Sword of the Lord Publishers, 1976.

Morgan, Jill, *A Man of the Word—the Life of G. Campbell Morgan*, London: Pickering and Inglis, 1951.

Murray, Iaian H., *The Forgotten Spurgeon*, London: Banner of Truth Trust, 1973, second (rev.) ed.

Nash, Ronald A., *The New Evangelicalism*, Grand Rapids, Michigan: Zondervan, 1963.

Needham, George Carter, *The Life and Labors of Charles H. Spurgeon*, Boston: D.L. Guernsey, 1883.

Northrop, Henry Davenport, *Life and Works of Rev. Charles H. Spurgeon*, Chicago: Monarch, 1890.

Orr, J. Edwin, *The Eager Feet—Evangelical Awakenings 1792 and 1830*, Chicago: Moody Press, 1975.

Orr, J. Edwin, *Evangelical Awakenings in the South Seas*, Minneapolis, Minnesota: Bethany, 1976.

Orr, J. Edwin, *The Fervent Prayer—the World-Wide Impact of the Great Awakening of 1858*, Chicago: Moody Press, 1974.

Orr, J. Edwin, *The Flaming Tongue—Evangelical Awakenings 1900-1920*, Chicago, Moody Press, 1973.

Orr, J. Edwin, *Good News in Bad Times—Signs of Revival*, Grand Rapids, Michigan: Zondervan, 1953.

Orr, J. Edwin, *The Second Evangelical Awakening in Britain*, London: Marshall, Morgan, and Scott, 1949.

Packer, J.A., *Fundamentalism and the Word of God*, London: Inter-Varsity Fellowship, 1958.

Pachter, Marc, (ed.) *Telling Lives—The Biographer's Art*, Washington, D.C.: New Republic Books/ National Portrait Gallery, 1979.

Payne, Ernest A., *The Baptist Union—A Short History*, London: Carey Kingsgate Press, 1959.

Payne, Ernest A., *The Free Church Tradition in the Life of England*, London: S.C.M. Press, 1951. 3rd. rev. ed.

Phillips, E.T., (ed.), *The View From the Pulpit—Victorian Ministers and Society*, Toronto, Can.: Macmillan of Toronto, 1978.

Pierson, A.T., *The Divine Art of Preaching*, London: Passmore and Alabaster, 1892.

Pierson, DeLavan, *A.T. Pierson*, New York: Revell, 1912.

Pike, G. Holden, *Dr. Parker and His Friends*, London: G. Fisher Unwin, 1904.

Pike, G. Holden, *The Life and Work of Archibald G. Brown, Preacher and Philanthropist*, London: Passmore and Alabaster, 1892*a*.

Pike, G. Holden, *Charles Haddon Spurgeon, Preacher, Author, Philanthropist*, New York: Funk and Wagnalls, 1892*b*.

Pike, G. Holden, *James Archer Spurgeon*, London: Alexander, 1894.

Pinnock, Clark H., *A Defense of Biblical Infallibility:* Phil., Pa.: Presbyterian and Reformed Publ. Co., 1967.

Pollock, John, *Billy Graham—The Authorized Biogrphy*, London: Hodder and Stoughton, 1966.

Poole-Connor, E.J., *The Apostacy of English Non-Conformity*, London: R.J. Thynne, 1933.

Poole-Connor, E.J., *Evangelicalism in England*, Worthing, Eng.: Henry E. Walter, 1966, rev. ed.

Poole-Connor, E.J., *Evangelical Unity*, Worthing, Eng.: Henry E. Walter, 1941.

Quebedeaux, Richard, *The Worldly Evangelicals*, San Francisco: Harper and Row, 1978.

Ramsey, John C., *John Willbur Chapman, The Man, His Methods, and His Message*, Boston: Christopher Publ. House, 1962.

Ray, Charles, *Charles Haddon Spurgeon*, London: Passmore and Alabaster, 1903.

Reardon, Bernard M., *Religious Thought in the Nineteenth Century*, Harmonsworth, England: Penguin Books, 1950.

Robinson, H. Wheeler, *Life and Faith of the Baptists*, London: Kingsgate Press, 1946.

Russell, C. Allyn, *Voices of American Fundamentalism*, Phil., Pa.: Westminster, 1976.

Sandeen, Ernest R., *The Roots of Fundamentalism: British and American Millennarianism, 1900-1930*, Chicago: University of Chicago, 1970.

Shelley, Bruce, *Evangelicalism in America*, Grand Rapids, Michigan: Eerdmans, 1967.

Shindler, R., *From the Usher's Desk to the Tabernacle Pulpit*, London, Passmore and Alabaster, 1892. (The Life and Labors of Pastor C.H. Spurgeon).

Smith, J. Manton, *The Essex Lad Who Became England's Greatest Preacher—the Life of C.H. Spurgeon*, London: Passmore and Alabaster, 1892.

Smith, Rodney E., ("Gipsy"), *Forty Years an Evangelist*, New York: George H. Doran Co., 1923.

Smith, Rodney E., ("Gipsy"), *Gipsy Smith, His Life and Work, by Himself,* New York: Revell, 1902.

Spurgeon, C.H., *et.al.*, *Autobiography,* 4 vols, London: Passmore and Alabaster, 1899.

Spurgeon, C.H., *et.al.*, as above, revised edition—Vol. 1—*The Early Years*, Vol. 2—*The Full Harvest*, London: Banner of Truth Trust, 1962.

. . . .*Great Pulpit Masters—C.H. Spurgeon*, New York: Revell, 1959.

Spurgeon, C.H., *Lectures to My Students*, Grand Rapids Michigan: Zondervan, 1954 reprint edition.

Spurgeon, C.H., *New Park Street Pulpit* and *Metropolitan Tabernacle Pulpit*, Sermon Volumes 1855-1917, London: Passmore and Alabaster, 1855 ff.

Spurgeon, C.H., *Revival Year Sermons, Preached in the Surrey Gardens Music Hall*, 1859, London: Banner of Truth Trust, 1959.

Spurgeon, C.H., *The Scriptures—5 Sermons by C.H. Spurgeon*, Pasadena, Texas: Pilgrim Press, n.d.

Spurgeon, C.H., *Speeches at Home and Abroad*, Pasadena, Texas: Pilgrim Press, 1978.

. . . .*Spurgeon, the People's Preacher*, London: Walter Scott, n.d.

Spurgeon, C.H., *The Treasury of Charles H. Spurgeon*, New York: Revell, 1954.

Spurgeon, Thomas, *Down to the Sea—Sixteen Sea Sermons*, London: Passmore and Alabaster, 1895.

Spurgeon, Thomas, *Fundamental Truths Re-Affirmed-Being Addresses Delivered at the Jubilee Year of the Pastors' College, April 15th-19th*, London: Passmore and Alabaster, 1907.

Spurgeon, Thomas, *God Save the King—Addresses Concerning King Jesus*, London: Passmore and Alabaster, 1902.

Spurgeon, Thomas, *The Gospel of the Grace of God—Sermons Delivered at the Metropolitan Tabernacle During his Father's Illness*, London: Passmore and Alabaster, 1884.

Spurgeon, Thomas, *Light and Love—a Series of Sermons Preached at the Metropolitan Tabernacle*, London: Arthur Stockwell, 1897.

Spurgeon, Thomas, *My Gospel—Twelve Addresses*, London: Arthur Stockwell, 1902.

Spurgeon, Thomas, *Scarlet Threads and Bits of Blue*, London: Passmore and Alabaster, 1892, (Poems).

Stevenson, George John, *Charles Haddon Spurgeon—a Sketch*, New York: Sheldon, 1858.

Thielicke, Helmut, *Encounter with Spurgeon*, Philadelphia, Pa.: Fortress Press, 1963, translated by John W. Doberstein.

Toon, Peter, *The Emergence of Hyper-Calvinism in English Non-Conformity*, 1689-1765, London: The Olive Tree, 1967 (published by private subscription).

Torrey, R.A., *Is the Bible the Inerrant Word of God?*, New York: Doran, 1922.

Thompson, Ronald W., *Heroes of the Baptist Church*, London: Carey Kinsgate Press, 1937.

Underwood, A.C., *A History of the British Baptists*, London: Kingsgate Press, 1947.

Varley, Henry, Jr., *Henry Varley's Life Story*, London: Holness, 1916.

Varley, Henry, Jr., *Henry Varley—the Powerful Evangelist of the Victorian Era*, London: Pickering and Inglis, n.d.

Vedder, H.C., *A Short History of the Baptists*, Phil., Pa.: American Baptist Publication Society, 1907.

Vidler, Alex. R., *The Church in An Age of Revolution, 1789-1971*, Harmondsworth, England: Penguin Books, 1971, rev. ed.

Wayland, H.L., *Charles H. Spurgeon, His Faith and Works*, Phil., Pa.: American Baptist Publication Society, 1892.
Whitley, W.T., *A History of British Baptists*, London: Charles Griffiths, 1923.
Williams, T., *London Preachers*, London: Eliot Stock, 1878.
Williams, William, *Personal Reminisences of Charles Haddon Spurgeon*, New York: Revell, n.d.
Wirt, Sherwood R., *The Social Conscience of the Evangelical*, New York: Harper and Row, 1968.
Woolley, Davis Collier, (ed.), *Baptist Advance*, Nashville, Tenn.: Broadman Press, 1964.
Yarrow, William H., *The Life and Work of Charles H. Spurgeon*, New York: I.K. Funk and Co., 1880.

b) *Volumes on Australia and New Zealand*

Blayney, Geoffrey, *The Tyranny of Distance—How Distance Shaped Australia's History*, Melbourne: Sun Books, 1966.
Bollin, J.D., *Australian Baptists, A Religious Minority*, London: Baptist Historical Society, 1975. (Private publication.)
Brown, Basil S., *Members One of Another*, Melbourne: Baptist Union of Victoria, 1962. (Victorian Baptist History 1862-1962.)
Clark, Manning, *A Short History of Australia*, New York: Mentor Books, 1969, rev. ed.
Clemens, Samuel, *Mark Twain in Australia and New Zealand*, Harmondsworth, England: Penguin Books, 1973. (Facsimile edition of 1895 work *Following the Equator*.)
Daley, Eric J., (ed.), *Great Is Thy Faithfullness*, Kerang, Victoria: Northern District Baptist Association, 1977. (Private publication.)
Dowling, Henry, *Incidents in the Life of Henry Dowling*, Melbourne: Fountain Barker, 1871.
Ebbett, Eve, *In the Colonial Fashion*, Wellington, N.Z.: A.H. and A.W. Reed, 1977.
Fisher, John, *Australians from 1788 to Modern Times*, Adelaide: Rigby Ltd., 1972.
Graham, Susan, *The Land I Love* (N.Z.), Wellington, N.Z.: A.H. and A.W. Reed, 1962.
Hughes, E. Escort, *The Story of Our First Hundred Years*, Adelaide: South Australian Baptist Union, 1937.
Kendon, W.A., *Souvinir Programme and Short History of the Auckland Baptist Tabernacle*, Auckland: Baptist Tabernacle, 1955 (in Tabernacle Archives). (Private publication.)
Lysnar, F.B., *New Zealand, The Dear Old Mauri Land*, Auckland: Bett Publications, 1915.
MacGregor, Miriam, *Etiquette and Elbow Grease*, Wellington, N.Z.: A.H. and A.W. Reed, 1976.
Manley, Ken R., and Petras, Michael, *The First Australian Baptists*, Eastwood, NSW, Baptist Historical Society of NSW, 1981 (Private publication).
Morris, E.E., (ed.), *Cassell's Picturesque Australia*, 4 vols, London: Cassell and Co. Ltd., 1889.
Pryor, Oswald J., *Australia's Little Cornwall*, Adelaide: Seal Books/Rigby Ltd., 1962.
Reed, Margaret S.F., *Henry Reed—An Eventful Life Devoted to God and Man*, London: Marshall Morgan and Scott, n.d. (assumed 1900).
Trollope, Anthony, *Australia and New Zealand*, Melbourne: George Robertson, 1873.
White, John E., *A Fellowship of Service—A History of the Baptist Union of Queensland*, Brisbane: Baptist Union of Queensland, 1977.
Wilkin, F.J., *Our First Century, 1838-1938—Baptists in Victoria*, Melbourne: Baptist Union of Victoria, 1939.
Williams, Muriel, *Charles Blomfield, His Life and Times*, Auckland: Hodder and Stoughton, 1979.

c) *Newspapers, Periodicals, etc.* (*op. cit.* unless indicated)

1. Australia
The Australian Baptist, Sydney.

The Australian Christian World, Sydney.
Ballarat Courier, Victoria.
Banner of Truth, Sydney: Baptist Union of N.S.W.
Baptist Union Enquiry, Report of Select Parliamentary Committee, Hobart, Tasmania: 1911.
Boort Standard and Quambatook Times, Tues. Dec. 23, 1969.
Day-Star, Hobart.
Geelong Advertiser, Victoria.
Launceston Advocate, Launceston.
Launceston Examiner, Launceston.
On Being Magazine, Hawthorn, Victoria.
Sydney Morning Herald, Sydney.
Tasmanian Baptist Church Chronicle, n.p.
Der Wahreitszeuge, (Queensland German Baptist newsmagazine), Ipswich.
Victorian Baptist, Melbourne.
Victorian Freeman, Melbourne.

2. Britain

Baptist Magazine, London: Houlston and Stonewall.
Baptist, London.
Baptist Quarterly, London.
Baptist Times and Freeman, London.
British Weekly, London.
Christian, London.
Christian Commonwealth, London.
Christian Endeavour World, n.p.
Christian Globe, London.
Christian Pictorial, London.
Christian World, London.
Christian World Pulpit, London.
Daily Chronicle, London.
Daily Graphic, London.
Daily News, London.
Daily Telegraph, London.
Echo, London.
Freeman, London.
Life of Faith, London.
Morning Leader, London.
South London Chronicle, London.
South London Press, London.
Sword and Trowel, London: Passmore and Alabaster—monthly newsmagazine of Metropolitan
    Tabernacle.
Word and Work, London.

3. New Zealand

Auckland Evening Star, Auckland.
Auckland Weekly News, Auckland.
The Baptist Builder, Auckland.
New Zealand Baptist, Wellington.
Thames Observer, Thames, (near Auckland).

4. United States of America

Baptist History and Heritage, Nashville, Tenn.: SBC Historical Commission.
Baptist Reformation Review, Nashville, Tenn.
Christian Bookseller, Colorado Springs, Colo.
Eternity, Phil., Pa.
Foundations, N.Y.
King's Business, Los Angeles.
Quarterly Review, Nashville, Tenn.: S.B.C.
Standard, Chicago.

d) *Unpublished Materials*

Baggott, Hudson Doyle, *A Study of Spurgeon's Preaching Method*, Louisville, Ky.: The Southern Baptist Theological Seminary, unpublished Th.M. thesis, 1951.

Bewsher, Don, *The Gibson Family*, unpublished manuscript, Tasmanian Baptist Archives, n.d.

Bewsher, Don, *Pastor Harry Wood, 1854-1935*, unpublished manuscript, Tasmanian Baptist Archives, n.d.

Bligh, Wesley J., *Altars of the Mountains*, unpublished manuscript, Tasmanian Baptist Archives, n.d.

.....*A Brief History of Deloraine Baptist Church*, 1859-1959, mimeod typescript in Tasmanian Baptist Archives, n.d.

Cramb, Geoffrey Arthur, *Taringa Baptist Church—The Early Years*, Brisbane: Baptist Theological College of Queensland, unpublished graduation thesis, 1975.

Crook, William Herbert, *The Contributive Factors in the Life and Preaching of Charles Haddon Spurgeon*, Fort Worth, Texas: unpublished Th.D. thesis, 1956.

Dixon, Helen C., *A.C. Dixon Memorabilia Collection*, Nashville, Tenn.: Dargan-Carver Library, Baptist Sunday School Board.

Edgar, Francis Smither, *Twenty-Three Unpublished Letters, 1834-1852*, Hobart: Archives Office of State Library.

Klose, Paul Charles, *The Preaching of Charles Haddon Spurgeon*, Chicago: Northern Baptist Theological Seminary, unpublished Th.D. thesis, 1956.

......*Minute Books*, (Deacons, Members); London: Metropolitan Tabernacle Archives.

......*Minute Books*, Auckland: Baptist Tabernacle Archives.

Nelson, Theodore F., *Charles Haddon Spurgeon's Theory and Practice of Preaching*: Dubuque, Iowa: State University of Iowa, unpublished Ph.D. thesis, 1944.

Potter, Sid, *When God Opened a Door*, unpublished handwritten manuscript in author's collection (assumed 1960s date.)

Powell, Michael J., *The Church in Auckland Society, 1880-1886*, Auckland: University of Auckland, unpublished M.A. thesis, 1970.

Lambourne, W. (Mrs.), *Personal Memories*—Transcript of Auckland Baptist Tabernacle, Aug. 17, 1955 address at Centennial Banquet— typescript in Tabernacle Archives.

Rait, Basel, *The Story of Henry Dowling*, unpublished manuscript page in Tasmanian Baptist Archives.

Rait, Basel, *Tasmanian Baptist History File*, Hobart: Archives Office of State Library.

Soundy, Ron, *J.T. Soundy Historical Collection*, Hobart: private papers.

Taylor, Arthur G., *Notes on the Gibson Family in Tasmania:* Launceston, typescript in local history archives of State Library of Tasmania, dated 1975.

Wood, Harry, *Early Years of Baptist Work in Tasmania*, unpublished manuscript in Tasmania Baptist Archives, dated 1907.

INDEX

Subjects, Persons, and Places

Entries which refer to quotations and the like within chapters and also to the endnotes are so quoted with the letter *N* and the reference number, thus:

Chap. 6/N. 57, 78

which means the reader should refer to reference numbers 57 and 76 both in chapters 6 *and* in the endnotes under the same numbers.

* * * *

266